BIRDING AROUND THE WORLD

Edwin Way Teale, winner of the Pulitzer Prize and John Burroughs Medal for distinguished nature writing, was one of Dodd, Mead's most popular and beloved authors. He was a great naturalist and a great writer, ranking with Thoreau, Burroughs, and Muir in their devotion and unique abilities to communicate a love for nature, a reverence for life.

It is fitting that Dodd, Mead, in its continuing dedication to natural history publishing, pays tribute to this popular writer whose many volumes are still favorite reading, treasured in many libraries.

This series, named **Teale Books,** is devoted to the celebration and discovery of nature. Symbolized by the green-winged teal, a small but hardy and fast-flying duck, **Teale Books** feature original works and are published in both paperback and hardcover editions.

Birding Around the World

A Guide to Observing Birds Everywhere You Travel

Aileen R. Lotz

DODD, MEAD & COMPANY
NEW YORK

No part of this book may be reproduced in any form
without permission in writing from the publisher.
Published by Dodd, Mead & Company, Inc.
71 Fifth Avenue, New York, NY 10003
Distributed in Canada by
McClelland and Stewart Limited, Toronto
Manufactured in the United States of America
Designed by Suzanne Babeuf
First Edition

1   2   3   4   5   6   7   8   9   10

Library of Congress Cataloging-in-Publication Data

Lotz, Aileen R.
Birding around the world.

(Teale books)
Bibliography: p.
Includes index.
1. Bird watching.   I. Title.   II. Series.
QL677.5.L65   1987   598'.07'234   86-29087
ISBN 0-396-08990-9

ISBN 0-396-09024-9 {PBK.}

CONTENTS

Foreword

Birds have held a special fascination for man since the earliest historical records. Anyone who has visited the pyramids of Egypt, or casually perused the heiroglyphics, might recognize some 30 to 40 species of birds (depending on his or her expertise) dutifully inscribed some 3,000 or more years ago.

Having spent the greater part of the past twenty years in the active pursuit of birds around the world, I was particularly impressed with the insight Aileen Lotz shows to the birding mentality.

Arnold Small and I had a long conversation during a birding break in Brazil recently about how fortunate we are to be living in the "Golden Age" of birdwatching.

At no other time in history have so many birds been available to so many bird watchers. Neither Arnold nor I, nor any of the other top birders in the world ever dreamed twenty years ago that we would see 5,000 birds or more in our lifetime. Yet the 6,000 mark has been passed, and 7,000 now beckons!

The advent of jet travel has brought the most remote spots on the earth within the reach of almost any determined birder. Places such as the Galápagos Islands and Sulawasi that took Darwin and Wallace respectively months or even years to reach and explore, are now easily reached by air from many metropolitan centers in a matter of hours.

The increase in communications at all levels has aided in our knowledge of the avifauna of these remote areas. As Aileen so aptly points out, hardly a place worth visiting ornithologically does not have a field guide or checklist of the appropriate birdlife.

Being a consumate lister, I don't feel it necessary to justify that part of my commitment to birding. Since no one will ever see every bird in the world, the challenge to the indomitable birder will always remain a lifelong challenge. Drop me off anywhere in the world, and I will find it exciting. I have never yet known a dedicated birdwatcher who was bored. Anywhere!

Birding goes beyond many people's concepts of the enjoyment and satisfaction we get from our sport. I have made close friends in the most remote places in the world, and have been welcomed into homes in almost every country I have visited by people who shared a kindred interest in their birds.

Birding transcends political boundaries as well. I can't imagine Orlando Garrido of Cuba, Efram Neyeri of Ethiopia, Weisu Hsu of China, Maurice Rumboll of Argentina or Tulendi Wodi of Indonesia caring the least bit about my political beliefs. We birded together and enjoyed one another's company . . . just as if we were two Californians who had met at Malibu Lagoon!

It has been an exciting twenty years. My life list is a treasure chest of memories of exciting times and places and friends. Who in their right mind could look at the "tick" next to Wallace's Standardwing and not get goosebumps remembering we were among the first people to see the bird since its discovery by Alfred Russell Wallace in 1858 on Halmahera Island in the North Moluccas?

Whatever you intend your level of participation in this exciting sport of birding to be, I can't think of a better apertif than this book. I sincerely recommend it for whetting your birding appetite.

James F. Clements

Preface

"World bird listing is the utlimate sport, a *lifetime Decathlon.*
One faces every terrain, disease, hassle, inconvenience, political tur-
moil, danger and culture on the planet as one wishes or doesn't wish.
Personal, financial, intellectual, physical resources all come into play;
the game ends only when one is forced to hang up the binoculars.
Each "lifer" is a rush of adrenalin, regardless of any number."

—Peter Alden, coauthor,
Finding Birds Around the World

The objective of this book is to help stimulate the adrenalin in the "early
birders" arteries, to encourage the pursuit of the sport of birding in some
of the most exciting and fascinating places on this planet. An equally important objective, is to encourage the traveler to look for tinamous as well
as temples, to visit the natural places of the world, to experience the excitement of seeing a beautiful bird winging through the forest, while bird and
forest still exist.

You will find in Part I hints to successful birding, with extra attention given to the knowledge that will help the happy hometown birder
graduate into the world birding class.

In Part II, you will find a quick rundown, arranged geographically,
of examples of common and uncommon birds likely to be found at the
other end of binoculars, at other ends of the world. Special habitats for
special birds suggest travel destinations beyond the "capital city circuit,"
for seeing chaffinches and cathedrals.

In Part III, you will find basic information designed to further your
interest in world birding. Resources are listed to help you enhance your
early interest in birding, to extend your knowledge of a fascinating field,
and to encourage both pleasure and passion for both birding and traveling.

No doubt people have been watching birds as long as people and
birds have inhabited the planet. World birding, as we know it today, is
a relatively new sport or hobby, one that is bringing to many people
challenges to last a lifetime.

Good birding!

Dedication and Acknowledgments

Most gratefully I dedicate this book to the men and women who enhanced my joy of birds and birding, and most particularly to those who opened up my mind to the endless fascination of finding new birds in new places around the world.

They changed my life, stimulated my enthusiasm for the world and its creatures, exposed me to exciting experiences, people and places, and enormously increased life's pleasures for me. What more could anyone ask?

First, I must thank four world birders who enabled me to achieve my objective of my Christmas 1980 expedition to Antarctica: to change my life in a way that would be significant for the rest of my years.

To Dr. James Clements, I express my appreciation for the exuberance he showed for every single bird we saw on the Antarctic voyage, for giving me my first world bird checklist, and for graciously writing the Foreword to this book.

To Dr. Arnold Small, I express thanks for his patience and dedication to encouraging the appreciation of birdlife that he shared with the handfuls of passengers visiting Antarctica, and which I know he shares with all who come in contact with him. I am grateful for his willingness to read and correct several chapters of this book in draft form and to come up with a couple of new Latin names for those of us addicted to the use of binoculars.

To George Venatta, I express my thanks for introducing me to some of the literature and to some of the places alive with beautiful birds, and to Stan Picher, who transmitted to me his excitement about Antarctica, its wildlife, and his admiration for the expertise of the world birders. Stan's life, too short, was devoted to preserving the natural beauty of land and its living things for generations to come in many areas of the California coast, most particularly the Audubon Canyon ranch.

Birding tour leaders are a very special "species." They are characterized by prodigious knowledge of bird life and an unending flow of enthusiasm. Foremost among several acknowledgments to these special people is that which goes to Peter Alden, author, tour leader, and the person who had the patience to review, correct, and edit the final manuscript for this book.

Theodore A. Parker III, Ted, so openly shares his knowledge and love of Neotropical birds with all who join his trips that it is difficult not to share the intensity of his concerns for the future of tropical forests and the rest of the natural world. I give special thanks to Ted for reviewing my chapter on South America and for his painstaking correction of my sometimes weird spelling.

Other leaders of birding trips each contributed in special ways to my growing love of world birding: David Bishop, Rafael G. Campos, Mort Cooper, Victor Emanuel, Jeri Langham, Steve Madge, Nigel Redman, Iain Robertson, Rose Ann Rowlett, Raj Singh, and Arnold Small. Dozens of companions on birding trips to many countries contributed wittingly, or unwittingly, not only to my knowledge of the world's birds, but to this book. My thanks to all.

Peter Carlton, in particular, performed a labor of love in reviewing so many chapters in their difficult early stages. Bill and Laurel Bouton graciously offered dozens of useful comments and corrections on an early draft. Maida Hodges provided some delightful twists for several chapters. Phoebe Snetzinger graciously shared with me many of her extensive birding experiences. Dr. Robert Kelly offered encouragement on early drafts, and Bruce Neville, whose knowledge of both birds and words is wondrous, were of inestimable help. Lorimer Moe kindly took time out from watching birds on Sanibel Island to edit, and enhance from his vast knowledge, the chapter on European birding. Thanks also to Pat Suiter, Rick Barongi, Ron Johnson, Ginny and Harry Hokanson, Wendy Wallace, and Gene Miller for their help, encouragement, and guidance. Jack Holmes earned my enduring appreciation for his patience during the painstaking review of the final draft and for his expert help on photograph selection.

A good editor/author relationship is imperative to the successful production of a book. These acknowledgments would not be complete without recognizing my great good fortune and enjoyment of my partnership with my editor, Mary Kennan. We chose each other, at different times, and I have been continually impressed with her encouragement and empathy for our joint project, and for her prompt, succinct, and judicious responses to my many inquiries.

In spite of invaluable assistance, I have inadvertently forgotten people, events, and information which I should have remembered; come to some erroneous conclusions, placed an occasional bird in the wrong habitat, or unwittingly given it a new name. For such errors, I humbly accept responsibility.

Credits

All photographs are by the author with the exception of the following: on pages 3 and 18, the photograph of the author is courtesy of Jack Holmes; and on page 197, the photograph of the Sooty Tern is courtesy of Joel Abramson. The original drawing on page 63 is courtesy of Laura S. Wiegert.

BIRDING AROUND THE WORLD

PART I

IN PURSUIT OF PUFFINS AND PENGUINS

🐦 One 🐦

Take Your Binoculars: Don't Leave Home Without Them

I encountered the world birders in the Cabo de Hornos Hotel cocktail lounge over a Scotch and soda. We were in Punta Arenas, that tip of Chile, port city on the Strait of Magellan, awaiting departure for Antarctica with intermediate stops in the Falkland Islands and South Georgia.

The conversation went something like this:

World Birder #1: Reading from a list, "I need a Chilean Swallow, a Chiloe Widgeon, a Fire-eyed Diucon, and a Chimango Caracara."

World Birder #2: "I need the Lesser Rhea."

World Birder #3: "I've seen them all and I know just where to take you." (World Birder #3 had been birding for three weeks in Tierra del Fuego and its surrounding areas.)

For the next three weeks, I followed these three outstanding world birders. They were: Dr. Arnold Small, staff ornithologist on Society Expeditions' ship, the M/S *World Discoverer*; Dr. James F. Clements, author of *Birds of the World: A Checklist;* and George Venatta, sometimes realtor, oftimes world birder, working his way toward the top of the "list."

Penguins, of course, were what they all wanted to add to their "world bird list."

"*What* is a world bird list?"

I had joined this Christmas expedition simply to *see* penguins. Must they be listed too? Oh, I knew something about bird checklists. Every time I visited Everglades National Park I checked off birds seen. Someone had given me a North American bird checklist; occasionally I remembered to make notations.

Quickly, I learned about world birders, world bird lists, life birds, and life lists. My vocabulary rapidly grew with words like "pelagic" (ocean birds), and "endemic" (in birding parlance, meaning restricted in range to a given island, region, or country). I was even exposed to sexual dimorphism without catching it.

First stop on the voyage was the Falkland Islands. Here, I encountered the sexually dimorphic Kelp Geese and discovered the term, in this case, means that the male is a different color from the female. In this case the male is totally white; the female dark brown. Both are easy to spot from a distance.

Chasing after the world birds, our little band of incipient world birders strode up the hill overlooking Port Stanley and down the road toward the airport, the road beside which Argentinian soldiers were to camp two years later. Walking briskly, our leaders were searching for a plover, a rather small brown bird, the Rufous-chested Dotterel. One of the world birders, having hiked way ahead, began waving wildly. As we ran toward him, I kept thinking, "The damn bird will fly long before we get there." It didn't. It sat there in a small field, just where Arnold Small had thought one might be found.

Arnold Small and Jim Clements, lifelong friends, had never before both seen a "life bird" together. They jumped up and down hugging each

Kelp Geese are an excellent example of sexual dimorphism: the male is all white, the female dark brown

other with the excitement you would have thought Stanley and Livingston might have displayed. Their enthusiasm, as we watched and photographed the bird, was contagious. On our return to the ship, it seemed only proper to order a bottle of wine to celebrate the occasion.

Welcome to the world of world birders. I had no idea there was such a species as "world birder" (*Terrahomo ornithogglus*), as Arnold later dubbed the kind. In Britain, the species could be known as *Homotwitchus ornitholistus*. (Small, 1986.)

It is safe to say that all 125 passengers on Society Expeditions' *World Discoverer* were traveling "to the ice," that Christmas of 1980, with some interest in seeing penguins. A few were backyard bird watchers. Others had but the mildest interest in birds. Some of us considered ourselves experienced bird watchers and always took along our binoculars. Maida Hodges had even taken a nature trip to Argentina and was one up on most of us—she had seen penguins before. Such was the mix of passengers visiting our most remote continent on both the *World Discoverer* and on the pioneering sister ship, the *Society Explorer* (formerly the *Lindblad Explorer*.)

BIRDING XANADU

This book is about world birding, and occasionally about world birders. It is for those who might like to do it around the world, in faraway places with strange-sounding names. It is also about traveling to those places.

"Birding is the best excuse for traveling," a young man remarked as we were bouncing about on an ocean, watching for birds and talking about traveling.

A few comments about what this book is *not*. It is *not* about "Where to Find Birds in Xanadu," in spite of the thought that Samuel Taylor Coleridge's legendary village where "forests ancient as the hills, Enfolding sunny spots of greenery" might have been a good place for *Kubla Khan* to bird as well as build a "stately pleasure-dome." There are many "where to" books on the market, some of which are listed in Part III. But this is *not* a book that will tell the ornithologist or the experienced birder anything new.

It *is* a book for travelers who have developed an interest in the world about them and who travel the highways, byways, and beyond, to experience the world, its antiquities, its architecture, its animals. Those whose idea of travel is only to visit relatives in North Carolina or to attend a Super Bowl game may find little of interest here.

"Birding" is a term that has almost outstripped Webster's dictionary. The term is defined as "the hunting of birds." The verb "bird" is defined as "to catch or shoot birds." Not only do hunters shoot birds, but ornithologists in days of yore shot birds for positive identification. High-powered binoculars, telescopes, high-quality photographic equipment, and the use of mist nets provide more acceptable means of identification now.

The terms "to bird," "birding," and "birder" have become commonplace enough for even *The New York Times*. My friends and I used to consider ourselves "bird watchers," a term still much in use. There is a *Bird Watchers Digest* read by many birders. A sort of professional organization of serious bird watcher/birders, known as the American Birding Association, publishes a bimonthly magazine, *Birding*. Call yourself what you will. The terms "birding" and "birder" will be used in this book to denote an activity and the person of more than casual interest.

BIRDING YOUR ITINERARY

World birding is a relatively new sport, or hobby, or window into the natural world. People have been actively watching birds since biblical times. More recently, in the eighteenth century, Gilbert White, Vicar of Selbourne in England, observed the birds that visited that small place. His *The Natural History of Selbourne* is a birding classic. John James Audubon, painter of birds rather than watcher, nevertheless popularized birds.

It was the dramatic improvement in optics that made it possible to really see birds. Roger Tory Peterson's field guides, utilizing stylized illustrations of birds to emphasize field marks, encouraged large numbers of ordinary people to observe and learn how to identify birds.

Only relatively recently have aids for world birders been published. Although there have been scientific listings of the birds of the world for many years, it was not until 1974 that James Clements first published what has become in the early 1980's the widely used way for North Americans to keep track of birds seen while traveling. The third edition (1981) of *Birds of the World: A Checklist* (really a book) is the edition referred to in this book. It beats all the bits and pieces of paper we once used for record keeping.

Following the success of John Gooders' *Where to Watch Birds in Europe,* first published in Europe in 1970 and in the United States in 1978, Peter Alden and Gooders coauthored *Finding Birds Around the World,* published in 1981. Such books broke from the strictly scientific tradition and were aimed at the traveling birder.

Since the 1950's and 1960's several organizations, such as the Massachusetts and Florida Audubon Societies, have met a rising demand by birders to see birds around the world. More recently, birding tour organizations have been formed expressly to take birders on organized tours led by expert birders. After birding North America first, birders wanted to see birds in the jungles of Mexico, Amazonia, Africa, and other special places throughout the world known for exotic birding.

In England and in some other European countries, similar organizations have formed. In the early 1980's, some of the British bird tour organizations began to advertise in North American birding publications and have begun to attract an international clientele interested in seeing birds in far corners of the world, difficult to reach by independent travel.

Birders have begun traveling to see birds, to see both toucans and temples. Travelers, some of whom were birders, by the thousands began seeking far-off places, partly as a result of the pioneer traveling of Lars Eric Lindblad. Zoos, museums, and universities began offering wildlife tours, and birders signed up.

Not only are people planning to see birds as they plan their itinerary, but they are also planning their itinerary in order to see birds. Most passengers on the *World Discoverer* decided first to travel to Antarctica, and second, while there, to see penguins. World birders reversed the priority: they wanted to add penguins to their list, and went to Antarctica to do so.

Many travelers visit western Canada and Alaska to enjoy some of the most beautiful scenery in the world. Having adopted the habit of taking their binoculars, they see many new birds. If they're very lucky, they may see a Great Gray Owl. That owl is one of the *most* wanted birds among North American birders. Aside from "selling their souls" to add it to their lists, birders would specifically include on their itinerary the places in western Canada and Alaska where they would be most likely to see the "Great Gray."

Some world birding leaders have become intensely fascinated with this relatively new activity. Peter Alden was one of the first of a group of young birding enthusiasts who, in the 1960's and barely out of high school, began circling the globe. His youthful enthusiasm and energy has made him one of the most knowledgeable birders in the world. Other young birders, who were budding naturalists in the 1960's when it became as acceptable for a young boy to be interested in birds as for a girl, are among the best birders today. They write books about birds, lead birding tour groups, and are respected authorities.

Not quite so young is James M. Vardaman, who celebrated his six-tieth birthday in 1981 by planning a spectacular ten-day itinerary that resulted in seeing 1,041 species of birds. Think what he could do in eighty days around the world! Well, in 1984 he clocked 2,532 species by August 27, a feat which set the "World Big Year" record.

HOW TO GET STARTED: EASING INTO WORLD BIRDING

"I wish I knew something about the birds I'm seeing," sighed a passenger on a *Lindblad* trip up the Gambia River in West Africa, as she watched the birders rush to the deck as someone shouted "New bird!" On the ferry between New Zealand's North and South Islands a regular passenger ex-claimed with a sense of accomplishment, "Oh, *that's* a Cape Petrel," as a world birder pointed out the black-and-white bird bobbing in the water.

Birders' enthusiasm is infectious. Nonbirders on a trip, if they're not completely annoyed with the dedicated purposefulness of the birders, often seek to understand why some otherwise sane people become so ex-cited about seeing a bird.

How does this interest in birds develop? Just the way your fishing, skiing, and golfing friends became interested in those activities. Often, friends ask, "Why don't you come along?" You do at the risk of getting hooked or sliced on fairways, slopes, or fishing ponds. At first, you're just a bumbling, stumbling companion. As you become proficient, you really begin to enjoy it. It is the same with birding. A friend invites you to go on a bird walk, and you see many birds that "weren't there before." Soon you become proficient at recognizing the common birds.

Or perhaps the world of birds just bursts upon you like a flash of bright orange. A Spot-breasted Oriole lands on a tree branch.

"What *is* that gorgeous bird?"

Or you find a bird fallen from a nest and nurse it into flighthood. You watch pelicans riding the invisible cushion of air and think how wonderful it would be to fly like that. Or you are real game hunters as were Bob and Mary Lou, but you revolt against the killing, and exchange rifles for binoculars. Thumbing through a friend's bird guide stirs your imagination, and you decide you'd like to know more about birds.

"I saw a very odd looking bird in the parking lot at the store," Edith told her husband as she unloaded groceries. He suggested buying a bird guide. Before making the purchase at the bookstore, Edith leafed through the book and quickly spotted the bird, a Killdeer. Pleased with that easy one, the book was purchased. Now, Edith never leaves home without her bird book and binoculars.

You go on an Audubon bird walk; such excursions are free, open to both novice and expert, and often occur in a local park or wildlife preserve. The leader helps you learn the birds. Struggling alone with her bird guide trying to identify shore birds on Virginia Key in Miami early one Saturday morning, a young, early birder suddenly is surrounded by members of the Tropical Audubon Society on their monthly shorebirds walk. She has never heard of Audubon, didn't realize that anyone but her brother was interested in birds. She is delighted to tag along with other birders eager to help her see new birds.

After you've explored the hometown habitat, any excuse to get away is an excuse to see new birds. Although you may have other ideas of what to do at a Club Med, take your binoculars anyway. Birds are attracted to the lush landscaping of these great vacation spots.

Birding may be a by-product of a camping trip to the Blue Ridge Mountains. In between hammering tent pegs, cooking breakfast on the camp stove, and breaking camp, dozens of birds may come by to investigate. If you're camping in the West, a Steller's Jay may treat you to a stellar performance of policing the camp for stray crumbs.

Business trips can be particularly useful for the birder. If the business meeting ends at Friday noon and you don't have to be back in the office until Monday morning, you may be able to stay over and see new birds and explore a new habitat. Seek advice from your local Audubon Society, check the local Audubon "hot line" in the place you are visiting, buy a "Where to find birds in. . ." guide, check the area for nearby wildlife refuges, state or national parks, and go.

This kind of birding is pretty laid back. It will quench the thirst of many birders. For others, it whets the appetite to go farther and to see more. Perhaps you will be inspired to go and see a particular bird in a particular place.

It was the wonderfully funny-looking puffin that lured me to Alaska. Ten days between two business meetings on the West Coast provided the opportunity. The puffin page in the bird guide had long fascinated me, and I was determined to see the puffins in the flesh. That was the first time a silly bird had determined my itinerary. It was a puffin orgy, first at Glacier Bay, later in the Pribilof Islands. Hundreds of Tufted Puffins and Horned Puffins, the Pacific species. Birds and snowcapped mountains are extraordinary in Alaska.

"What could possibly be more exciting than puffins?"

You guessed it. Penguins.

Travel-birding is an addictive habit. Planning a trip, you automatically include with your bathing suit and sunscreen, your binoculars and bird guide. With some birding experience you may even include a particular locale on an otherwise birdless itinerary in order to see a particular bird.

Author unwittingly took her first step toward world birding when she landed at Gustavus Airport, Alaska, in search of puffins in Glacier Bay

As enthusiasm grows, travel objectives often change from places to see *things* to places and opportunities to see *birds*.

Pat Suiter, vice-president of the Tropical Audubon Society in Miami, tells how she eased into world birding. "With my anthropology background, I wanted to see some of the famous ruins in the world. That need satisfied, I wanted to see the great animals of the world, and I went to India and Kenya. That was wonderful. I began seeing the birds too, and I decided to take some birding trips."

World travelers will have the Taj Mahal at the top of the "must see" list. Most birders want to see such magnificent sights too. With teary eyes, they wonder at its marvelous symmetry and incredible beauty. They photograph. But walking through the lovely garden surrounding the world's most famous temple of love, they also enjoy the pretty Yellow-legged Green Pigeon, and other birds flitting from tree to tree. Wandering around the marble terrace surrounding the Taj, one sees the Taj from beautiful angle to more beautiful angle. Down below, shorebirds on the Yamuna riverside, and the Dusky Crag Martin, will especially delight the birder. There are birds everywhere.

Senegal and The Gambia in West Africa are not high on most travelers' travel-priority lists. However, when an unusual opportunity arose to go birding there with Peter Alden, one of the world's most peripatetic and knowledgeable birders, those little-known countries zoomed in seconds to the top of the list. Visiting that part of Africa, brought to the world's attention by Alex Haley in *Roots,* getting to know the people as well as the birds, was a remarkable experience. I might have missed it if I had not been pursuing new birds.

BEYOND THE CAPITAL CITY CIRCUIT

A traveler/explorer who has spent a lifetime doing his thing around the world spoke at a meeting of the local Sierra Club awhile back. At the end of a fascinating slide-lecture on a recent trip to Borneo (an island southwest of the Philippines), he was asked,

"You've seen so many places in the world. Where else is there to go?"

"I haven't seen *most* of the world," he responded.

Some travelers specialize in the capital cities of the world. Tour operators specialize in the "Capital City Circuit." Sometimes they play the game, "How many capital cities can we fit into two weeks?" For some, the game tires quickly. They long to see more of a country than broad boulevards, equestrian statues, art museums, and fancy restaurants.

"I'm tired of cities and all the hubbub. I think I've seen every museum and cathedral in Europe!"

Opportunities for traveling adventures are countless. A serious interest in birding can open up to the active imagination places hardly dreamed of. There's a whole world beyond Paris, London, and Rome. London to the Farne Islands' seventh century bird sanctuary. Beyond Bangkok, there's a rainforest getaway, the Khao Yai National Park, the northern city of Chiang Mai, the mountainous border area, Doi Pu Muen. After Lima, the Abra Malaga, high atop the Andes. After Bombay, the ancient city of Madurai. Kuala Lumpur (Malaysia) and then Malaysia's famous Taman Negara National Park, reached by dugout canoe. The mountainous Szechwan province in China. Beyond Istanbul, ancient Cappadocia. Rio de Janeiro to the beautiful forested hills of Itatiaia National Park. After Kenya, Namibia and Botswana. Leave Panama City and go up to the mountain rainforest of the Chiriquí. Bolivia, Bali, San Blas—all beckon.

Birders travel to see birds in places such as these. For more and more birders, their hobby expands horizons. Travelers who bird along the way have added an extra dimension to their travels, one that adds extra interest to any trip no matter where the destination or what the primary purpose. Those travelers can be spotted with binoculars around their necks, a bird guide in their flight bag.

"Hell, I don't want to take another Caribbean cruise. I was bored stiff last time."

Birding cures boredom. Ask any birder. Birding around the world cures it more. It adds a fillip, "something that serves to excite or stimulate."

Each person makes a choice of how to spend time and money. Maida Hodges, who visited the Antarctic, for years had no finished flooring in her Vermont house. The cost of a trip to the Antarctic would buy the finest flooring available. Looking at carpet samples one day, she thought about the whales in Baja California; and the bare boards went uncovered for a while longer.

Although birding can be one of the most inexpensive of hobbies, if it is to be combined with extensive traveling, one needs both time and money. A few birder/travelers manage to combine such an avocation with a vocation, even a mid-life change. A physician who decided that medicine was really not what was going to give him a satisfying and happy life gave a new twist to his knowledge of biology. He began to lead nature trips to exotic places around the world, places he wanted to go anyway.

WHAT, WHY, WHO, WHERE, WHEN?

WHAT is Birding?

Ben King, one of the world's top birders, in *Birding* magazine said, "Birding is a leisure-time activity which is done for fun."

It is elbow-bending, hoisting binoculars and looking at a bird. Once you've seen the bird, observed its characteristics of appearance or behavior, you identify it, generally with the aid of a bird guide. You may simply remember its name or you may write it down on a piece of paper, on a bird checklist, or in the bird guide.

Birding is seeing birds where you are. World birding is going someplace—close to home or on the other side of the world—to see more birds. Birding is an active interest in the birds of the world, just as snorkeling is an active pursuit of the underwater world.

WHY Do People Bird?

Birding is fun without being fattening or sinful. How many of your activities fit that definition? People get into birding for many reasons. Birding gets you up early in the morning and, while the early bird gets the worm, you get the bird. It's a socially acceptable activity although traditionally considered somewhat odd. Nobody, however, wonders at the sanity of the golfers who arise early to get a good starting time, or at the jogger who wants to do five miles before going into the office. (Well, some of us wonder about joggers.)

Such activities are engaged in because people think they are fun, as well as being good physical or intellectual exercise. Some people bird, others golf, dive, ski, fly, or collect stamps. They do it because they enjoy it.

Birding is one of the healthiest "sports" you can take up, for both brain and brawn. You have to go out of doors into the sunshine and fresh air. Fresh air is good to breathe. You have to walk, an excellent exercise all by itself. For the serious birder there are long hikes, sometimes climbing up and down hills to locate special habitats, and an occasional slog through a swamp. Identifying birds is a challenge, like fitting together the pieces of a puzzle.

Birding wipes away the cares of the world, literally with flights of fancy. Sometimes it is personal tragedy that leads to the need for a new emotional outlet. A recent widow on a South Texas birding trip had always enjoyed the out of doors and thought that birding might be a good activity to add new interest to her life. A widower on a Jamaica birding trip had traveled much of his life without ever noticing birds. He too was seeking an absorbing interest and found that the challenge of identifying new birds opened up new worlds for him.

Phoebe Snetsinger, one of North America's most respected birders, was told several years ago that she had only a few months to live. She already was an active birder and decided that if she had only a limited time left, the thing she most wanted to do with the rest of her life was to see the birds in the rest of the world. Five years after her surgery, doctors found no further spread of the melanoma. "I've won my game," Phoebe says. She beat the medical odds—she topped 5,000 world birds on a trip to the Philippines in January 1986, to hold the women's "championship" title, and came home to plan to see the Kagu in New Caledonia in 1986 and Antarctica in 1987.

Certainly, birding can't cure cancer. The passion for birding exhibited by many world birders can go a long way toward overcoming some permanent or temporary pain.

Arnold Small, suffering from a foot ailment, nevertheless went on a thirty-mile hike (each way!) to see one of the great birds of the world, the Horned Guan, at El Triunfo in Chiapas, Mexico.

WHO Are Those Crazy Bird Watchers?

There are some crazies and some "little old ladies in tennis shoes." It is likely, however, that the lady (of indeterminate age) is wearing hiking boots and the tennis shoes are worn by an eager, young lad. Seeking to dispel the common image, Maida and Rachel on one of their Plum Island jaunts to catch the migration, decided to project a more "macho, heavy-metal biker image."

"Rachel wore a black motorcycle hat and we always had a six-pack of beer conspicuously in view. Upon spotting new birds we swore and swigged as much as possible." Lots of people watch birds. Probably several million, including a real "macho" fireman on another Plum Island visit.

An Audubon Society field guide to the birds of eastern North America sold a million copies in ten printings. Peterson's most recent *A Field Guide to the Birds East of the Rockies* made *The New York Times* best-seller list. *Publishers Weekly Yearbook,* in its 1983 list of "All-time Hardcover Best Sellers: Adults' and Children's Books," reported that the Peterson guide ranked thirty-second out of eighty-eight titles; a whopping 1,408,605 copies had been sold. The American Birding Association, founded in 1969 by Jim Tucker and a handful of friends, now has 7,000 members. These tend to be the "hard core" birders. *Living Bird Quarterly,* the membership journal for the Cornell University Laboratory of Ornithology, reports that Lab membership has grown rapidly from 3,000 in 1982 to 11,000 in 1985. The National Audubon Society has a half-million members.

Birders are businesspeople, realtors, teachers, college students, retired just-about-everythings, bankers, lawyers, nurses, printers, chemists, actuaries, astronomers, dietitians. Birders come in every conceivable size, shape, sex, age, race, nationality, or handicap. A man with withered legs, confined to a wheelchair, nevertheless became an expert birder, overcoming his reluctance at having people stare at him as he was being wheeled up the Himalayas.

WHERE? Birders See Birds Everywhere.

Prince Philip, the Duke of Edinburgh and a founder of the World Wildlife Fund, was being interviewed by Norman Myers for *International Wildlife* magazine. In response to the question, "Do you try to find time to look at wildlife now?" the Duke replied:

> Oh Lord, yes. I always travel with binoculars. If I stay at an embassy, it nearly always has a garden, and if I go out for an hour in the morning, I can usually find something interesting to look at—largely birds, I suppose, because there are more of them and they are so much easier to watch. If I go to Balmoral Castle in Scotland, I usually drive around to see what birds there are, because if you go to the same place frequently, you get to know that this is here and that is there. So you go out to see whether the grey wagtails are there or whether the last of the plovers have left for the winter.

Birders see birds everywhere; the places to see them are vitually endless, as experienced birders know. There are few activities in which one can engage that will not produce a bird or three, if you're looking. Even a golfer can see more than a birdie. The rafter splashing down the Nenana River in Alaska will look up (while hanging on tightly) to see Golden Eagles circling overhead.

Fields and Forests. Of course, look high in the canopy; low in the undergrowth. Walk across a stubbly field, and you may flush a quail. Coming through the woods, be alert to chatters of a feeding flock of mixed species; you might see a dozen species in a minute or so.

Roads and Expressways. Even driving in the fast lane can be productive. Along the expressway shoulder in Miami, you spot a Smooth-billed Ani amongst a group of grackles; an Osprey circling high overhead. Glancing quickly out the window, you see a Great Blue Heron flying over a pond. A stoplight at an intersection may be an occasion to spot birds on wires, perhaps a Budgerigar among the European Starlings in west coast Florida.

Pull off the road if you want to get a good look at that hawk overhead. Don't try this on the interstate, however. Getting a good look at a Swallow-tailed Kite may be your top priority, but the state road patrol does not consider birding an emergency. On a country road, stop where there is a pond, trees, a marsh, or scrubby field. Keep the windows open and *stop, look,* and *listen.*

Listen all the time. You will hear the call of a bird you want to see. Or you may hear some birds "mobbing"—angrily screeching. When you investigate you may spot an Eastern Screech Owl or a Sharp-shinned Hawk up in the live oak tree.

Even adversity can provide rewarding birding. Good looks at Sandhill Cranes have resulted from car trouble. Driving north on the Florida Turnpike, it was a faulty radiator that delayed the first leg of a vacation trip. There in the distance, under a patch of sabal palms, were three stately cranes, a life bird.

My first Long-billed Curlew also owes its sighting to a radiator problem: the gas station attendant in Raton, New Mexico, forgot to replace the cap. Heading across the Oklahoma panhandle, we boiled over. Boiling our ice on the camp stove was the only solution to producing water in that arid land, but looking across the grassy field was my "lifer."

On safari in Africa, flat tires are a common occurrence. Rather than being a disaster, it provides the opportunity for everyone to get out of the minibus and stretch. If you're looking for birds, you may spot a Vitelline Masked Weaver building its ball-shaped nest in the nearby acacia tree.

Trains and Buses. The alert birder will be scanning the fields from train or bus. Birders, quick of eye, spotted a half dozen life birds on the train trip down the lovely gorge, following the Urubamba River on the trip from Cusco to Machu Picchu in Peru.

Traveling by bus in England, we passed a field full of startling black-and-white birds with plumed crests, Northern Lapwings. Although the bird is common on farmlands throughout Britain and Europe, a nonbirder friend, taking the same route, said she never saw any birds.

Cities. Even in cities, there are opportunities to bird, although the cityscape will not normally be the birder's favorite habitat. The nearby park is likely to produce more than the ubiquitous park pigeon. Walking to the park also provides an opportunity to see more of the city. You get out of the stuffy hotel and find out what a beautiful day it is. Check out the hotel grounds. Many a "lifer," a bird never seen before, will be found. Although North Americans consider it one of their own birds, the beautiful Vermillion Flycatcher was a first for me at my hotel in Quito, Ecuador.

Looking out the hotel window is a good place to look for birds. In Miami, it may well be a Fish Crow. In Nairobi, it will be the Pied Crow with a white neck. In London, it will be the crow with the grayish nape, a Jackdaw. At the Imperial Hotel in Tokyo, it may be the Azure-winged Magpie. In Port Moresby, New Guinea, they are likely to be Rainbow Lorikeets.

These may be life birds for you. On a recent trip to London, having to catch an early morning plane, I was up at first light, looking out the hotel window to the adjoining field. My first partridge—actually a pair—poked their way through the high grass in pursuit of breakfast.

The only place where I didn't see a single bird—not even a crow or a House Sparrow—within walking distance of a hotel, was at Anaheim, California, within sight of Disneyland. There must be some irony in that. A little boy in a water taxi crossing a real lake on the way from Disneyland back to the campground pointed to a real island where a Great Blue Heron stood motionless. "Is it *real?*" he asked his mother.

Don't even assume that a city street is devoid of bird life. Check the top of the next building—you might see a Kestrel or a Peregrine Falcon perched on the roof. A Peregrine Falcon living on the thirty-third floor of the U.S. Fidelity and Guaranty Building in Baltimore made the September/October 1985 issue of *Bird Watcher's Digest.*

Cemeteries. These are often great places for bird-finding. They have trees and flowers and grass, and they're quiet. Check out the historic Key West cemetery and maybe find a rarity. Wander through the cemetery in North Yorkshire in England and look for the Tawny Owl. Try the Mount Auburn Cemetery in Cambridge, Massachusetts, superb for spring migrants.

Airports. Definitely not quiet, the vast stretches of flatland on which airports are built are attractive to certain kinds of wildlife like jackrabbits and Burrowing Owls. The Key West and Marathon airports are good places to see, and especially to hear, the Antillean Nighthawk. David Keys was astounded to spot a California Quail when he landed at Auckland, New Zealand.

Peter Alden explains that in many lands, airports are among the few refuges, free from hordes of hunters. Many birds of the grasslands find safety there. Watch for bustards at Spanish airports. Do, however, be aware of security. Peter, being poked by a bayonet in the stomach, was probably taken for a spy when all he was doing was checking Sand Grouse from the top of the gangway at the Kuwait Airport.

Garbage Dumps and Sewage Ponds. These are among the best places to see birds. Just don't breathe. A birder/traveler could compile a substantial bird list by visiting such places. If you're driving through a strange town, ask, or follow the sign to the landfill. At the sewage treatment plant on Virginia Key in Miami, along with a fantastic collection of shorebirds, you are likely to see Smooth-billed Anis and maybe a Bald Eagle. The Brownsville, Texas, dump is famous among birders. Great varieties of birds are there in the wintertime. One of them will likely be another tourist, the Mexican Crow.

Highway Rest Stops and Picnic Areas. These are often good birding areas. Watch a Cactus Wren fish a piece of bread out of the trash can at a rest stop in New Mexico. A recent trip along the interstates in California and Arizona produced a rest stop "list" of thirty-three species in eight stops, including a Golden Eagle, and a ground squirrel chasing a Greater Roadrunner.

Zoos. Zoos often have fine aviaries. Some provide good introductions to birds you may be seeing on your travels. Metrozoo, south of Miami, has a beautiful display, the Wings of Asia. Beautiful as these birds are, they're in cages, even if the cage is a huge walk-through aviary. Often, wild birds will be attracted to zoos and will help the birds and animals with breakfast. While you're wandering around the San Diego Wild Animal Park, watch for Black Phoebes, Lincoln's Sparrows, Audubon's Warblers. Golden Eagles have also nested there. The New Delhi Zoo grounds seems to have comfortable nesting places for the striking Painted Storks. Perhaps seeing local and exotic endangered species, such as the California Condor, increasingly being bred in zoos, will renew your dedication to conservation measures.

WHEN? Birders do it in the Daylight and the Dark.

Though some of us groan at the thought, the best time to see most birds is early in the morning. This is particularly true for tropical birds; they're active very early, and tend to rest in the heat of the day. However, you can walk into the forest in the middle of the day and you will still see birds. They may not be the same ones, but there are always birds around.

Be alert to birds that fly away from their roost to feed during the day. You'll want to catch them before they leave the roost, or in the evening when they return. Scarlet Ibis returning to their mangrove roosts in Caroní Swamp in Trinidad; Roseate Spoonbills to their roosts in the Ding Darling Wildlife Refuge on Sanibel Island, Florida—these are among the most spectacular sights in the natural world. Parrots, raucous and colorful, are favorite evening sights wherever they occur.

Do it at night if you want to catch owls, frogmouths, potoos, pauraques, and the like. A well-placed flashlight beam is generally needed. Some birds, like nighthawks, will be seen just before dark.

Whenever you have time, grab your binoculars and search wherever you happen to be. Have a layover of a few hours at the airport? You may have time to take a taxi or arrange with a birder friend to stretch your legs in a nearby birding area. Coming into Kennedy? Head for the Jamaica Bay Wildlife Refuge for lots of water birds and perhaps a rarity. If the layover is in Rome, take advantage of Alitalia Airlines' free offer and go on the Graffiti archaeological tours to historic places nearby. Never mind that you aren't interested in ancient digs; in such places there are bound to be birds.

BIRDERS SEE MORE THAN BIRDS

"At any rate, even though the birding was disappointing, we saw fabulous numbers of animals. The final count was something like two dozen moose, 15 or so caribou, 4 grizzlies, four-dozen or so Dall sheep, 1 muskrat,

1 very big beaver, and 1 enormous porcupine, slowly waddling across the road in front of us while we were walking one night." Mary and Tom Wood were writing to friends about their Alaskan adventure.

Alaska is wildlife heaven. Puffins in the Pribilofs are almost upstaged by Northern Fur Seals—hundreds of thousands of them—stunning and snorting nonstop. Seals also go with penguins on Antarctic beaches. Southern Fur Seals, Crabeaters, Weddell Seals, enormous Elephant Seals, and slinky Leopard Seals, scouting the shoreline for a tasty, if hapless, penguin. Killer whales arching out of the water in tandem. Whales and porpoises of all kinds are spotted on ocean voyages and pelagic birding trips. Perhaps more than hunters, birders see animal life few people see outside a zoo: foxes, wolves, reindeer, marmots, porcupines, antelope, badgers, monkeys in the treetops, coatimundi, agouti, tapir, alligators and crocodiles, bats, salamanders, snakes, and spiders.

Birders see mountains, valleys, forests, swamps, deserts, bogs, seas, and shores. They see their own neighborhood, the parks and wildlife preserves, their country. World birders see parts of the world the "Capital City Circuiter" is blind to.

Birding is an "ever new" experience. One sees new sights every time. New birds, new things about old birds, orchids in the treetops, "stuff" on the beach, tracks of tiny feetlike necklaces in the sand, the magic of early morning mist.

For some people, traveling is a way of life. For some people, birding is a way of life. For people who catch both the traveling and the birding bug, the world has virtually unlimited horizons. Just remember to take your binoculars.

Author never leaves home without binoculars (but always leaves the cat behind)

BIRDERS' JARGON

Birders, like persons in most specialized endeavors, develop their own jargon, often confusing to beginning birders. Some terminology is colloquial, but as birders meet other birders, the jargon spreads. As you encounter birders around the world, you may find these phrases and terms helpful. More serious definitions will be found in the Glossary in Part III.

Common phrases

It just flew. By far the most common phrase uttered by birders worldwide. Also *It just dropped. There it goes. It's gone.*

Going away from the boat. Similar to above.

I saw where it flew from. Easier to see where the bird's been than where it is now.

It's at nine o'clock about two feet in from the edge of the branch. You need to know your "o'clocks" (nondigital) to spot birds. Visualize the tree ahead of you as the face of a clock; train your binoculars on where nine o'clock would be; then move them in toward the trunk about two feet.

Straight ahead, flying right to left. Gives you an idea of where to start looking.

You should have been here yesterday—the trees were alive with birds. Of course today, you're watching starlings and House Sparrows.

Common terms

Banding. Nothing to do with marching to music. It is the attachment of a small identification ring to a bird's leg so that its travels can be charted as others report the identification number. Birders must have permission from appropriate wildlife agencies to do this. The British call it *Ringing.*

Big Day. Not a day with more than twenty-four hours, but a race, fairly common among competitive North American birders, where they see how many species of birds they can see in one twenty-four-hour period. It's catching on in other countries.

Bins. Not rubbish containers. British shorthand for binoculars.

Bird guide. Same as *bird book* or *field guide.* Generally refers to a pocket-sized book, easy to carry into the field, which provides brief descriptions of birds, along with drawings or photographs to aid in identification.

Blew it. Not as a gunner blows it away. It refers to a bird you were supposed to "get," but you took the wrong path, got there too late, etc. Similar to *hosed* (your expectations were drenched).

Blind. Does not refer to birder's eyesight, or that of the bird. Is a structure to allow the birder to remain hidden from the bird's view but with peepholes through which to see or photograph the bird. The British call them *hides.*

Broad-bill. "Sophisticated" birders often refer to a bird by an adjective, but don't be fooled by this one. If you are sure of where you are, you'll know which one is being discussed. If you're on an Old World beach, it will be the Broad-billed Sandpiper. If you're in an Asian forest, it will be a member of the broadbill family, Eurylaimidae. On the other hand, if you're on a Pacific island, it will be an Old World Flycatcher such as the Guam Broadbill. See *TV* below.

Checklist. List of birds to be found in a particular area with a place for the birder to put a check mark upon seeing the bird. Sometimes checklists are included in a field guide; often they are separate folded lists on card stock that fit neatly inside the field guide. Extensive checklists often are pamphlet or even book-size.

Christmas Count. Doesn't mean counting Christmases in a pear tree, but rather the annual Christmas Bird Count sponsored by the National Audubon Society, in which volunteers all over North America, and occasionally elsewhere, count the number of birds of each species that are seen in the course of a day. Lists are later published and used for year-to-year comparisons.

Chum. Not a good buddy, but bits and pieces thrown overboard on pelagic trips to attract fish to attract birds, e.g. pieces of fish, popcorn. Participants suffering from *mal de mer* are also said to be "chumming."

Clements. As in, "I've checked it in my Clements." Common practice of using the name of an author as a "thing;" shorthand for, "I've checked it in the *Birds of the World: A Checklist* by James Clements." Same shorthand applies to well-known authors of field guides: "Did you bring your Peterson?"

Confusing fall warblers. Roger Tory Peterson coined the phrase; refers to look-alike warblers that have lost their distinguishing breeding plumage. The Peterson North American guides arrange them on separate pages to help you figure them out.

Crippler. Not a stumble that breaks your leg, but an exciting species you see for the first time, or a real rare bird for some time or place. British twitchers love cripplers.

Dipped out. British term indicating that you failed to find the bird you were looking for. Similar to *gripped off,* which means that someone else saw the Mountain Tailorbird in the tall bush next to the stream, but when you got there it was gone.

Dropped. Hopefully does not refer to your binoculars but to the bird that was in sight but just dropped down into the bushes.

Dude. British term describing a "bird watcher," impeccably dressed, binoculars neatly stored in unblemished case. Should be avoided by "real" birders.

Early birder. Maybe a person who arises at dawn to go birding. In this book, it is a birder at the early stages of birding.

Field mark. Doesn't mean you've marked a field for further study. It is the characteristic marks of a bird seen in a field, e.g. black cap, white wing bars, that help identify it. Peterson field guides have pointers to important field marks.

Flying gas hog. Plane in air.

Got/have. Among the most useful words in a birder's vocabulary. "What have you got?" "I got three life birds in that one field." "Get anything?" "We had a Sungrebe in Peru." Translates as "see."

Hot line. Nothing that will burn you. May refer to the North American Rare Bird Alert, a national system of finding out, or being notified, of where rare birds are being seen; or to informal systems where one birder simply calls another birder to identify where a special bird may be found. May also be called a "grapevine."

Jizz. Not a new form of music, but a vague combination of a bird's characteristics—size, shape, behavior—that can help the observer identify a bird at a distance when field marks are not visible; particularly useful for seabirds and hawks. May be subconscious identification.

Kettle. No, not for boiling water. Describes a formation of migrating or soaring birds spiraling around warm thermals.

LBJ. Short for "Little Brown Job." Describes a small nondescript bird that probably was not identified. In some circles, known as a *COK*, "Christ Only Knows," or simply a *UFO*. Similar to *BVD*, "Better View Desired." Quite the opposite is a clear identification of a special bird known as a *BGB*, "Bloody Good Bird"—British, of course.

Life bird or *lifer.* Not the bird of a lifetime or a person incarcerated for a heinous crime; it refers to a bird that the birder has never before seen, i.e., first time in your life you've seen that species.

Life list. A list of all the birds that a birder has seen to date. Inveterate listers will update this list with their "lifers" after each birding trip. To "list" means to keep a list or to check off on a printed list the birds you have seen.

Lumping. Nothing to do with moguls on the ski slope. Refers to a decision of ornithological arbiters that what had been two separate species, are now one. Opposite is *Splitting.*

Migratory trap. Doesn't have steel jaws, you'll be glad to know. A place where migrants are forced to congregate in abnormal numbers due to surrounding inhospitable terrain.

Mobbing. Might seem to apply to the way birders rush to spot a rarity, but it really means the tendency of some birds to scream and fly at predatory birds or even snakes. Crows' or Blue Jays' mobbing noises may signal an owl nearby.

Need/want. Does not refer to Maslow's hierarchy of human needs. It is used to identify a species the birder wants to see in order to list it: "I need a Painted Redstart."

Paddy bashing. When you do it, you're not hitting an Irishman on the head, but walking through rice paddy fields looking for birds.

Peeps. General terminology for the small sandpipers heard "peeping," often difficult to identify.

Pick up. Does not refer to a date. Translates to, "Add a species to the list," as in, "I want to pick up an Indian Black Eagle."

Pishing. Refers to silly sounds birders sometimes make while standing in front of an absolutely birdless bush. They hope some hiding bird will pop out to investigate the "pshh, pshh, swhh, swhh," thinking it might be an invader. Noted birder/author Peter Alden says pishing has nothing to do with attracting birds, but is just the sound bird leaders make to vent their frustration at not being able to show birds to the group. Sometimes it does work, though. Also try kissing the palm or back of your hand. Or try a mechanical "squeaker." May also refer to "pishing in the bushes."

Raft. This one is not the one that floats you down the river, but a large bunch of seabirds resting close together on the water surface.

Rare bird alert. Don't listen for the siren to go off when a bird, rare to a particular habitat, occurs. In North America it includes a national computerized, telephone-access system by which birders may find out about rare birds, or be notified of their presence. Most urban areas and states have a tape-recorded message one can call to find out about recent important sightings.

Shank. Used more in the rest of the world than in North America. Refers to Redshanks, Greenshanks, Lesser Yellowlegs, all *Tringa* sandpipers. Also learn "greensand," not an unusual geologic occurrence but another *Tringa,* the Green Sandpiper.

Skin(s). Not off your nose. Refers to preserved dead birds, in museum or university collections, that are studied by ornithologists and serious birders seeking help in identifying a difficult bird, or seeking to learn about a bird's plumage.

Smart bird. Does not refer to a bird's intelligence but to a bird's attractive appearance. Mostly a British term.

Split/splitting. Does not refer to firewood or infinitives. Is the opposite of "lumping," meaning that a heretofore single species has been divided into two or more separate species. Listers get a bonus bird.

Spuh. Articulation of "sp.," short for "species." Used to indicate that the bird was clearly a member of a genus containing several lookalike species such as the *Empidonax* flycatchers or the *Phylloscopus* warblers, but that the species was not determined.

Stickbird. Also "twig bird," "leaf bird," etc. Means the birder has sighted something that looks like a bird but on checking with binoculars finds it has turned out to be just a stick. "Falling leaf birds" are common in deciduous forests, diverting the birder's attention momentarily; occasionally being confused with butterflies, another common distraction.

Stringy. Doubtful identification. A *Stringer* is a birder with a reputation for stringy calls. Common British term.

Stuff. Has two meanings: "There's a lot of stuff in that tree" means, "It looks like there are a lot of birds in that tree." "It dropped into the stuff at the bottom of the tree" refers to weeds, sticks, rubble on the ground under the tree.

Tick. Mostly a British phrase, only partly translatable into American. To "tick" a bird is generally equivalent to checking the species on a checklist. Using the word as a noun usually means the birder has just seen a life bird: "That was a good tick." In North America, ticks bite.

Trash bird. Humorous reference to a long-sought-after or rare species that suddenly turns up in unexpected numbers. A first sighting of a Bald Eagle on a birding trip is generally cause for some excitement, but after the tenth sighting, it might be referred to in a kindly way as "the trash bird of the day."

Twitcher. Common British term describing the person who is more interested in "ticking" off a large number of birds than in knowing much about them; twitches with the excitement of seeing a new bird, rushes off to twitch again. Often drives long distances between twitches.

TV. One of the most commonly used abbreviations in New World; stands for Turkey Vulture. Acronyms are common among birders. Easier to say GBB or JEEB than "Greater Black-backed Gull." In Latin America, the ubiquitous Tropical Kingbird is the TK. Birders also frequently drop off the noun, assuming that everyone knows that "Great Blue" means Great Blue Heron. Ditto for "Little Blue." If you're seeing several "Buff-breasteds" along the beach, it will be the Buff-breasted Sandpiper. Beginning birders should not hesitate to ask, "Buff-breasted what?" British birders often give combined names to a bird that might be one of two similar-looking species: "Comic" is not a funny bird, but probably a Common or an Arctic Tern. "Shagrant" stands for Shag or Cormorant; "Barwit" stands for Bar-tailed Godwit.

Wag. Not what a dog's tail does, but what the bird's tail does. Short for any of the widespread species of wagtail.

Window. Has two meanings: "It's just above the window in the tall tree," means "Look for an opening in the tree branches through which you can see the sky," a window. White patches on the wings of soaring birds are sometimes also referred to as "windows." Look in your bird guide at the white patches on the wings of the skuas and some raptors.

Wiped out. Doesn't mean exhaustion from wiping windows, but success in seeing all the birds of a category: all three species of skimmer in its family *Rynchopidae* (Black, African, and Indian); a representative species from every family of birds.

AUTHOR'S NOTE: Although many birders on many trips have unwittingly contributed to this list, special thanks are due to Peter Alden, Peter Carlton, and Bruce Neville for getting into the swing of definitions.

ᚹ *Two* ᚹ

Tools of the Trade: Essential Equipment

Getting started in the sport or hobby of birding costs less than many others. No special clothes or really expensive equipment is needed. Essential equipment: binoculars. Perhaps only the cane-pole fisher can get by with fewer bucks.

Binoculars are essential. British birder Peter Carlton appears always to be permanently attached to his "bins"

World birding, however, is another story. World travelers content to enjoy birds in the palace gardens in London or Tokyo would be spending money to see those cities anyway. But if you decide you must see penguins in Antarctica, the cost of birding quickly escalates. World birders find that as they add more and more birds to their list, it costs more and more for each new species.

Sometimes working out the price on a unit/cost basis can be a psychological salve. Although a trip to Antarctica is very expensive, you do see lots of penguins. On a unit/cost basis, my trip turned out to be three cents per penguin. Cost per species would have been quite another matter.

Maida Hodges has some creative approaches to costing out her birds. She suggests a graduated scale from an LBJ to a two-color, three-color, or rainbow-hued bird. She would add extra points for unusual crests and wattles. Identifying herself as a "sophisticated world birder," she says, "I, for one, like pretty birds, bigger than a bread box, easily seen, that fly close and stay put, and also contrast nicely with their ambient background."

Dreamer!

As is the case with most hobbies or sports, you can keep it simple and inexpensive, or you can get terribly involved.

Although Shirley, my roommate in the Pribilof Islands, was on a nature tour with borrowed binoculars, that's not a good idea. (Nor is it a good idea *at all* for a couple to think they can share binoculars.) Shirley, who showed up ten years later at Machu Picchu, assured me she had since bought her own.

A close second to binoculars in essential equipment required is a field guide to the birds in the area where you live. You can enjoy birding for years, as many do, with these two pieces of equipment.

Some additional equipment costs only pennies. A small notebook and pencil are a good idea in order to list species, maybe numbers of birds seen and perhaps to make notes of unusual habitat or weather. In this wondrous electronic age, you might even decide to dictate your notes on a small tape recorder—not expensive to buy today.

If you want to bird watery habitats, or those where the birds are far away, a spotting scope will be in your future. Perhaps you've already "outgrown" your first binoculars and want to upgrade to better, more expensive glasses.

If you really get turned on to world birding, you'll invest in additional bird books: field guides, where-to-find guides, a bird dictionary or encyclopedia, and more general books that will meet your specific interests. To become more proficient in "spotting" birds with your ears, you may want to buy records, tapes, or videocassettes to help the identification process. Graduates into the "hot shot" category, particularly if they're doing tropical birding, may feel the need for a tape recorder with a continuous loop tape to call in birds with an owl's call, or to tape and play back the elusive antbird hiding in the forest shadows. A selection of current aids to better birding will be found in Part III.

BINOCULARS

Wading through a lot of technical information about binoculars may be confusing to the person simply seeking guidance. (I speak from experience.) It is hard in the beginning to get the numbers straight. Some of us agonize over the right choice of binoculars; others rush out blindly and make a bad purchase. This brief discussion may help you get going, but do follow up with one of the recent and much more thorough articles identified in Part III.

Two numbers will be found on all binoculars: 7×35 and 10×40 are examples. The first number indicates the power of the binoculars. A seven-power binocular magnifies your view of the bird seven times; it seems seven times closer than you know it is. A ten-power binocular is more powerful; the bird appears ten times closer.

The second number measures the diameter of the "objective lens," the end of the binocular you don't look through. It controls the amount of light that enters the lenses. The importance of this number is critical in low-light birding; it doesn't make much difference on a bright day with the bird basking in the sunlight. Binoculars with an objective lens of fifty lets a lot more light in than one that measures twenty-five.

If this is confusing, don't worry. Many people who have owned binoculars for years don't understand the numbers. They are important, however, so give it a try.

Another very important consideration for birders is "minimum focal distance." Most binoculars allow you to view the moon and beyond, but if you can't focus on the bird in the nearby bush you're in trouble. Buy binoculars that focus closely, surely under twenty-five feet, and as far under as possible. Some brands are close-focused at the factory; others can be adjusted by experts.

Probably the question most often asked by the budding birder is, "But what binoculars do you use?" To answer this question, a questionnaire was mailed to my companions on a birding trip in April 1985, to the Dry Tortugas off the mainland of Florida. Thirty responses were received, probably close to 100 percent, as some couples may have filled out a single questionnaire. Participants had been birding anywhere from three years to forty-five years and represented an accumulation of 431 years of birding experience.

Several questions were asked, eliciting responses that may help you make a decision. Binoculars with seven-power or eight-power ranked equally at the top of recommendations to a new birder. Top North American birder Benton Basham's response probably summed up the recommendations best: "Choose a 7×35 or an 8×40 under one hundred dollars." The make of binocular did not seem very important to respondents; more than half did not even specify a manufacturer. Another respondent said, "Buy the best you can afford."

Predictably, most respondents started with 7×35 binoculars and believe they chose correctly. For the beginning birder this is a good choice; they are fine for normal birding conditions. Only two of the respondents said they were now using a 7×35 for most or all of their birding. All respondents had upgraded, often going through a succession of glasses, either to a higher power or a better make. (One respondent admitted buying his first with Green Stamps!)

What do these birders use today? Leitz binoculars were the most popular in this particular group. Respondents were nearly equally divided between the Leitz Trinovid 8×40 and the 10×40. Zeiss 10×40 binoculars came in second with one person opting for the Zeiss 10×50. The Nikon was the third most popular brand, seven, eight or nine-power. Nearly all respondents had backup binoculars, sometimes more than one, of a different power, for use under special light conditions, or to keep in the car. The 10×40 was the favored power in upgrade binocular.

My own experience is probably fairly typical. I started out with inexpensive Tasco 8×50's and birded with them for many years. Then came the mercifully lightweight Nikon 9×25. That was fine for South Florida's bright light conditions.

In the low-light understory of the Peruvian jungle I could see a tiny dark brown bird but not the black face of the Black-faced Antbird that leader Ted Parker assured us the bird had. A quick look through Ted's Zeiss 10×40's, and I saw that the bird was not only there, but indeed had a black face and a gray breast. I realized how much I had been missing and vowed to upgrade. After sampling both Leitz and Zeiss binoculars, offered to me by group members for my research, the balance tipped to the Zeiss 10 × 40.

A special note to wearers of eyeglasses. Most binoculars today are equipped with a rubber eyecup that folds down. When you do that, it puts the pupil of your eye the correct distance from the binocular lens.

In summary, don't spend a lot of money until you're sure you want to spend a lot of time birding. Angie was worried about already having invested in fairly expensive binoculars, but they weren't good enough for the dim Thailand jungle. She liked the idea of stowing them under the car seat for emergency purposes when she upgraded.

SPOTTING SCOPES

A spotting scope, often just referred to as a "scope," is particularly useful for birds way out on the mud flat in Sanibel Island, Florida, or in the Great Indian Desert (in northwest India). Actually a telescope, it should be mounted on a tripod. Choose a "flip-lock" tripod that quickly and simply sets up and down. If most of your birding is done from your automobile, the car door or roof makes a satisfactory rest for the scope. Unless there is stationary support, a scope is virtually worthless. The magnification, generally from twenty times to sixty times, requires steadiness for clear viewing.

In the binoculars survey, birders were also asked if they owned a scope. All but three said they did. A Bushnell scope was by far the favorite, with the Bushnell Spacemaster 20–45 topping the list. Numbers here refer to magnification: seeing the bird as if it were from twenty times closer to forty-five times closer. You can go up to sixty or eighty, but heat waves or the slightest movement blur the bird.

Scope and tripod on a trip can be just extra baggage. On a birding trip, leaders will have one or more scopes. Traveling birders make a decision on taking a scope based on the type of birding anticipated, and their eagerness to see every bird close up as quickly as possible.

SOFTWARE

Binoculars in hand, the other essential equipment required, even for the backyard, is a field guide. If your local bookstore does not have the bird guide you want, there are a number of mail-order book dealers listed in Part III who would be happy to hear from you. Some field guides cover a whole continent, e.g. North America. Others are guides to tiny, remote or special places such as Tikal, the magnificent Mayan ruins in Guatemala.

Characteristically, a field guide is small enough to easily be carried on a bird trip, often fitting into a jacket pocket. Most basic guides carry illustrations and brief text identifying important characteristics of the bird

Serious world birders generally find that it's worth the extra effort to bring scopes. Don Bailey and other members of the Birdquest group scoping shorebirds at Khao Sam Roi Yot National Park, Thailand, 1986

you are looking at. Roger Tory Peterson's first *Field Guide to the Birds* pioneered the use of relatively simple illustrations with markers pointing to important characteristics: a yellow rump or a white eye-ring. Typically, a field guide will provide a brief introduction, a labeled drawing of the basic bird, sometimes a checklist, and sometimes helpful information about how to get started. Basic field guides are listed in Part III.

Important for birders who are looking for particular birds, or who want to visit good spots for birding as they travel, are the where-to-find guides referred to in Chapter 3 and listed in Part III. Eager birders may also make use of birding "hot lines" or may subscribe to the North American Rare Bird Alert in order to get up-to-the-minute information on rare sightings. Further information will be found in Part III.

TO LIST OR NOT TO LIST?

A good question. Not all birders are listers; not everyone on a birding trip keeps a list. A list is certainly not essential to the enjoyment many people derive from seeing and identifying birds. George, birding in Thailand, makes a point of not being a lister.

Some birder friends have a mental list of the birds they have seen but, by nature, they simply aren't listers. That aspect of birding just doesn't interest them. They are interested in the variety and beauty of the birds they see on trips around the country or the world. They often view the lister as being someone who cares more about numbers of birds seen than about the birds themselves.

Most serious birders do keep lists. For some, numbers are very important. "I have more marbles than you have." For most, the list is a record, a way of preserving the names of the species of birds. Sometimes it's fun to play the numbers game.

The bird checklist is considered one of the most important pieces of equipment for most serious birders. Most persons who call themselves world birders keep one or more bird lists. Local Audubon Societies and bird clubs often develop their own lists, and most state and national parks and preserves have bird lists. It's a good idea to pick one up. It will help in the identification process. You'll be pleased to find out that the Colima Warbler is in fact found in Big Bend National Park. Keeping the local bird list also helps when you transfer the information to some master list after you get home.

Checklists range in size and complexity, from a simple typed list developed by the director of a local nature preserve to book-sized world checklists. Some field guides contain checklists. Bird checklists can be fairly elaborate affairs and may suit you if you like bookkeeping. In addition to checklists for particular areas, the American Birding Association (ABA) publishes an up-to-date booklet listing all the birds that have been identified in the North American continent.

As in other bird lists, species are listed in taxonomic order. (See Chapter 4 for further information.) This sequence, and the species listed on the ABA list, conform to the North American ornithologists' "bible," the "AOU checklist," updated and revised from time to time. Few amateur birders use this list (a large volume) compiled by the internationally respected American Ornithologists Union. Inevitably, there are computer programs that enable the avid lister to keep the life list current. The Clements Checklist, used by many North American birders, includes a computer coding system

Each birder will answer in an individual way the question, "To list or not to list?" For the inveterate lister, the numbers and kinds of lists are limited only by one's imagination, time, and energy. Some birders keep lists of birds seen at home ("yard lists") or at a nearby nature reserve or park. Some keep county lists and state lists. Then there's a North American list, and finally a world list. The ultimate in listing is the life list.

Periodic lists are another possibility: a separate checklist for every visit to Sequoia National Park; a trip list for the summer vacation; an annual yard, county, state, etc. list. Sometimes during migration an unusual number of different species will be seen on a particular day. This may stimulate the creation of an October 1, 1985, list. Birders can get so caught up in this kind of listing that they will keep detailed records day by day, month by month, year by year.

Bruce Neville is a lusty lister. Bird trip leader for the Tropical Audubon Society (TAS) in Miami, he officially began to count species for his life list on January 1, 1979. Some of us gave ourselves a head start by checking off all the birds we remembered seeing as we were growing up. Bruce, a biologist, has evolved an entire system based on the "Grinnell system" developed by Joseph Grinnell of the Museum of Vertebrate Zoology, University of California, Berkeley.

1. Journal. Into this he transcribes his field notes from every birding trip. He describes the trip and lists all birds seen. (Not satisfied with just birds, he records notes on bugs, rocks, flowers, weather, and even, occasionally, stars.)

2. Notebook of species. There is a page, in taxonomic order, for every species he's seen. He transfers the information from the journal and records date, location, and any unusual characteristics of the particular bird seen. This record not only includes birds seen on birding trips, but those seen on a daily basis. If he saw a Swallow-tailed Kite on his way to work, it would be listed in the notebook.

3. Numerical list. This is his life list. No. 483 is the Purple Sandpiper seen on a trip to Jacksonville, Florida.

4. Book record. He notes the date and place of each new species, or unusual occurrence, in his field guide, a relatively common practice.

5. Year list. Kept in the handy ABA Traveler's List booklet. This list is broken down into several categories:
   a. North America by years
   b. Florida by years
   c. Other states where he has done substantial birding
   d. Trips
   e. Local
      (1) Everglades National Park
      (2) Fort DeSoto Park near St. Petersburg
   f. County (including graphic maps)
      (1) birds seen in each of the sixty-seven counties in Florida
      (2) counties by bird
      (3) number of counties in which each species has been seen

6. Foreign list. Bruce does not yet consider himself a world birder, but he has birded in Ecuador. Obviously, he has an Ecuador list.

This would seem to approach the ultimate in listing. Aside from his compulsiveness about listing, Bruce, who is otherwise a normal human being, uses this information as background material on his birding walks and for a monthly column he writes for the TAS bulletin.

Most of us have a very simple system, keep some list purely for our own satisfaction. The lister may be interested in comparing this year with last year, or building up a personal life list. For many, this is sufficient.

"I'm within ten birds of beating my last year's record of total birds seen."

"My goal is 500 species by the end of the year."

"The spring migration wasn't anywhere near as good as it was last year."

Some birders enjoy ticking off the families of birds as they see a new species representative of that family. In 1986, Miami's superbirder Joel Abramson lacked only two families. Having recently seen the nearly extinct Kagu, the only member of the family Rhynochetidae, on the South Pacific island of New Caledonia, he was planning to take off for Madagascar to see a ground roller (there are five species) of the Brachypteracildae family. But alas! Friend Peter Kaestner of Washington, D.C. made it to the top before the end of the year with the Rufous Gnateater, member of the little-known family, Conopophagidae, confined to South America.

Birders joining organized birding trips will quickly be exposed to the listing phenomenon. Usually a list of anticipated sightings will be sent in advance of the trip. Each day during the trip, a listing session will be held in the evening to check off species seen. After the trip, participants will receive a list of group sightings.

For the competitive soul, there's a national "game." *Birding* magazine, published by the American Birding Association, records the national competition among birders. Each year the magazine publishes a list of birders according to either the number of birds they have seen in one year or the total number on some life list.

There are approximately ninety different categories in which a birder might choose to be listed although the number of categories per birder is limited. One could choose both an annual list for the preceding year and the life list category. One could choose to be listed for total number of birds seen in the world, faunal region, continent, country, or state. Names are listed within each category in numerical order according to the number of species reported. There are rules, of course, and a threshold count that must be achieved before your name can be published.

In 1985, P. Norman Chesterfield was No. 1 with 6,162 birds on his life list, Arnold Small was No. 2 with 5,719, and Miamian Joel Abramson was right behind with 5,691. Phoebe Snetsinger saw 1,713 birds around the world in 1985, putting her in the No. 3 spot on the annual world bird list. She jumped to No. 7 on a world life list with 4,879 birds, and No. 3 on her Missouri list with 324 birds seen in her home state. World bird list author James Clements was among the champion listers in the No. 10 spot for world totals. George Venatta has been working his way up that list and was No. 9 with 4,702. It's like batting averages for birders.

Who are these competitive birders? Some are ornithologists. Some teach ornithology or biology. Some are professional trip leaders. And some are ordinary people who go to work every day but spend their vacations, holidays, and weekends chasing birds instead of golf balls. Joel Abramson is a doctor; Benton Basham, an anaesthesiologist; George Venatta, a realtor.

Big listers, some of the top birders in North America, often participate in a version of "can you top this?" In what is known as a Big Day or Big Year, they seek to top their own or someone else's record number of species seen. In 1984, big lister for a Big Year was birdman James M. Vardaman with 2,800 birds. To reach such a phenomenal total requires time, money, and the assistance of the best birders around the world to guide the big lister to the best places.

All kinds of versions of the listing game have evolved over the years, and appropriate rules have been developed by the American Birding Association (ABA). Sometimes teams compete against each other; results are usually published in *Birding* magazine. Those who become members of the ABA will learn about the latest "Big" events.

In addition to this kind of serious listing, there is a lighter side to the game. You could have your own Big Day List. Or a Going-to-Work List. Or a Railroad Station List. Or a Birds-Seen-on-TV List. A Birds-on-Christmas-Cards or Stamps List. One friend has an Animals-Petted-During-Birding-Trips List. Patting whales in the Sea of Cortez comes up high. Some character even came up with a Tinkle List. That could put a damper on the whole thing!

"Can I list birds I see at the zoo?"

"Can I count the bird that killed itself when it flew into the sliding glass door?"

You can count or list anything you want to. But if you want to be accepted in the birding community, you will scrupulously follow some well-accepted rules. (Only you will know how honest you are.) The ABA published the first "rules" in 1972 and clarified them a decade later. They answer some common questions.

If the bird is in a cage—placed in the cage—at the zoo, you shouldn't count it. It should be "wild" to be counted. If the bird is nibbling a free lunch outside the cage, count it. Occasionally, a wild bird will sneak inside the cage. If you know it's a sneak thief, count it.

Not only must it be wild, it must be alive. If you saw the bird fly into the door, count it. The ABA frowns on counting birds caught in mist nets. The trick is to watch it after its release, and if it is flying normally, count it. If you are cleaning up a Short-tailed Albatross after an oil spill, by all means count it. If you spilled the oil on it, no-no.

BUSTARDS AND BASTARDS: PROPER BIRDING ETIQUETTE

Everyone brings to an activity certain mind sets and attitudes, their own personal equipment. Most birders are unfailingly courteous and helpful. However, occasionally a real "rudie" comes along. Friends birding in England recall being in a small group watching a rare shorebird. A car drove up and a couple of avid "twitchers" jumped out, pushed their way to the front of the group, spotted the bird they had come to see, made their way back to the car, and roared off. At this point the bird everyone had been watching flew.

Another type of bastard shows up in a tight viewing space and insists on getting in front of you, effectively blocking your view of the bird. So, when you spot your first Kori Bustard on your African safari, don't be so excited that you forget there are others in the van. Be sure you're not blocking someone else's view. If you're on a birding trip and only the leader has brought a spotting scope, don't hog the eyepiece. Many leaders will call out "quick look, quick look." After everyone has looked and seen the bird, have a second-helping look, if the bird is still in sight.

There is a birding bastard who excels at keeping the bird a secret. The bird is spotted and studied by this bastard, who will only announce to the group that it was there after the bird has flown. That bastard lists it, while others fume.

Sometimes the bird you are seeking is on private property. Most owners don't object to birders, and many may welcome them if approached politely. Always seek permission to bird private property. Sometimes it will be farmhands who are visible; let them know what you want to do and where on the property you'd like to bird. Most likely they will allow you to bird and will let you know when they're ready to close the gate at the end of the day.

In recent years, prevalent use of tapes to call birds has led to abuses, not of other people so much as of the birds. Artificially altering the bird's environment by repeated playing of tapes of owls or other predators, or of a supposed invader of the territory, can truly distract a bird, particularly during nesting season. In extreme cases, it can cause nest abandonment. Respect the rights of birds as well as people.

Sometimes nesting areas on beaches or other places where people are apt to go are cordoned off to protect nesting sites of such ground nesters as Least Terns or Black Skimmers. Be attuned to the bird sounds around you. A scolding bird may be scolding you, telling you that you've come too close to a nest for the bird's comfort.

Birders who use a birding jaunt as a social occasion and can't refrain from talking to the person next to them are often considered bastards. Silence frequently is vital, particularly on a forest trail. When in doubt, close your mouth.

We've all been bastards at one time or another so don't lay a guilt trip on yourself. Improving your birding skills includes improving your birding etiquette.

THE HOUSE SPARROW IS EVERYWHERE

Another kind of personal equipment that every birder carries along is the accumulation of prior experience in birding. Even when birding on another continent, there are ways of making sense out of the new array of birds. Starting out on your first serious world birding trip doesn't mean you will be baffled by every bird you see. Many birds will be the same as those with which you are familiar; others will have useful similarities.

Almost without fail, the first bird I see in a new place is the House Sparrow. In Punta Arenas before embarking for Antarctica, the first bird was old familiar himself, a widespread immigrant in most of the world.

Your visiting British birding friend sees a familiar duck in the wildlife refuge and exclaims, "Oh, there's a teal," pleased to see a familiar feather.

"That's a Green-winged Teal," you reply, secure in your knowledge that it is a different teal from the Blue-winged Teal.

There are teals on every continent but Antarctica. The Common Teal, *Anas crecca,* is common on ponds and lakes in lots of places around the world. The one North Americans call the Green-winged Teal is a bit larger, actually is a subspecies, *Anas crecca carolinensis.* (For your second lesson in Latin, see Chapter 4.)

While on that safari, look for the bird that looks like our meadowlark singing in the low thornbush. It looks familiar, but has an odd name, the Yellow-throated Longclaw. It behaves somewhat like our meadowlark but is in a different family, that of wagtails and pipits. And in the faraway Falkland Islands is the Long-tailed Meadowlark. Doesn't bear much resemblance to the North American varieties for it has a red breast and lacks the characteristic black V on the breast. But it belongs to the same family, in fact the same genus. More about family, genus, and species in Chapter 4.

The Cattle Egret, which arrived in Florida in the early 1950's, has rapidly spread across much of the world in suitable habitats (where cattle, other grazing animals, or even tractors stir up the bugs in the grass). It's a nice familiar bird to see in a foreign environment.

People know crows and crows evidentally know they're birds. These Common Crows are "cawing" the birds of one of the Everglades National Park's well-known ponds

Even nonbirders know crows. That's a start when you see a large black bird in many places around the world; at least you know where in the bird book to look. And on the page with English crows, you quickly figure out that the crow may be a Rook.

Flycatchers, among the most numerous species of birds in the world, have similar characteristics although it's often difficult to distinguish one species from another. There are two different families, New World fly-catchers and Old World flycatchers. They all feed on flying insects. The Phoebe you learned in childhood is a New World flycatcher. "It acts like a flycatcher," you'll say as you check the flycatcher page in your Mexican bird guide.

"It looks like a robin," you'll think as you're on your way to identi-fying the Mistle Thrush on your trip to England. By knowing that the American Robin is a thrush, the identification is easy. But on that trip to England you discover their "robin" looks different; it's smaller with an orange breast. It too is a thrush. The "robin" in Australia may have a pink or yellow breast. It's actually an Old World flycatcher. Although "robin" is a common bird name, different robins come from different families.

When you first became interested in birds, you discovered that some "gulls" were actually terns. You learned the differences in shape and behavior. Gulls are gulls and terns are terns around the world; some species are found worldwide. Otherwise it's just a case of figuring out which species of tern is flying over the Ganges River.

Herons, ibis, egrets, ducks look pretty much the same around the world. From your knowledge of North American or European species, you're on your way to identifying similar species in North Africa or Australia. Osprey and Peregrine Falcon, wherever they occur, are the same species.

Snowy Egret on photographer's favorite perch at Mrazek Pond, Everglades National Park

From familiarity with the common House Wren with its perky uplifted tail, you easily identify as a wren the Canyon Wren of the American West (the much larger Cactus Wren may fool you). Instinctively you think "wren" when you see the little blue bird with the incredibly long, cocked tail in Australia. That "wren" is in a different family, the Old World warblers, but when you look up "wren" in the Australian field guide, you'll find it.

World birders quickly learn there are hemispheric differences between birds found in the New World and in the Old World. Many species and families of birds are found either in the New World or in the Old World but not in both. Motmots are fairly widespread in tropical New World, not elsewhere. Bee-eaters are found only in the Old World. Old World warblers are mostly over there, but gnatcatchers and kinglets, members of that family, are found in the New World. Barbets are widespread in both "Worlds."

Woodpeckers have many different appearances both in North America and where they are found elsewhere. They all have the same characteristic—they peck wood. If the bird is probing rather than pecking, it may be one of the large number of woodcreepers—different family, different order.

OBSERVATION SKILLS

As important as having binoculars is knowing where to point them. Your eye and your visualization skills are essential in helping others see and identify your bird. The Indian Peacock sitting on a branch right in front of you is no test of your skills. But try describing the Elegant Trogon's nesting hole, high in a tree in the middle of the forest. It's like missing the tree for the forest.

One of the most important locational tools is visualization of the face of a twelve-hour clock. Learn to pick up field marks of the scene in front of you and identify something obvious, then talk your companion to the bird: "Three o'clock in the biggest dark green tree to the left of the boulder."

"Seven o'clock from the red flowers, about two feet from them."

"Follow the twisty vine up to where it meets the second branch coming out from the right; follow along that branch to where the light green tree in back meets it; then drop (your binoculars!) down two feet and the bird is sitting on a tiny twig with his back to us."

"To the right of the sky—in front of the sunlight—left of the 'bulbul' tree."

Move from the known to the unknown. Does the new bird look like any bird you are familiar with? Does it act like a known bird? Where is it in relation to something else? The system won't work for all birds, of course. Barbets, cotingas, curassows, mousebirds, jacamars, manakins, birds of paradise, and many others just won't look like anything in North America. Some birds are so far back in the thicket that only you, because you saw it fly in, can see it.

Welcome to the fascination and challenge of world birding.

🐦 *Three* 🐦

Birders Do It Alone or in a Group

Some birders do it alone. Some birders do it with an organized group. More and more birders are doing both.

Birding is an ideal activity for the person who enjoys doing things alone. The bird doesn't need a big audience; in fact it may perform better for a single, silent soul. Peter Alden, author and widely known leader of birding trips around the world, says,

"The ideal number of birders on a forest path is one!"

Nineteen eager birders were ready to snake along after Alden down a narrow, twisting path through a dark Gambian forest in West Africa. Quiet though we were, our sheer mass scattered birds before even Peter could spot them all. On the other hand, thirty-eight eyes spot more birds than do two eyes.

Birding is ideally adaptable to either singular or group pursuit. Although the focus of this chapter is on the relatively recent development of birding group tours, it is necessary to recognize that some people react negatively to the idea of a group tour; they prefer birding alone or with a spouse or friend, if at all possible.

Lots of birders have spent a lifetime of birding on their own and have never given thought to taking an organized group birding trip. Sometimes, however, one has virtually no choice but to temporarily become part of a group in order to see birds of particular places. Such places may be off-limits to the individual birder, or may require vast personal resources to get there.

Birders, with developing enthusiasm for birding, have recognized the many advantages of seeing the maximum number of birds in the shortest amount of time; of being part of a group of persons who share the same interests, and of having an experienced guide.

DOING IT ALONE

There is much to be said for the lone Indian-type quietly slipping through the trees, stealthily coming around a bend in the trail to catch a fleeting glimpse of a Little Tinamou before it vanishes into the undergrowth beside the path.

For "loners," birding is a perfectly respectable outdoor activity. One can decide to get up early on a Sunday morning, be in Everglades National Park at first light, and walk the boardwalk at Anhinga Trail in blissful peace and quiet. You may ignore another "loner" if you wish, or speak, as the spirit moves. Birders do tend to be communicative even if alone.

"Have you seen anything?"

"We saw a Barred Owl at the end of the boardwalk."

"At the top of the Royal Palm tree way over there is a Pileated Woodpecker. See it?"

You don't need a partner as you do in tennis or chess. You need not be tied to someone else's schedule. You can travel the country alone, as wildlife artist Lydia Thompson did a few years ago seeking her personal essence of the birds.

Birding is a great activity for a single person or for a spouse whose marital partner is into golf. The single birder, whether really single or not, can readily join up with another birding aficionado and be perfectly comfortable.

Many birders pursue their hobby for years and build up substantial lists without ever joining an organized tour. It can be a lot of fun to do it on your own, to figure out for yourself what that bird is.

Maida, expressing the satisfaction many birders find in doing it alone, once said, "A bird that is my very own is the one I've found by myself, figured out on my own, and or I've had some time to savor, and to let it etch itself into my mind's eye."

"It's got to be a Semipalmated Sandpiper—its bill just isn't long enough for it to be a Western."

If you're with a birding group, your leader calls out, "Semipalm," and moves on down the shore-line for a better view of a flock of Red Knots.

Mary and Tom Wood belong to the self-help species of birder. They just don't think of themselves as "groupies." They started birding in Everglades National Park by themselves or with a friend or two. While meandering around South Texas at the right time of year, they were able to find, without expert help, 105 different species in one day.

Sometimes the birding territory is such that you can't avoid being part of a group even though you're alone. The flight out to the Pribilof Islands in the Bering Sea off the coast of Alaska can be booked on an individual basis, but you automatically become part of a group when you get there. You all stay at the same hotel, the King Eider, its name more elegant and evocative than its actuality. If you're single, you've an automatic roommate. You all eat together in the dining hall down the hill. The old school bus picks you all up every morning for the ride to the seal beaches and the bird cliffs. Other members of the group *may* be birders; some may be botanists perpetually photographing the wild flowers; others may be casual sightseers.

It's possible and indeed feasible to get out by yourself to Fort Jefferson on the Dry Tortugas, at the other extreme of the United States. It is accessible by boat or plane from the Florida Keys. Whether with an organized group or not, you'll be looking for special birds, perhaps the Black Noddy. In the spring of 1985, it was Wilbur and Harriet Davidson, well-known North American birders, camping by themselves at Fort Jefferson, who spotted the Black Noddy and led a tour group to it.

Antarctica is another place where a real "loner" would be written up in the *National Geographic*. You may be traveling alone, but there's a host of other people on the ship that takes you there. Same thing with the more likely destination of the Galápagos Islands. You can do it solo, but the vast majority get there by boat or ship, partake of the knowledge of the government-licensed guides (who may or may not be knowledgeable of the finer points of the Darwin's finches), and participate in at least a modicum of group activities. At that minimum, you will probably be randomly assigned to ABC groups (albatross, boobies, or cormorants), for purposes of getting you ashore in small boats.

Birding alone, rather than in a group, is relatively easy in most of North America and Europe. The prevalence of where-to-find guides helps the birder with very specific directions. No birder should travel much of North America without the Pettingill books: *Finding Birds East of the Mississippi* and *Finding Birds West of the Mississippi*.

At a somewhat more specific level, the many *A Birder's Guide to . . .* by James Lane, and others of similar vein, have led birders to drive 1.6 miles down highway 105, turn right at the first dirt road, and then go 0.7 mile to a stand of Douglas fir. There, the guide will tell you, you will find Steller's Jay, Pygmy Nuthatch, and Lazuli Bunting. The Lane guides provide a useful chart indicating where and when, in the area covered by the guide, you are likely to see particular birds, lists of rarities, simple maps, and sometimes lists of mammals. If you want to see the birds of a particular "hot spot," don't leave home without your Lane guide.

Most of the best birding spots in North America have been covered by similar publications. Some books may cover a whole state, a part of a state, a county, or even a city. Ask the local Audubon Society, bird club, or newspaper nature reporter.

Even more detailed, but not providing as comprehensive coverage, is the two-volume *Bird-finding Guide* published by the American Birders Association. In loose-leaf notebook form, it provides detailed descriptions by ABA members about how and where to locate some rare or unusual birds. Take out appropriate pages to guide you if you think you'll get bored lying on the beach in Barbados, if you expect a free afternoon during your conference in New Orleans, or if you want to be sure to see the Cave Swallows when you take the kids to New Mexico's Carlsbad Caverns.

These guides will lead you down the straight and narrow path, across the railroad track, to the oak grove where, sure enough, you'll find your bird. It's absolutely amazing how the same species will be found in the same places year after year. Generally, there are hand-drawn maps, some so detailed that x's will be drawn in to show exactly where to look for the Henslow's Sparrow.

Such books are "guides," not the gospel truth. Birds are highly mobile, and they may change their minds about where they like to be. Change of habitat is a more likely explanation. If the weedy field has been plowed and planted, you won't find the White-collared Seedeater on your visit to South Texas. If, since the guide was published, a dam has been built and the area flooded, the guide to where the birds *were* will be useless. Unusual climatological conditions may change migration patterns. Check other local sources before you make a time-consuming trip to see a particular bird.

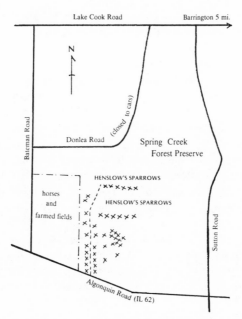

Detailed ABA maps are extremely useful in finding an elusive sparrow

North American and European birders have many good sources for guidance on those continents for nonorganized birding. Some other areas of the world have good guides to help the individual birder.

For starters, the world birder will want to look at *Where to Find Birds Around the World* by two brilliant and peripatetic birders, Peter Alden and John Gooders. They narrowed the world down to 111 key locations, centered around main cities, national parks, and especially good birding areas. It is particularly useful to birding travelers on the Capital City Circuit: Washington, D.C., Mexico City, Guatemala City, Panama City, Quito, Lima, London, Vienna, Nairobi, New Delhi, Sydney, etc.

"Alden and Gooders revolutionized my travel plans," a frequent traveler said recently. "I now plan an extra day when I have to take a business trip to a place like Singapore because I now know I can see some good birds there."

For the European traveler, Gooders' book *Where to Find Birds in Europe* is a necessity. Elsewhere, coverage by such books is spotty. Current books will be found listed in Part III.

Jetting about the world on business, or for birding or nonbirding vacations, the birder will carefully check the airline schedule. Sometimes a few hours between planes or the necessity for a layover will provide a good opportunity to bird the countryside via taxi, rental car, or public transportation.

In Shanghai, Alden and Gooders remind the traveler of the People's Park within the city and suggest several other good birding areas nearby. In Hong Kong, the Peak Tram will take you to the top of Hong Kong Island for a variety of birds. The birder there will make an effort to see some birds found nowhere else in the world.

Popular tourist objectives like Iguaçu Falls in South America, Victoria Falls in Africa, and Mazatlán in Mexico all have good birding nearby. Birders making plane connections in Miami can quickly get to Coconut Grove or Miami Springs to see the Canary-winged Parakeet and other current exotics.

Birders opting to see the world and its birds on their own will probably want to rent a car at their destination and head for the hills. Major rental car companies will be found in most major cities. Off the beaten track, the airport into which you fly is likely to have a rental car desk, even though it has a strange name. You will need a major credit card (sometimes more than one if you anticipate a hefty bill—some smaller agencies have limits on what can be charged to one card). In most countries you will need an International Driver's License *and* your regular license. U.S. residents can call the nearest American Automobile Association for information (you need not be a member). Check with your travel agent for any special requirements such as insurance.

DOING IT TOGETHER: INS AND OUTS OF BIRD TOURS

On the flip side, traveling alone in a foreign country isn't always easy, feasible, or possible. Independent travel may be discouraged. Birds you most want to see may be in remote locations and difficult to reach. You may be uncomfortable if you don't know the language. You may have limited time and you want to maximize it—see the most birds in the shortest amount of time. You may not be safe in some areas, so remember there is safety in numbers of fellow birders.

There are two kinds of tour operators of interest to birders. (See Part III.) The *nature tour operator* provides itineraries that appeal to a broad spectrum of travelers seeking to experience the natural world. Leaders may not be expert birders. Such tours go to interesting places and involve people in interesting activities: trekking in Nepal, hiking the Inca trail in Peru; snorkeling and whale watching in the Sea of Cortez. These kinds of destinations are good for birding too.

Such a trip might be at the right time, going to the right place, with an announced interest in birds. For some, this kind of a trip may be more attractive than the more intensive birding expedition. You may see more of the sights of a country. George Venatta, an experienced world birder accustomed to the "go-go" pace of most birding trips, found one such trip too "laid back." Audubon Society (local, state, or national) tours tend to appeal to a broad interest in the cultural and natural environment and may not provide concentrated attention on birds. The Massachusetts Audubon Society is a notable exception; they have long specialized in birding trips.

More tuned in to birder's special interests are *birding tour operators.* Many have been organized in the last decade or so to meet the rapidly growing demand of birders to pursue their hobby around the world. Leaders of such trips generally are highly skilled birders. Some are authors of bird guides to the place of their interest. The reputation of the trip leaders is one of the most important factors in choosing which trip to take.

Although birders typically have a wide-ranging interest in the natural environment, it is birding they most want to do. It is birding that the bird tour operators provide from dawn to dusk. And after dusk, they take you "owling."

George Foster, a lifetime bird watcher, had never before been on a birding trip. With good humor after dinner at the hotel in Chiang Mai in Thailand, he observed that "birding is the most single-minded activity I've ever known. You're birding ten or twelve hours every day, spend the evening going over the bird list, and then still have enthusiasm when you get up early the next morning."

"Indefatigable" is the word often applied to birders. If the minibus brings them back to home base while there's still daylight, they will scout the garden or scan the ocean.

This enthusiasm is the reason increasing numbers of birders are turning to organized tour operators to meet their world birding needs. It is safe to say that birders will see more birds in a given amount of time on an organized birding trip than they can possibly see and identify on their own.

Like everything else, you get what you pay for. On an organized birding trip, you are paying for the birding knowledge of the experts who *know* the birds. They know just where to go, at what time of day. Their tours are scheduled for the right time of year to take advantage of migration, breeding, or other events that make a birding trip productive.

As on local Audubon or bird club walks, you'll find both beginners and experts on most organized birding trips. On a scale of one to ten, there won't be many tens, or experts. Most of your fellow birders will be in the five-to-nine range; some one to four. Jean admitted she didn't know much about the birds of her native England. She had begun to get interested in the birds on a recent trip to Australia, then spent three weeks in India on an intensive birding trip because "I'd always wanted to see India." You don't have to be a "hot shot" birder to both learn and enjoy.

Let's assume you have gone well beyond the local park system in your birding; you probably have purchased more than one field guide; you've extended business trips to include birding the vicinity; you've just upgraded your binoculars; and you're eager for some intensive birding with the experts. Your vacation dates are known, and you have some idea of how much money you are willing to part with and some destinations in mind.

You have obtained brochures from some of the tour operators listed in Part III, and you zero in on the trip that best meets your needs. Best to plan ahead. Spur of the moment necessitates a phone call. Although birding trips are becoming more and more popular, not every trip is full. Sometimes there are last-minute cancellations, so don't hesitate to ask. Be alert, however, to the time required to get necessary shots, a visa, update your old passport, etc. (Any respectable world birder has a valid passport, valid for several months after the trip ends.)

For your first birding trip you may choose a North American destination where, the literature tells you, a considerable variety of birds new to you assuredly will be found. It may be southeast Arizona, where you know accommodations will be good and where you'll see some Mexican species that regularly cross the border. Or perhaps it's Churchill in Manitoba, with the added faint hope of seeing an early polar bear.

You'll be part of a small group of persons whose primary objective is the same as yours: to see new birds and to polish up general bird identification skills. Members of the group will be men and women, old and young, tall and short, expert and novice. Heterogeneity is characteristic of birding groups.

If you hanker for faraway places, you might choose Costa Rica or India or Japan for your birding trip. The whole world is out there, and each year new places are being opened up by enterprising birding tour operators seeking to satisfy the tandem desire of world birders for new birds and new places.

Before you sign up, however, think about some of the facts of bird-tour life. Birding trips can be somewhat strenuous; typically there's little free time. On a birding trip in India our day's schedule often looked like this:

5:30	Wake-up call
6:00	Breakfast
6:30	Begin field trip
1:30	Return for lunch
	Rest
3:30	Go out for late afternoon birding
6:30	Return for wash up and dinner
7:30	Dinner
8:30	Do bird list (go over checklist with leader to check off all birds seen during the day)
9:30	Night walk to look for owls and Jungle Cat
10:30	Fall into bed

A full and typical schedule.

Any free time is spent bringing one's own list up to date, checking the field guide for descriptions, or discussing questionable identifications with other members of the group. It's bird, bird, bird, bird. Shopping for gifts and souvenirs may be "on the hoof," quick purchases from vendors as you board the bus. Museums probably will be out. There will be little or no time for lolling by poolside, except in hot areas with little midday bird activity. Peter Alden and Alec Forbes-Watson keep a birds-seen-from-the-pool list in East Africa, jumping in when a Bateleur flies over or a Red-cheeked Cordon-Bleu flies into a nearby bush.

Well-known tourist attractions, such as the ruins of Machu Picchu or the Taj Mahal, are normally included on the itinerary (there are birds everywhere). Ordinary sightseeing will be limited; the purpose of a birding trip is to bird. Some participants will take time off from birding to poke around the ruins or get into the city to shop. Ted Parker, leading a Victor Emanuel Nature Tour trip, "excused" those who wanted more time to photograph Machu Picchu by saying that he would have passed up local cultural institutions when he was younger (he's still young) but now he believes that this is part of the total experience of being in a foreign environment, perhaps never to return.

Most of the time, you will be outside the large cities. This is an advantage in some countries, but it may limit what you perceive to be some cultural adventures. It may also limit the choice of accommodations. Accommodations in the main cities will range from adequate to luxurious, depending on the tour operator and on the city. In the hinterland you may have to rough it a bit.

Roughing it takes several forms. In Nainital in the lower Himalayas in India, it meant an ancient hotel, probably luxurious a half-century ago. One could almost smell fifty years of dust. Worn oriental rugs covered successive layers of worn and torn oriental rugs. One could get smoked out of the room with an open fire, lit every evening if you wished, or suffer the cold and too few blankets.

In tropical jungles, if accommodations are to be found within a reasonable distance of the forest for purposes of dawn birding, they may be reminiscent of scout camp. For some, sleeping on mosquito net–covered mattresses on the platform of an open-air structure with thatched roof is delightful and slightly nostalgic; for others it is mental and emotional torture.

As you might surmise, plumbing outside the United States and Canada can be an affront to personal sensibilities. Even in North America or Europe, one will be lucky, in some out-of-the-way places, if the bath is "down the hall." In some places in the world, wash and shower water simply drain out of the bathroom into a trough.

In the jungle, one often finds some nice privies at the tourist camps. They are luxurious if they have self-contained toilet paper. Plumbing in some countries, especially during time spent in the field, is literally that— the field. Tour leaders will identify mens' and ladies' bushes. If a rest stop isn't suggested, you can always tell someone you are off to search for a "lark's nest."

Hot water may be a singular luxury, one to be savored like silk sheets. Lots of us never learn to appreciate the spartan virtues of a cold shower, even in the hot jungle. Electricity in remote locations is often scarce. The generator, if there is one, often runs only a few hours a day. Few birders would survive in one piece without a flashlight.

On a typical birding trip, food is plentiful, may reflect local cuisine, but rarely could be termed gourmet. Generally there is little choice; sometimes there is an exclusive reliance on one meat and often a dearth of frest fruits and vegetables. In some tropical areas where fruit abounds, you may get to mango or banana heaven. Veteran birders take along their own snacks to ward off starvation on the trail even though some bird tour operators do an excellent job of anticipating such needs.

Good wines are seldom available, but local beer often is. Stronger stuff is generally expensive to unavailable. Soft drinks are available everywhere, although you may never have heard of the local cola. Listen to your tour leader's advice about both ice and water. Some tour operators will provide water purification materials; others will advise tour members on what to bring.

Sometimes the only feasible way of providing food to a group is to arrange for a box lunch; or the fixings for a picnic will be brought along because there will be no restaurants where the group will be during the day. Occasionally a picnic breakfast must be provided because no coffee shop is open as early as birders need to get started. One of the least appetizing ways to start a day that I experienced was a predawn tailgate breakfast in the parking lot of a motel in Kingston, Jamaica. It included the inevitable hard-boiled egg and a sardine sandwich as the "pièce de upchuck."

Most birding trips involve a good bit of hiking, sometimes climbing: best to be in good shape. Transport may be elemental. Forest paths may be wet, so be prepared for wet shoes. Narrow logs bridging a stream may be the only alternative to wading. Each path through the forest is an adventure.

With these caveats, a birding tour can be a real blast. You'll see places far from typical tourist traps. You'll be in virgin forests, on deserted beaches, working ranches, wildlife refuges with a wealth of animal life, remote wilderness as peaceful as paradise. You will pass through small villages where native folk work and play and live their lives, often as they have been doing for centuries.

The more birders see, the more they want to see. They may see lots of fresh air and sunshine, to say nothing of an occasional nourishing rain. Birders do it in the rain too. As in any group of persons who share an interest, the opportunities for companionship and new friendships abound. There's an excitement in watching the bird list grow day by day, even hour by hour, and of sharing with other members of the group.

"I got three life birds before breakfast."

"Twenty life birds, and it isn't even lunchtime."

"Wiped out a family with that bird."

There's an excitement in silently padding through a dark forest, try-ing not to crackle a leaf or, for heaven's sake, to sneeze! The group may sit without a word for an hour waiting for a glimpse of the laughingthrushes we know are nearby; theirs is the only sound to split the silence. Sitting shoulder to shoulder in a tight viewing space, one doesn't dare stretch a leg for fear of scaring the tiny Chestnut-headed Tesia that has just come into view at the edge of the little pool of water. That evening, the tesia will be a "write-in" on the bird list.

There's a different kind of excitement when the birding leaders have scheduled a reconnaissance trip to a new area where they've never birded before. Birdquest did this on a Thailand trip, taking participants up to an area near the Burma border. Roger said it was one of the reasons he signed up. Although the birders rode in an open truck that kicked up enormous clouds of red dust on the way, group members dusted each other off and enjoyed the adventure. Not knowing what to expect, seeing the Burma mountains in the distance after our long climb to a vantage point, hearing the heavy artillery of a border skirmish in the distance, and seeing the Gould's Sunbird all made the trip very special. But it's not for everyone.

Like most general interest tours, the bird tour operator will send you full information: detailed itinerary; weather probabilities; suggested clothes and equipment; suggested reading list; and most important, a bird list com-piled from previous visits to the area. You will study this list to get an idea of what birds to expect.

One of the most important traditions of birding group tours is the trip bird list. The tour operator will have provided a checklist of birds seen previously in the area or expected to be seen. Each evening, either before or after dinner, the leader will go over the entire list with the group, each member checking off the birds seen by the group and those personally seen or heard. This is a relaxed time after a full day in the field, a time when comradeship develops, and it often is a time of hilarity as birders recount funny experiences.

Each birding group develops a language of its own that makes the group experience special, a bonus beyond the birds. While going over the bird list in the evening, someone in the group questions where some bird was seen. The answer might be, "On the feather trail." (That's the road where we walked, picking up the feathers of the Green-winged Pigeon that the "Hill People" had been plucking and dropping.) Reference to "Peter's bridge" reminds the group that's where we saw all the Rose-ringed Parakeets. The "Drongo tree" is not a species of tree but reminds us of the place where we saw so many drongos.

Most people interested in the birds are also interested in the bees and the butterflies and the rest of the bounty Mother Nature offers us. Sightings of other creatures are often included at the end of a bird list to round out the activity: mammals, snakes, alligators, crocodiles, and whatever else might draw particular attention.

Follow the Leader

If a birding trip appeals to your sense of adventure and your interest in expanding your world bird list, one of the secrets to its success will be the ability of the individuals in the group to follow the leader. A good leader will constantly be concerned about the welfare of the group. It is equally important for group members to be alert to the leader's commands. On a forest trail, watch the leader's hand commands: Come ahead—stay back—crouch down—keep quiet. If the leader is forced to voice commands, the bird may disappear.

Stay with the leader, but don't "hog" the leader. Don't try to second-guess the leader by staying back to try to see some little bird. If the leader moves on, it's probably because the bird isn't worth waiting for or will be found later. Your delay could delay the group or cause you to lose the group. On the other foot, don't act like the leader's shadow; give other members of the group the opportunity to closely follow the leader. Let's face it, on a forest trail the persons in the front of the line see more birds than those at the rear. Changing places is common courtesy, actually a common characteristic of most birding groups.

Although the organized birding tour probably is more expensive than doing it on your own, if time is money to you, it may be a better decision. You won't waste time beating the bushes for some elusive sparrow better seen a mile away in back of the water tank. You will definitely see more birds and utilize your time more efficiently when you go with an experienced birding leader. You will sample more habitats, see more species, and maybe have more fun!

POSTSCRIPT—DOING IT ALONE: EXCERPTS FROM A TRIP DIARY

A good opportunity for birding on one's own is a cross-country trip. Today's interstate system in North America affords a good, safe way of seeing the country, getting to special birding areas. Most of those birding areas, of course, are not going to be right on the interstate; you generally have to get off to see the birds. In the spring of 1985, longtime birding friend Emily Barefield joined me for an on-and-off birding trip between Miami and San Diego.

May 12. After spending first night with friend in Tallahassee, we zigzag across North Florida heading for I-10. Wow! A Wild Turkey crossing the road in front of us, disappearing into the piney woods of the Okaloosa National Forest. Have been looking for him for a long time. Armed with the pocket-sized *Traveler's List and Check List For Birds of North America* published by the American Birding Association, we check off the turkey—"tick the turkey" as the British would say. Across the panhandle we "tick" common water birds. Alabama flashes by, but few feathers.

May 13. Little birding in Louisiana. Following the advice in Pettingill's *Finding Birds West of the Mississippi,* we leave I-10 at a little town and drive up on a dike; good look at a nice deep forest but few birds more exciting than a cardinal.

Main objective today is Anahuac National Wildlife Refuge east of Houston. We leave I-10 and drive into town of Anahuac. We head for flooded rice fields. Scope set up, we quickly spot a Hudsonian Godwit. Great view of Wilson's Phalarope in breeding plumage. An "old coot" stops for some conversation, thinks we might be trying to spot Errant Husbands. He establishes his wildlife credentials telling us about seeing very rare Red Wolf at a nearby waterway. Following his directions we find pleasant area, enjoy lovely sunset and late afternoon refreshments. No Red Wolfs, but otters, Black-necked Stilts, Black-crowned Night Herons, and a pair of Spotted Sandpipers engaging in courting ritual.

May 14. Early morning arrival at wildlife refuge, leisurely drive over gravel roads surveying wet prairies and vast coastal marshes. Birders flock here in April, take buggy rides to see the Yellow and Black Rails. We miss them but enjoy King Rail and Willet, each tending to four chicks. Rabbits abound and nutria crisscross road between one pond and another. Lots of common ducks and gaggles of Snow Geese. Pleased to see Orchard Orioles, Pine Siskins, and Dickcissels.

Leaving refuge, we pass more flooded rice fields. Again, scope and binoculars attract attention, this time from Mr. Schultz, owner of the fields. He wants us to verify his sighting of the Wilson's Phalarope, then invites us to drive through the fields for better views of the thousands of shorebirds feasting on tiny creatures surfaced by the flooding. Enormous flock of Ruddy Turnstones slowly leads our car down road.

We're too late for mass of migrants that drop down at High Island, on the coast, and note from bird list posted in Murdock's Grocery that there's not much bird life around. Good view of Black Tern in breeding plumage flying over beach. Back on I-10 we crawl through Houston and push west to Flatonia (a real place!). Western Kingbirds on the wires in back of the motel, Cliff Swallows swirling across the field.

May 15. Arrive in San Antonio in time to lunch on famous Riverwalk. Join animated luncheon throng, watch water taxis coursing the Rio Grande, and enjoy Mexican lunch enclosed between the city's famous Marguerita cocktail, and Marguerita pie made with pretzel crust. Pettingill is our guide for afternoon birding. We find touted sewage treatment processing plant. Man in charge encourages us to drive along dikes but "be careful of Water Moccasins." Nice collection of birds including what we're almost sure is Western Meadowlark. No doubt about first Roadrunner of trip.

May 16. Leave I-10 to take scenic route out of San Antonio and are rewarded with Painted Buntings in nearly every tree. We're heading for Johnson City, headquarters of Lyndon and Lady Bird territory, high on Edwards Plateau. Objective is typical birder's objective: not historic sights but Golden-cheeked Warbler. At Pedernales Falls State Park, walk down path to see falls cascading down boulder-strewn gorge, peering through the woods as we go. Another birder says he's looked unsuccessfully for three days for warbler. We stand around the parking lot undecided which way to walk next, when Emily spots the coveted bird—a pair. We work edge of parking lot, spot second pair. Good birding!

Just west of Johnson City is Fredericksburg, unexpectedly delightful layover. Settled by German pioneers in mid-1850's, town has preserved much original architecture and culinary flavor.

May 17. Friendly motel owner urges us to visit Enchanted Rock State Natural Area north of town to see massive pink granite outcropping. Schedule doesn't permit hiking the many trails, but we see good sampling of bird life, including Yellow-billed Cuckoo, Bewick's Wren, Golden-fronted Woodpecker, more Painted Buntings. Pick up bird checklist and put this spot on list for return visit. Proceeding west, meet up again with I-10, which takes us to Fort Stockton.

May 18. Difficult to pass up Big Bend National Park, great birding hot spot. I had been there years ago (before I knew about the Colima Warbler). Take loop road south of I-10 down to Ft. Davis and through Davis Mountains State Park. See Montezuma Quail and are delighted with lingering look at Gray Fox.

May 19. After picnic breakfast in McKelligan State Park overlooking El Paso we scramble about rocky hillside in search of Black-throated and Black-chinned Sparrow. Glad to add former to list. Not far west of El Paso, leave I-10 again for Silver City, New Mexico. Stopping at a roadside rest area on the way, Chihuahuan Ravens watch us eat picnic lunch. Center of great birding territory, Silver City is location of Bear Mountain Lodge run by venerable birder Myra McCormick. Black-chinned Hummingbirds at feeder, Gambel's Quail and Brown Towhees scuttling about under the bushes, Common Poor-will calling at dusk, and egotistical Painted Redstart in a nearby forest.

May 20. After birding Silver City area in morning, head back south, cross I-10, and proceed down Route 80. Armed with the Lane *A Birder's Guide to Southeastern Arizona,* we turn east into Portal, Arizona. This hamlet is birders' HQ. "Have you seen the trogon and the tanager?" asks the owner of the little general store. No question, we are in Birder's Heaven. Heading for Cave Creek Canyon we find trogon's nest high in tree leaning over stream. A dozen birders standing about or sitting on boulders at stream's edge, monitoring hole in tree. Word has it that it's about time for Elegant Trogons to "change the guard." Soon male comes, perches momentarily on edge of hole while female emerges and flies off to gather food for presumed chick or chicks.

Great is camaraderie of these birders, all eager to share information. They saw the Flame-colored Tanager (a brand new bird that spring for North America—we see it next day). They tell how many life birds they saw in one day up at Rustler Park, whether they've spotted the Lucy's and the Grace's Warbler. Then there's exclamations over early morning and late afternoon lighting in Cave Creek Canyon as sun rays set orange cliffs on fire, bathing them with liquid gold. It is spectacular.

May 22. Enjoy rugged beauty of Chiricahua Mountains for couple of days, breakfasting in and birding Cave Creek Canyon each morning. Get to know Bridled Titmice flitting among trees, really see yellow eye of Yellow-eyed Junco, become acquainted with Bronzed Cowbird near motel, list new warblers. A trip to car at night produces tiny Elf Owl on the branch overhead. At the research station see Black-chinned Rivolis and Blue-throated Hummingbirds, later Steller's and Gray-breasted Jays. We bird Rustler Park high above the Canyon with Lydia Thompson, budding wildlife artist, and her father. Find Mexican Chickadee, Olive and Hermit Warblers, Band-tailed Pigeon, but miss the Red-faced Warbler. Today we move on to Ramsey Canyon and Nature Conservancy's Mile Hi Lodge. Visit too brief, but long enough to get good looks at Sulphur-bellied Flycatcher and Strickland's Woodpecker at nest hole.

May 24. With a day driving out of Arizona, pick up I-10 again in Tucson with stops to bird along way, we reach San Diego in evening to visit for few days with relatives. Highlight of trip across hot, flat Imperial Valley were Burrowing Owls perched on fence posts, guarding vast fields of vegetables. On return trip we were to count fourteen of them on south side of I-10 within twenty-mile stretch near El Centro.

May 28. Several pleasant days in San Diego produced more family activity than birding except for seeing Elegant Terns near marine biological station. Returning over rugged desert mountains, we resume our birding in the fast lane. Surprising rest stop near El Centro produces screaming Black-necked Stilts, Killdeer, and egrets, birds not often seen on interstates.

May 30. Return trips often hasty, this no exception; just plain running out of time. Because we missed it on trip out, a stop at Arizona-Sonora Desert Museum and nearby Saguaro National Monument has high priority. Museum is exception to birder's rule that you don't see live birds in museums. A marvelous outdoor introduction to flora and fauna of Sonora Desert, museum grounds also attract variety of "countable" birds, those found in the wild. Gila Woodpecker pecks for breakfast as we cook ours. Towhee-like bird with distinctive "necklace" greets us on museum steps. Check bird book, is interior race of Brown Towhee.

Yesterday's highlight, with no side trips, was I-10 rest stop with couple of Scaled Quail, Northern Oriole, and Cassin's Flycatcher on nest during picnic lunch. Decide to start "Rest-stop List."

Today we detour north of I-10 into Guadaloupe Mountains then on to Rattlesnake Springs, a lovely grove in Carlsbad Caverns National Park. See Vermillion flycatchers, Summer Tanager, American and Lesser goldfinches, Ring-necked Pheasant with hen and chicks, Lark sparrows, Ladderback woodpeckers. Slanting down to southeast, pick up I-20 for different route back across Texas.

May 31. Detouring again south of I-20 to picnic at Abilene State Recreation Area. Knock off another trip objective: Mississippi Kite, not just one—four. So common in this park is this handsome gray hawk with deeply-forked tail that it graces cover of park checklist.

June 3. Home after visiting friends in Dallas and Ocala. Total bird species: 205, a not particularly impressive list. Dedicated birders could easily have doubled it. (But they might not have taken time to savor Marguerita pie.) Trip combined birding, sightseeing, visiting friends and relatives, as such a trip often does. Alas, friends and relatives often don't know a catbird from a mockingbird.

Observations

Birding in the fast lane through the south (North Florida, Alabama, and Louisiana) at that time of year does not offer great birding unless you've never before seen Great Egrets.

Texas topped our state list at 127 species. Such a total by no means is reflective of all the birds one might see with more time to stray from the beaten interstate. For anyone contemplating a cross-Texas birding trip there are many other good birding areas that should not be missed, some of which are mentioned in Chapter 5.

New Mexico birding tends to be overshadowed by the magnificent birding in its neighbor state to the west. However, we were pleased with a total of fifty-seven species in not much more than one day. We particularly enjoyed the flashy Acorn Woodpecker, Canyon Wren, Phainopepla, Warbling Vireo, Black-throated Gray Warbler, Black-headed and Blue Grosbeaks.

Arizona lived up to its billing as one of the best birding states. Our few days there didn't do it justice; southeast Arizona deserves a minimum of a week during spring migration particularly. Our total of eighty species would have been boosted considerably had more time been spent there.

🐦 *Four* 🐦

Learning to Love Latin

You didn't have Latin in school? Not to worry. Most of us didn't. We all recognize, however, that it is the international language of science. Few birders have the scientific background qualifying them as ornithologists, but a general knowledge of the scientific ordering of birds and of their scientific names can be very helpful. It is virtually essential for birders who pursue their hobby around the world.

Most of us began to bird in English—that is, we paid little attention to the Latin or Latinized names of the different species. Nor did we concern ourselves with which family a particular species was in. Our main concern was the identification of the little whitish bird with the brownish back scratching in a snowy field as a Snow Bunting. Besides, the Latin named seemed unpronounceable, *Plectrophenax nivalis*. Our bird guide may not even have identified its family name, Emberizidae, that family of sparrows, buntings, cardinals, grosbeaks, a few finches, etc.

BIRDING IN LATIN

Our bird watcher friends would certainly not ask us,

"What is the difference between a *Cyanocitta cristata* and a *Calypte anna?*" Imagine!

No birder of sound mind would ask such a question. Any dummy knows that the Blue Jay and the Anna's Hummingbird are terribly different. But the Latin gives no clue to the uninitiated about what birds are being discussed. Were your friend to ask, "What color is a *Cardinalis cardinalis?*" you could hardly miss the answer; not even good enough for Trivial Pursuit. A few Latin names are virtually identical to the common name. *Vireo philadelphicus, Parula americana, Jabiru mycteria.*

If you asked your bird watcher friend,

"Are any *Myiarchus* flycatchers around here?" the response is likely to be,

"A *what* flycatcher?"

Birding in Britain, Nigel identifies a small yellowish bird as a "Phyllosc," short for *Phylloscopus*, the genus of Old World leaf-warblers. We might wish things were simple, that warblers would be warblers all over the world. But they're not. Most North American warblers are wood warblers in the family Parulidae. The Old World warblers belong to a much larger family, Sylviidae.

One can bird a lifetime in North America, and many do, without ever feeling the need of paying attention to a bird's Latin name. Birding beyond the borders of North America is what quickly turns a birder's attention to Latin names.

Beginning to keep a world bird list is an eye-opener. North Americans using the Clements *Birds of the World: A Checklist* (often referred to as "the Clements"), will notice immediately that the Latin name is listed first, is in boldface, and is easier to read (if not to pronounce).

Secondly, you'll begin to wonder whether a particular bird you saw in one country is the same one you saw somewhere else. Could the Crested Caracara in the Falkland Islands possibly be the same caracara you saw near Lake Okeechobee in Florida? It is. A look at the Latin name, *Polyborus plancus*, confirms it.

Might the Greater Ani of South America be called the Groove-billed Ani that comes from South America up to parts of southern United States? No, the Latin names are different.

Is the Common Kingfisher in India the same species as the bird known simply as the Kingfisher in Britain and Europe? Yes, their Latin names are the same: *Alcedo atthis*. The Yellow-vented Bulbul you saw in Thailand looks different from the bird of the same name you saw in Kenya. It is different; it's Latin name is *Pycnonotus goiavier*; the one commonly seen in East and Central Africa is *Pycnonotus barbatus*, also known as Common Bulbul.

All birds—from albatross to Zenaida Dove—have Latin names. All other living things have Latin names too. Not all names have Latin roots; some have Greek roots, some are neither. Regardless of the origin of the name, they are all Latinized. It's the worldwide system of identification using a common terminology, regardless of the name in English or Russian or Swahili.

Birding around the world makes some knowledge of the Latin names very useful. The serious birder will want to know whether the American Robin is in the same family with the European Robin encountered in Britain and Europe. Checking both the North American and British field guides, or the Clements, we discover that these robins do belong to the same family, Muscicapidae. They are of different sub-family and genera. Our familiar robin is *Turdus migratorius;* their familiar little bird with the orange breast is *Erithacus rubecula*.

Why must we know this? Very simple. Sometimes the same species of bird is known by one name in one country and another in another country. A bird may be known by the same name in different countries, yet be a different species. British birders are more likely to refer to birds by their Latin names than are North Americans. Perhaps it's because they bird in Europe with its many different languages.

Efforts have been made in recent years to clear up the confusion among the common names, but unless you're using an up-to-date bird guide for the countries you are visiting, the new clarifying corrections may not be found. Early Peterson field guides simply said "robin" in North America and "robin" in the field guide for Britain and Europe. But as we've seen above, they are different species. Now, the robin found in North America is known universally as the American Robin; the robin found in Europe is officially the European Robin.

Just to make world birding especially challenging, the confusion about robins doesn't end there. All robins are now considered members of the same family, Muscicapidae, a huge family into which several previously separate families have been lumped as sub-families. Thus the family Turidae became the sub-family, Turinae, one of the two largest sub-families. Notice the *inae* ending. Many robins, be they called Bush-robins, Robin-chats, or Magpie-robins are thrushes, but the Ajax Scrub-Robin of New Guinea is a logrunner (it really is a bird), and the Eastern and Western Yellow robins are Old World flycatchers found in Australia.

Thrushes are a particularly good reason to develop a passing acquaintance with Latin names. In addition to the American Robin, other thrushes particularly well known in North America include the Wood Thrush, Hermit Thrush, Veery Thrush, Swainson's Thrush, and Gray-cheeked Thrush. Now, on your visit to Jamaica, you saw the White-eyed Thrush. When you come home and begin to enter your Jamaican birds in your Clements, the fun begins. If you look up the common name "thrush" in the index, you will find that the thrushes of the Turdidae family are found on pages 323–40 (in the third edition). That's a lot of pages to go through, a lengthy process because they're listed in taxonomic not alphabetical order. But look up its Latin name, *Turdus jamaicensis*. There are only four pages of *Turdus*, a much quicker search-and-find job.

Learning to love Latin a little will go a long way in saving time for the lister. In fact, some of the printed checklists have only the common name. That means a two-step operation. If you saw the endemic Rufous-tailed Flycatcher on your Jamaica trip, you'd go crazy trying to find it by looking up "flycatcher" on your world bird list. There are nearly forty pages of flycatchers in three different families. Best solution is to look in the field guide for the Latin name, *Myiarchus validus*, then quickly run down the *Myiarchus* flycatchers on two pages in your Clements.

If, during your travels to other countries, you talk to natives about their birds, you may find they have their own colloquial names. Some bird guides identify the different names by which a bird is known. The Bahama Woodstar is locally known in the Bond field guide as God Bird or simply Hummingbird. The Vervain Hummingbird of Hispaniola and Jamaica is also known as God Bird. Its other locally created names include Little Doctor Bird, Bee Hummingbird, Zumbadorcito, Zumbaflor, Ouanga-Négresse, Secefleurs. In Jamaica, the Smooth-billed Ani goes by the name of Long-tailed Crow along with a half dozen others in local dialects.

Some explanation of the Latin origins and designations will help place the Latin names in perspective. It was Karl von Linné (usually Latinized as Linnaeus), the Swedish botanist in the eighteenth century, who devised the system of classifying living organisms. Linné had a remarkably global view, and the Linnaean classification system, outlined in a mighty tome, *Systema Naturae*, in 1758, is the basic system used today.

This classification system is "binominal," that is, it gives to every animal and plant two names. The first is the generic name (Latin, *genus*, race or birth). This name is always a noun and it is always capitalized. *Parus* is Latin for titmouse, member of the family, Paridae, which includes tits, titmice, and chickadees, friendly visitors to gardens in much of the Northern Hemisphere.

The second name is specific to that species of bird and is generally an adjective; it describes the kind of *Parus* it is. The second name is never capitalized, is always lower case. *Parus carolinensis* is the familiar chattering Carolina Chickadee of the southeast United States. Both names are always italicized.

Latin names of the birds form an international language, understood by naturalists—and by many birders—all over the world. A scientific text in Japanese would still use Latin names for birds, flowers, or other living things. Rules for naming and sometimes renaming animals are complex. The rule-making authority rests in an organization of scientists known as the International Commission on Zoological Nomenclature. That august body keeps things organized.

Latin or Latinized names, derived mostly from Latin or Greek, may be descriptive of geography, size, shape, coloration, a particular characteristic of the bird, or the favorite person of the naturalist who names it, or it may have no significance at all. *Anas bahamensis* is the Bahamian Pintail, a duck first found in the Bahamas; *Tetraogallus himalayensis* is the (guess what?) Snowcock.

The African Fish Eagle, a superbly handsome bird, is also a very noisy one, as you might guess from its Latin name *Haliaeetus vocifer*. The Rufous Songlark found throughout most of Australia is the *Cinclorhamphus mathewsi,* named after G. M. Mathews, an early Australian naturalist. *Melospiza lincolnii* is a sparrow named not after a president, but after a companion of Audubon. The Rev. John Bachman, a close acquaintance of Audubon's, is memorialized in the Latin names of the American Black Oystercatcher and Bachman's Warbler, *Haematopus bachmani* and *Vermivora bachmanii.*

Then there are the names that tell you little. The well-known Laughing Kookaburra of Australia is identified in Latin as *Dacelo novaeguineae.* Some kingfishers are in the genus *Alcedo*. The genus, *Dacelo*, of the Laughing Kookaburra, whose common name derives from its laughing call, is an anagram of the Latin name for kingfisher.

Some Latin names are easily translated: *Turdus olivaceus* is of course the Olive Thrush. *Turdus philomelos* has a more romantic meaning. *Philos* is Greek for beloved, dear; *melos* is Greek for song. Hence a song lover or Song Thrush.

Few people ever know the Latin names well enough to rattle them off at a cocktail party. Few birders "speak" Latin. However, it is a good idea at least to look at them when you're looking up something about birds.

On a pelagic trip (to see the oceanic birds), you may hear your leader say,

"There's a good chance of seeing *Pterodroma*s today." You may remember that is the genus of so-called gadfly petrels. At least you might guess it is the Latin name of a bird, not a turtle, and you can sneak a look at the book to verify what to look for.

"There's an Alcid on the water, dead ahead."

It could be any member of the family Alcidae: a Common Murre, a Kittlitz's Murrelet (you should be so lucky!), or maybe a Tufted Puffin.

The genera of Tyrant Flycatchers are often referred to by their Latin names. The genus *Tyrannus* includes all kingbirds, such as the Eastern and Gray Kingbirds. *Myiarchus* includes look-alikes such as Great-crested and Ash-throated Flycatchers. *Empidonax* (known familiarly as "Empis") includes a whole group of look-alike, difficult-to-identify flycatchers. Hawks, too, often are referred to by genus. "It's an *Accipiter*" may be the first call that identifies the Sharp-shinned Hawk. "It looks like a *Buteo*," someone says of the Red-shouldered Hawk sitting on a far tree branch.

There's more than method here. Open your bird guide and look at the generic names of some birds you like. Maybe American wood warblers. Look at the plates of the *Dendroica* warblers and notice the similarities among the genus. Once you get a fix on the genus, the species is easy: *townsendi*, Townsend's Warbler, *graciae* Grace's Warbler, etc. Then notice the difference in appearance between the *Dendroica* warblers and the *Oporornis* warblers. It's a new dimension for some birders.

Becoming familiar with a representative member of a genus will give you some idea of the appearance of other members that someone may be describing or looking for. Having an impression of a *Myiarchus* flycatcher in this country will give you a head start in identifying similar-looking birds throughout tropical America. It also quickly narrows down the confusing field of flycatchers.

Occasionally a bird's common name will also be its Latin name. Our Anhinga, familiar to visitors of southern swamps, is the *Anhinga anhinga*. (Just to emphasize the point!) The other species of the genus are known as darters.

LEAFING THROUGH THE FAMILY TREE

Many birders get a kick out of adding a new family to their list of families, or of seeing all the species in one family. In addition to keeping a species list, some birders keep a family list. The ultimate objective of that might be to see a representative of each of the approximately 170 families. It's particularly satisfying to "wipe out" a family in which there is only one species. The Secretary Bird, so exciting to see running across the plains in East Africa, is the only species in the family Sagittariidae. Such families are known as monotypic; they contain only one species.

Before leafing through the bird family tree, a brief rundown on the animal kingdom will be helpful. It will show us where everything fits. Most of us have played the children's game "animal, vegetable, or mineral."

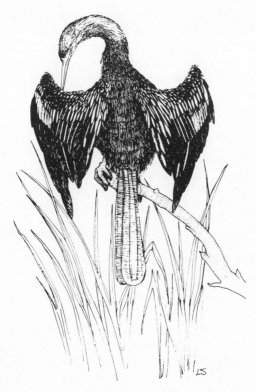

Anhinga anhinga, North American species of widespread family, Anhingidae

Well, we're talking here of everything in the universe that isn't vegetable or mineral. We'll trace the friendly Carolina Chickadee, *Parus carolinensis,* through the universal classification used for all animals.

> *Kingdom*—Animalia, all animals.
> *Phylum*—Chordata, meaning "provided with a back string." Here birds, humans, other mammals, and vertebrates are located. (Other phyla cover all the lower forms of life.)
> *Subphylum*—Vertebrata, the vertebrates: birds, man and other mammals, fishes, amphibians, reptiles.
> *Class*—Aves. Here the birds, aves, break away from everything else.
> *Order*—Passeriformes, the perching, or "sparrow-like," or songbirds.
> *Family*—Paridae, the titmouse.
> *Genus*—*Parus*, Tits, titmouse, chickadees.
> *Species*—*carolinensis.*

You will see that the name of the order above ends in *iformes.* This ending is how you tell if it's one of the twenty-eight orders. Falconiformes are vultures, hawks, and falcons; Strigiformes are owls. Orders are another grouping you can tick off if you are interested. You'll also note that the name of the family ends in *idae.* Trogonidae is the family of trogons, Psittacidae of parrots. Some families are divided into subfamilies; you can tell if the ending of the word is *inae.*

If we had chosen the Ostrich, *Struthio camelus,* as our example, it would have been monotypic three times over. It is the only species in the genus *Struthio;* the only species in the family Struthionidae, which is the only family in the order Struthioniformes. So there!

Below the level of family and subfamily are two subdivisions, repeated here for emphasis:

> *Genus* (plural, *genera*) Latin for "race" or "kind." The genus designation is always the first word in the Latin name, and it is always capitalized. Our Chickadee is a *Parus.*
>
> *Species* (both singular and plural) is the specific name of the bird. Thus the Carolina Chickadee is known as a specific chickadee, *Parus carolinensis.* It is the species that constitutes the basic identification in all bird guides. There are approximately 8,600 extant species of birds in the world. Generally a bird guide will introduce the species with a brief description of the family of which it is a member.

Scientists group birds into order, family, genus, and species on the basis of the bird's anatomy. They also take into account where the bird lives, what it eats, and other characteristics, particularly its breeding behavior. Groupings are sufficiently permanent for the birder's intellectual comfort, but scientists do agree from time to time on changes, taking advantage of new scientific knowledge. Even the Latin or Latinized names are changed occasionally.

Subspecies, or races, are a further refinement of the system. We find that there are three races of Ostrich, the Somali, North African, and the Masai, located in three geographical areas. A species can be subdivided into one or more subspecies. Subspecies have a third word added to their Latin name. Thus the Green-winged Teal in Chapter 2 becomes the *Anas crecca carolinensis.* The Common Pheasant, *Phasianus colchicus,* thus is known as the *Phasianus colchicus formosanus* in Taiwan.

Periodically, ornithologists get together and, on the basis of new information, particularly breeding habits and range, change species designations. In birding parlance this is known as "lumping" and "splitting." In North America, it is a committee of the American Ornithologists Union (AOU) that does this. To date, there is no corresponding international committee.

Sometimes heretofore separate species are combined as subspecies of a single species. In birders' parlance, this is known as "lumping." For example, the Dark-eyed Junco, *Junco hyemalis,* lumps into one species what previously had been considered at least four separate species: the Slate-colored, Oregon, White-winged, and Gray-headed Juncos. What formerly were considered separate species are now known as races of the same species. When this happens, strict listers "lose" birds. Instead of listing four species of Juncos, they now list only one. The Bewick's Swan is now considered conspecific with—same species as—the Whistling Swan. The "new" swan was renamed Tundra Swan.

However, there are rewards as well as penalties. The Red-breasted and Red-naped Sapsuckers formerly were considered races of the Yellow-bellied Sapsucker. All three are considered "good" species now, such that birders who took note of seeing these subspecies in the past gain up to two "new" species on their life lists! This is known as splitting. Ornithologists sometimes get put into two camps: the lumpers and the splitters. Birders love the splitters, despise the lumpers.

Sometimes just the name is changed without changing the species designation. Catbird is no longer plain old "Catbird." For clarity, the Catbird of North America is now known as Gray Catbird to distinguish it from Black Catbird, a different species, on the Yucatán Peninsula. Then there are bowerbirds in the South Pacific that are called "catbirds." It *is* a complex world.

Recent field guides reflect the latest decisions on splitting and lumping at the date of publication. They also reflect changes in common names, most of which are made to reduce confusion for the world birder. Now "American" is put in front of Tree Sparrow, *Spizella arborea*, to distinguish it from the tree sparrow in Europe now identified as the Eurasian Tree Sparrow, *Passer montanus*. They're not even in the same family, leading Peter Alden to question the wisdom of new designations suggesting they are related. He'd like to see the American Tree Sparrow called the Winter Sparrow. Are we having fun yet?

The beginning birder is urged to buy the latest edition of a bird guide in order to learn the latest designations of species. Not to worry about what happened in the past; just know that sometime in the future there will likely be more splits and lumps and name changes. Scientific knowledge is turning up new information all the time, and new information is coming to light on the relationships of families, genera, and species to each other. Biochemical work utilizing radioactive DNA experiments may, in the future, take some of the guesswork out of the ordering of birds.

SKELETONS IN THE CLOSET

Most of us, if we search, can find a few family skeletons in our closet. We use the term to describe some relative or ancestor accused of some misdeed or general notoriety. In the bird world, we are referring literally to skeletons, the skeletons of extinct birds. Although our overwhelming concern is for the birds of the world today, the bird family tree would not be complete without mentioning the bird ancestors.

The granddaddy of all birds known today is the Archaeopteryx of the order Archaeopterygiformes (OK—"Arky.") Fossil remains of this creature indicate that it was the evolutionary link between reptiles and birds. On the time chart it goes back to the Upper Jurassic time, 130 million years ago, give or take a million, when it shared the earth with dinosaurs. A little later an order of toothed marine birds evolved, known as Hesperornithiformes, fossils of which have been found in North America. Another order, Ichthyornithiformes, developed at about the same time. Several other ancient orders are totally extinct; some have some living species.

Many people are initially confused about the arrangement of birds in the bird guide. At first glance there doesn't seem to be rhyme or reason. However, the orders are in the somewhat rough sequence of the geologic age of the bird. Authors of some bird books begin by talking about ancestral and extinct orders. They then move on to orders in which there are living species.

The ostrich is thought to be the most primitive of living birds. It would appear first in a world bird book. It is the first bird in an East African bird guide. A little later on came penguins and loons. The loons, called divers in Europe, are the first birds in North American and European field guides. Vultures, hawks, and falcons—Falconiformes—came even later. Passeriformes are the last order in bird guides. They are considered to be the most recent of the evolutionary lineage.

One final word about extinction. It is forever. Among early orders of birds some families are extinct; others survive. Among surviving families, some species are extinct. Among the loons order, for example, there are two fossil families. Of the surviving family, eight species have been described from fossils.

The moment of extinction is almost impossible to determine. Thus birds now thought to be extinct such as the Carolina Parakeet are still listed in recent bird guides. Who knows, birds thought to be extinct for hundreds of years do occasionally turn up, and we would want to be able to identify them.

The Passenger Pigeon was included in bird guides for many years after the last one died. The Eskimo Curlew is thought to be extinct, but birders still occasionally report them. (For a poignant story about *his* passage, read *Last of the Curlews* by Fred Bodsworth, Dell Publishing Co., 1955.) A pair of Ivory-billed Woodpeckers apparently was discovered in Cuba in the spring of 1986, bringing hope that the great bird is not yet gone. Modern bulldozing of specialized habitats, the use of lethal chemicals, the clearing of forests for home and farm, the introduction of "foreign" animals on islands, all raise warning flags. "Nuclear winter and current population trends alone or together will cause wholesale extinction of birdlife," believes Peter Alden.

THE ORDER OF ORDERS

Having rattled the bones of the bird world's ancestry, we can move on to sketch the order of birds as they are listed in most bird guides.

Very roughly following the evolutionary ladder, bird orders appear as follows in most bird guides and checklists. Deviations from this order are usually explained by the author.

Struthioniformes—Ostrich
Rheiformes—Rheas
Casuariiformes—Cassowaries and Emu
Apterygiformes—Kiwis
Tinamiformes—Tinamous
Gaviiformes—Loons (Divers)
Podicipediformes—Grebes
Procellariiformes—Albatross, Shearwaters, Petrels
Spenisciformes—Penguins
Pelecaniformes—Pelicans, Boobies, Cormorants, and kin
Ciconiiformes—Herons, Storks, Ibis, and kin
Phoenicopteriformes—Flamingos
Anseriformes—Ducks, Geese, Swans
Falconiformes—Vultures, Hawks, Falcons
Galliformes—Grouse, Pheasants, Turkeys
Gruiformes—Cranes, Rails, Bustards, and kin
Charadriiformes—Jacanas, Plovers, Gulls, and kin
Columbiformes—Pigeons, Doves, Sand Grouse
Psittaciformes—Parrots
Cuculiformes—Cuckoos, Coucals
Strigiformes—Owls
Caprimulgiformes—Frogmouths, Nightjars
Apodiformes—Swifts, Hummingbirds
Coliiformes—Mousebirds
Trogoniformes—Trogons
Coraciiformes—Kingfishers, Bee Eaters, Hoopoes, Hornbills, and kin
Piciformes—Jacamars, Honey Guides, Woodpeckers, and kin
Passeriformes—perching or sparrowlike birds (half the species of the world)

Birders, in the process of becoming world birders, will find that a knowledge of Latin names, Latin expressions, and family and species names will actually make life simpler and more enjoyable. It will be easier to determine if a bird of one name is the same species as a bird of another name. It will facilitate finding the species in a world bird list.

Use of some Latin expressions is common among world birders; it's their common language. Some of those expressions relate to the various families of birds and is a sort of shorthand. Instead of saying, "I know that bird is in the family of orioles, blackbirds, meadowlarks, and bobolink," experienced birders will say simply, "It's an icterid."

In getting a handle on the birds of the world, Peter Alden suggests it is most important to learn the unifying characteristics of the larger genera. "Remember that a genus *unifies* like creatures, while species *separate* like creatures." *Sterna* unifies terns that basically look alike; the different species, e.g. *fosteri*, *aleutica*, separate one species from another.

SPEAKING LATIN

The following are some of the commonly used Latinized words North American birders may use to identify birds:

Alcid	Family Alcidae, Auklets, Murres, Guillemots
Accipiter	Family Accipitridae, Osprey, Hawks, Eagles, Genus *Accipiter*
Buteo	Family Accipitridae, Genus *Buteo*
Corvid	Family Corvidae, Jays, Magpies, Ravens, Crows
Empidonax	Family Tyrannidae, Tyrant Flycatchers, Genus *Empidonax*
Fringillid	Family Fringillidae, Finches
Icterid	Family Icteridae, Orioles, Blackbirds, Meadowlarks, and Bobolink
Myiarchus	Family Tyrannidae, Tyrant Flycatchers, Genus *Myiarchus*
Pterodroma	Family Procellariidae, Shearwaters, Fulmars, Petrels, Genus *Pterodroma*
Passerines	Order Passeriformes, perching birds
Raptor	Latin for Bird of Prey (usually diurnal, not owls)
Turdus	Family Muscicapidae, Genus *Turdus*, thrushes
Tyrant Flycatchers	Family Tyrannidae

British birders more commonly use Latin or Latinized terms. They will frequently refer to the species in a genus by the genus name, particularly when there are quite a number of species in the genus. *Mergus* is the genus of a number of ducks known as "sawtooths," such as the Red-breasted Merganser. *Hirundine* comes from the family Hirundinidae, swallows. *Phylloscopus* is the genus of considerable numbers of confusing Old World warblers.

PART II

CONQUERING THE CONTINENTS: SAILING THE SEAS

INTRODUCTION

World birders tend to think of their activity in continental terms.

"I've birded on every continent."

"Have you done any South American birding?

The organization of this book reflects this thought process. There is a chapter on each continent, one on islands, and one on ocean birding. Such organization, however, poses some problems for birders. Many migrating birds span two or three continents.

World birders also quickly become aware of another way of viewing the world: major faunal regions. Birders who have not yet focused their binoculars across continental boundaries may not be familiar with faunal regions.

Clements' world bird checklist in hand, North American birders write in the date and place of their first sighting of a Common Redshank. The fine print says it is "widespread in Palearctic, Ethiopian, and Oriental regions." Checking off the Red-breasted Merganser, we find it is "widespread in the Holarctic region." The Brambling, often encountered in Europe, is "widespread in the Palearctic region."

Look at the inside cover of the Clements checklist. It all begins to make sense. A generalized map of the world shows seven major faunal regions. It is important to know them because world birders refer to them as they discuss the birds of major geographic areas. Field guides may also refer to them.

Faunal Region	*Includes*
Nearctic	North America, including Greenland, down to about mid-Mexico.
Neotropical	South America north to mid-Mexico, including the West Indies.
Palearctic	Europe, Asia north of the Himalayas, North Africa down to the Sahara Desert, and most of Arabia.

Holarctic	Nearctic and Palearctic combined.
Ethiopian	Africa south of the Sahara, Southern Arabia, and possibly Madagascar.
Oriental	India and Southeast Asia, to Bali and Sulawesi.
Australasian	Australia, New Guinea and some nearby islands, Tasmania, and New Zealand.
Oceanic	South Pacific Islands. (Some experts don't use this designation.)

Faunal or zoogeographic regions are major areas of the world where plant and animal species are more closely related to each other than they are to species in other faunal regions. Factors that delimit faunal regions have to do with ocean barriers, amount of rain, air temperature, or major topographic features such as mountains.

Although the organization of this book relates to the seven continents, some modifications have been made with respect to faunal regions. As an aid to the reader, brief definitions of the organization of Part II are provided here.

North America and South America

A look at the atlas shows that our continental geography includes the lower forty-eight states, Alaska and Canada, Greenland, Mexico, Central America, the Greater Antilles, and the West Indies. For birders, the term "North America" has not, until recently, included that portion of the continent south of the Mexican border nor the island communities in the Caribbean.

The southern half of Mexico and the islands lie south of the Tropic of Cancer, and those habitats are "tropical." Although many birds familiar in North America spend their winters in the tropics and some Mexican species regularly cross the Rio Grande into South Texas, New Mexico, and southeast Arizona, the birding community for years has found it convenient to use the Mexican border as the dividing line.

The American Ornithologists Union (AOU) provides the authoritative definition that most bird guides follow. North American birds in the past have been considered to be those found north of the Mexican border, including Alaska, Canada, Greenland, and Bermuda.

However, the sixth edition (1983) of the AOU checklist corresponds better to the geographer's North America and includes all of Mexico and Central America, including Panama. The Hawaiian Islands, Bermuda, and the West Indies, except for islands adjacent to South America, are also included. This new definition better integrates geographical North America with the Nearctic faunal region.

The older definition, i.e. Anglo-American, has been chosen for this book. Birding in Mexico and Central America is included in the Latin American chapter.

Europe, Asia, and Africa

British bird guides often include birds found in the Middle East (geographically part of Asia) and Northern Africa in order to more closely relate these guides to the Western Palearctic. Because the USSR transcends the Europe/Asia continental division, discussions of Russian birding occur in both Chapters 7 and 8.

Australia

New Zealand and New Guinea are included in this chapter to conform to the Australasian faunal region.

Islands

Chapter 12 includes both islands on the Oceanic faunal region and others that either are not closely related to major continental land masses or that are unique in their bird life.

♫ *Five* ♫

Bird America First:
Birding North America

WHEN DOES A BIRDER BECOME A WORLD BIRDER?

We surmise that birding at home doesn't qualify us as world birders. If "home" means the backyard and the local park, true. If you've birded just Ontario, Canada, for the past fifteen years, you really don't qualify as a world birder, even though you may be the best birder in the province. But venture forth across the continent in pursuit of over 700 birds, and you have taken the first step toward world birding.

For North Americans, birding America first may be an insidious lure to unveiling the wonders of birds around the world. World birders generally are well familiar with birds on their own continent. British birders take advantage of the fine birding opportunities just across the channel. Then they look across the North Atlantic and wonder how those long-lost colonies are doing. To find out, they begin ticking their North American bird list.

Some really good birders are so challenged by North American birding that they have little interest in the rest of the world. Besides, the habitats are diverse and the scenery magnificent. Listers may set their sights on seeing 500 species, not too great an accomplishment for a birder with casual-plus interest. Twenty-six avid birders in 1985 saw that many birds in one year according to the American Birding Association's (ABA) annual tabulation. The 1985 ABA list incluces 810 birders who listed 500 or more birds on their life list, a 16 percent increase over 1984.

Out of several million estimated watchers of birds in North America, that's peanuts. Of course there are more. Some people don't keep lists. Lots don't belong to the ABA. Some don't want to be listed; some of us just haven't gotten around to filling out the paperwork. There are a lot of birders out there who still have a lot of North America to see, lots of new birds to delight the eye and mind.

Between the 400 and 500 species mark, birders will notice a change: the birds stop crossing their path. They need now to make a conscious effort to cross the bird's path of flight. They begin to make lists of species they *haven't* seen and plan to go where they are likely to find them. This is when birding really gets interesting, when the birding bug becomes contagious.

Moving from 500 to 600 is tough. Birders become goal-oriented. The ABA reported that 439 birders counted 600 or more birds on their North American life list in 1985. From 600 on it's uphill all the way and requires a dedication, and often a pocketbook, that few birders can muster. Some birders will call it quits at 600. A few "pros" will push on toward the goal of 700, reached by only forty-four ABA listers in the 1985 report—a 50 percent increase over 1984!

"After reaching 700, my listing goals sort of disappeared," said Bill Bouton, member of the amorphous "700 club." He was then trying out tropical birding in Peru.

North America's top lister in 1984 (three others beat him for the top spot in 1985) and greatest birding booster was Benton Basham, who has at this writing combed the continent for 753 species.

As you might guess, some top birders are professional bird tour leaders, but some, like Basham, an anesthesiologist, have full-time careers. You might say he is addicted. He hears from the grapevine about every rarity reaching our shores. He jets around the country spotting the bird, greeting his fellow rarity-seekers with a deceptive laid-back geniality, sometimes hitting several birding "hot spots" in one weekened. His enthusiasm for his avocation is catching.

A real fraternity has developed among birders in the 600 and 700 range. They tend to show up most anywhere within hours of a rarity's occurrence. Friends were visiting the Nature Conservancy's Mile Hi Lodge at Ramsey Canyon in Arizona a few years ago when, in the afternoon, the identification of a rare hummingbird was confirmed. Early the following morning a carload of birders from Sacramento arrived. They had driven all through the night in the hopes of adding a new bird to their list.

Pelagic trips, still not common, often bring together birders who have met on other trips. Even though they may have seen all the ocean birds they are likely to see, hope springs from the waters that a vagrant will fly by. This happened in the fall of 1985 when Shearwater Journeys passengers, out of Monterey, California, spotted the Short-tailed Albatross, rare in North American waters. The sighting even made a public broadcasting news report.

Serious North American birders even have their own "professional" organization, much as do civil engineers, city managers, doctors, and lawyers. It is the American Birding Association (ABA). It publishes a magazine, *Birding,* concentrating, but not exclusively focusing on, North American birding. It provides a forum for the ranking of listers and holds a biennial convention.

The distinguished initials ABA even lend a certain aura to the organization, and occasionally a little confusion. Theodore A. Parker III, author, preeminent authority on the birds of Peru, and active member of the appropriate ABA, tells a hilarious story about a lengthy telephone conversation between his lawyer father, Theodore Parker, Jr., a member of the American Bar Association (ABA), and a naturalist who thought he was talking to young Ted.

"Is this Ted Parker of the ABA?"

"Yes."

Fill in your own ending.

The Audubon Society's *Encyclopedia of North American Birds* lists a total of 847 species of birds that live on our continent at least part-time or that have been spotted on or flying by our shores. With new sightings and species splits, ABA in 1986 listed 853 birds.

In sheer numbers of species, North America does not compare with many other areas of the world, particularly the tropical world. North America's 800-plus species are but a shadow of the 1,600-plus species found in several South American countries, including Peru, a country roughly twice the size of Texas. Mexico, our neighbor to the south, counts over 1,000; India, more than 1,200; Southeast Asia (Burma, Malaya, Thailand, Indochina, and Hong Kong), more than 1,100.

THE HABIT OF HABITATS

Many birds are restricted to specific habitats. If the particular habitat does not provide the food or variety of foods required, the bird normally will not be found. If the forest is not sufficiently large to provide not only a variety of food, but of cover, nesting material, and location, the bird will not be found there. If the swamp is filled and replaced by a housing development, waterfowl and other birds requiring a watery habitat will not land or nest.

Protection of particular habitats is essential to the perpetuation of the objects of the birder's attention. Fortunately, the United States and Canada have preserved large tracts of lands in parks, national forests, and nature preserves.

Major vegetational associations in North America are often classified into life zones or biotic communities. From north to south, or higher elevation to lower, major life zones are:

Arctic
Hudsonian
Canadian
Transition
Upper Austral, known as Sonoran in the west
Lower Austral/Sonoran.

These zones reflect differences in temperature and humidity that affect plant life and therefore bird life. Each life zone represents approximately 400 miles of north-south distance in North America or roughly 2,500 feet in elevation.

Each zone supports slightly different biotic communities. As you move from one life zone to another you will notice differences in the flora and fauna. As you climb a mountain or move from low to high elevation within a short distance, you will observe the same kinds of changes.

Just within the southwest New Mexico/southeast Arizona area, famous for its variety of bird life, all life zones except the Arctic can be experienced. When you start out in the desert, you are in the Lower Sonoran zone. It's hot and dry with cactus and desert wildlife. Moving higher, there is more rain, it's cooler, pinyon and juniper trees abound. Higher and cooler still is the Transition zone with its ponderosa pine and Gambel's oak.

Above is the Canadian zone with Douglas fir and aspen. In the Mogollon Mountains in Arizona, above 9,000 feet in the Hudsonian zone, it is cold, wet, and during the winter snow falls on the Englemann and blue spruces. Bird life reflects this diversity.

Biotic communities as definitions of habitat are more explicit. They define the diversity of this continent from the "Arctic" of far northern Alaska, Canada, and Greenland, to "tropical" areas of south Florida and "southern desert scrub" areas, extending north from Mexico into parts of the southwestern United States and Baja California.

Sometimes the biotic name shows up in the name of the bird; thus the chickadee of much of Canada, the Boreal Chickadee, is found in the "open-boreal coniferous forests" of Canada. In the "pinyon-juniper" biotic community we find the Pinyon Jay. In the description of its habitat we learn from the National Geographic field guide that it is found in the "pinyon-juniper woodlands of interior mountains and high plateaus."

Very large biomes, such as the grasslands of the states east of the Rocky Mountains, the "eastern deciduous forest" of much of the eastern United States, and the "northern coniferous forests" of much of Canada are familiar without definition to anyone who has been seeing America first. Some bird guides list the biomes and show them on a color-coded map.

Many North American birds are found only in particular biotic communities. Some species are widespread across the continent. Others migrate from one part of the continent to another; some migrate long distances, even to other continents. Thus, the birder seeking to know the birds of North America must pay close attention to the places where particular birds are to be found and often to the time of year. The White-headed Woodpecker is easily spotted in open coniferous forests above 4,000 feet from Washington to southern California, rarely elsewhere. Downy Woodpeckers on the other hand are quite widespread throughout the United States and Canada.

Other birds are east-west oriented, and several bird guides are separated into separate volumes covering birds of eastern North America and western North America. Generally the east-west boundary line is considered to be the edge of the semi-arid Great Plains on a line running north and south from mid–North Dakota along the 100th meridian. The American Dipper, the bouncy little gray bird playing around in rushing mountain streams, is only found in the West. The Brown-headed Nuthatch is only found in the East (southeast).

Some birds such as meadowlarks have eastern and western counterparts reflecting distinct species: the Eastern Meadowlark and the Western Meadowlark. There is a sizable area where their ranges overlap, and the birder may be hard-pressed to distinguish between them except when they sing. The Boat-tailed Grackle common along southeast coasts, particularly in Florida, meets the Great-tailed Grackle at about the eastern border of Texas. In such areas, greater attention to details is required in order to be sure of the identification. Other birds will be found nearly everywhere on the North American continent in suitable habitats, as shown on the distribution maps in most bird guides.

Coastal areas are home for many common water birds. Sometimes these birds are found on beaches, sometimes in water areas inland from the coast. Rice fields and other agricultural fields near coastal areas are good when they are being flooded. Many familiar coastal birds breed in the far northern limits of the continent up toward the North Pole and on the shores of Greenland. If you want to see the often drab sandpipers in their breeding plumage, journey in June to Churchill, on the shore of the great Hudson Bay in Canada.

Great Egrets are "bigger than a breadbox" and therefore easy to see along most coastal areas in the United States

MIGRATORY MIRACLES

Some birds are only found in North America in summer after they have migrated from Central or South America. Although North Americans think of many of the migrating warblers as "their" birds, some spend most of their time south of the border. These migratory birds provide us with close links with our Latin neighbors to the south. North Americans become aware that they must share the concern of naturalists throughout the world over the deforestation of much of South America. Loss of habitat there means fewer birds returning to enhance the North American springtime with their lovely songs.

Many migrants are found in very limited breeding grounds; others are more widespread. The Golden-cheeked Warbler, which winters in Mexico, is found in summer on the Edwards Plateau in a relatively small area of Texas west of Austin. The Rose-breasted Grosbeak summers in the northeastern and north-central United States and Canada, while the Black-headed Grosbeak is a common summer resident in the West. Both migrate south for the winter.

Most modern bird guides include distribution maps that will guide the birder on when and where particular birds are likely to be found. Be warned, however. While these maps are extremely useful in identifying birds and in showing where they may be found, they aren't infallible. Birds sometimes ignore them.

The Purple Gallinule, the iridescent chickenlike jewel of swampy areas in South Florida south to Argentina, summers in a limited range in parts of the southeast United States. Imagine my surprise to find a Purple Gallinule in April in a park pond south of Denver where snows were just receding. Distribution maps don't show the Black Scoter anywhere near South Florida, but many of us saw one bobbing in the surf close to the Sanibel Island beach in the winter of 1981–82. The scoter may be irruptive—that is, known to move occasionally beyond its standard territory in search of food. That same winter, a Common Eider was seen south of Sanibel in Naples, Florida, way beyond its normal range.

Many migrants touch down in border areas on their way north or south. Thus we may see the Rose-breasted Grosbeak in Everglades National Park in April, winging north. The Worm-eating Warbler rests in the Dry Tortugas on its way north. Wilson's Phalarope is common in Texas rice fields in May. None of those touchdown points show on guidebook maps, which often note only breeding and winter ranges.

Shorebirds are highly migratory. Most of the world's shorebirds breed in the far north near the Arctic Circle. It is here that they are found in their more colorful breeding plumage. As they approach their wintering grounds along southern coastal areas, their plumage may be variable. Some may still have remnants of their rich brown coats, but as winter approaches, their color turns to grayish and they blend in with the sandy habitat. That's the way most birders see them.

Chancing along the Atlantic or Pacific coasts in spring and fall may bring to you a windfall of birds. Both pelagic and land birds use these flyways. The Arctic Tern, greatest traveler of all, will be spotted from its breeding grounds in Alaska and northern Canada, down the coast of California and Mexico, down the South American Pacific coast, to finally reach Antarctica.

The central flyway is also busy with avian traffic. Birds travel from Alaska and northern Canada, and even from as far away as Siberia, across North America's grasslands. They cross Alberta and Saskatchewan, flying down through Montana, Wyoming, the Dakotas, and south to coastal Louisiana and Texas, a favored route for waterfowl.

These flyways provide many birding "hot spots." Many wildlife sanctuaries have been established along these routes by the U.S. government, sometimes by state and local governments. They provide safe breeding grounds, stop-over spots for birds needing bed and breakfast, and wintering grounds in which they may gather strength for that springtime trip back up north.

Other birds are confined year-round to a particular latitude. Some have adapted to survive the whole year under sometimes difficult climatic conditions. If you're waiting for a ptarmigan to migrate through southern California, you will wait forever. Ptarmigans have learned how to find food year-round in northern Canada and Alaska. If you want to see them, you must go there.

HIGHS AND LOWS

Elevation is another key factor in finding birds. The generalized biotic communities relate to some extent to elevation, but within such designated areas there are often finer differences in lifestyles. The Mountain Chickadee of the Rocky Mountain area will be found in high-altitude coniferous forests during nesting but at lower altitudes during winter. The Clapper Rail, found in coastal salt marshes (at or close to sea level), is unlikely to be found on a high cliff.

North America's topography provides a great diversity of altitude: from high alpine Mount Denali, reaching to over 20,000 feet in Alaska, to Death Valley in California, sinking 282 feet below sea level. Birders travel for many hundreds of miles in the wintertime to see millions of birds found at sub–sea level Salton Sea, a migratory "trap," a good place for the birds to find food and water.

WHETHER THE WEATHER IS GOOD OR BAD

Weather can also make a difference in what you see, and where. If you're checking on your vacation home on a Florida coast after a hurricane, look for birds blown in from the storm. You might find a Bananaquit from the Bahamas. Birders are among the few who eagerly anticipate a good hurricane, as all sorts of seabirds get blown from normal flight paths.

A late summer or early winter in the north may mean an early or late, strong or weak migration of birds through Florida. It is not an idle epithet that designates the annual flood of tourists to South Florida to see the "snowbirds." Experienced birders know that northbound songbirds along the western Gulf of Mexico can encounter severe head winds, forcing millions down into sparse coastal vegetation along the coasts of Texas, Louisiana, and Alabama—a birder's bonanza. Watch the weather, and remember that a good storm may blow in some good birds—even rarities.

BIRDING "HOT SPOTS"

For the person suffering a seizure of birding fever, there is another system for building up your North American list as quickly as time and pocketbook allow. Benton Basham says, "See the tough birds first, and you'll see all the rest along the way." He's devised a code system for classifying North American birds. A Code Five is a real toughie—accidentals that reach our shores. He says chase them fast. A Code One is likely to be found anytime you walk into the right park. Members of the "700 club" have to see a lot of Code Fives and Fours. Basham identifies 610 birds in the Code One and Two categories, likely to be seen while running after the others. In the middle is a Code Three bird, which requires you to be in the right place at the right time to see it. This code is included in the third edition of the *ABA Checklist,* available from the American Birding Association.

Particular places to see particular birds are known as birding "hot spots." Some such areas are good year-round, some are great at only one season, while others become a temporary "hot spot" if some rarity is discovered. Several guides are available that describe in detail many of these places. (See Part III.)

South Florida is a "hot spot" with year-round attractions. It is famous for big birds. They're easy to see close to road, path, or boardwalk, particularly in Everglades National Park. Brown Pelicans, only recently removed from the endangered species list, are everywhere in coastal waters. Huge American White Pelicans with striking black wingtips sail in formation over Florida Bay during winter months.

Large white birds festoon the mangroves like lights on a Christmas tree. Egrets, ibis, and herons are all over the place. Great Blue Herons are in abundance, consorting with Little Blue and Louisiana Herons, occasionally a Reddish Egret.

Roseate Spoonbills splash their incredibly pink wings across the bright blue sky. Mistaken by many nonbirders for the more famous Flamingo, the spoonbill can perhaps best be seen close at hand in the Ding Darling Wildlife Refuge on Sanibel Island (offshore from Fort Myers, Florida), where it swings its long, flat bill like a vacuum cleaner picking up tiny mollusks in the shallow water.

Refugees from the cold and snow find South Florida more than one kind of "hot spot" in winter. It's a good place to warm up to the birds. It is also the place birders come to get some of their "most wanted" birds: the endangered Snail Kite, the Purple Gallinule, the White-crowned Pigeon, the Mangrove Cuckoo, the Smooth-billed Ani, and a few exotics like the Red-whiskered Bulbul and the Canary-winged Parakeet.

One of the best birding drives anywhere is Route 41, the Tamiami Trail, between Miami and Naples. Snail Kites, Limpkin, Black and Turkey Vultures roost in the cypress early in the morning; Red-shouldered Hawks cap telephone poles; Bald Eagles and Wood Storks fly overhead. Great and Snowy Egrets and White Ibis look like ghosts in the dark forest and gracefully wing from one side of the canal to the other. Little Blue and Louisiana Herons do the same. Great Blue Herons stand like statues close by, Sandhill Cranes in the distance. Double-crested Cormorants and Anhingas hang their wings out to dry. Robins and an occasional Eastern Bluebird keep the kingfishers company on the wires. These birds were all seen on one winter two-hour trip.

Texas birding is so good that Roger Tory Peterson wrote a whole field guide for that great state. Graceful Scissor-tailed Flycatchers perch on nearly every utility wire. Roadrunners do it with regularity.

South Texas around the Brownsville area in winter and spring is great both for wintering North American species and for its resident Mexican species. Ringed and Green Kingfishers regularly fly across the Rio Grande for a look at *El Norte*. Probably the most famous garbage dump in the United States is the one at Brownsville, a good place to look for the Mexican Crow. If birders have a favorite dam, it's likely to be Falcon Dam, where with some effort they will find the Ferruginous Pygmy-Owl.

Anahuac National Wildlife Refuge, on the north coast of Texas, and surrounding areas have scads of species, particularly in the spring. Anahuac runs a buggy service in April to see rare Black and Yellow Rails. Dickcissels abound. Nearby flooded rice fields in May provide an astounding variety and quantity of shorebirds, including the Hudsonian Godwit. God Wot! High Island down on the Gulf of Mexico is a haven for migrating birds reaching the shoreline in the springtime. Land ho! They just drop down out of the sky to give their wings a rest and grab a bite to eat.

Aransas National Wildlife Refuge is best known for its winter population of the seriously endangered Whooping Crane. That won't be the only new addition to your list—Aransas claims the largest number of any refuge, 350 species.

Big Bend National Park, though way off the beaten path, reports 425 species of birds, more than any other park in the United States. Common western and uncommon birds abound. This is the only place north of the border to see the Colima Warbler. For the beginning birder, it offers a satisfying variety of western bird life; for the experienced birder, the chance to flesh out the life list.

Texas has been the site of many firsts of the North American birding world. One of the more interesting in recent times was the sighting on the famed King Ranch in 1971 of the Jabiru, the largest of the three storks found in the New World. Such a sighting, of course, makes history and good copy.

Located on the eastern edge of the Edwards Plateau in Austin is the home of the American Birding Association and several bird tour organizations, and focal points for fine birding. The delightful town of Fredericksburg directly west of Austin is a good base for exploring surrounding parks. Enchanted Rock State Natural Area has hard-to-miss Black-chinned Hummingbirds, Golden-fronted and Ladder-backed Woodpeckers,

Bewick's Wren, and Lark Sparrows. Nearby Pedernales Falls State Park is a good place to find the Golden-cheeked Warbler during the breeding season.

Southeastern Arizona in the spring and summer is legendary among birders because of the likelihood of finding strays from across the border. You might even see a bird new to North America as some of us did on a western birding trip in 1985. The hot news then from Cave Creek Canyon in the Chiricahua Mountains was the appearance of the Flame-colored Tanager, which had never before been seen north of Mexico. A couple of years earlier it was the Crescent-chested Warbler making its North American debut in the nearby Huachuca Mountains.

The Sonoran Desert, which stretches from Mexico up into southern Arizona, is a must for the birder passing through. It is a "rich" desert (don't read "dessert"), filled with life. The saguaro may be the most impressive of cactus species. It marches up and down hills and across the desert floor like a stiff-backed soldier. Pock-marked with black holes, it is home to Western Screech and Elf Owls, Cactus Wrens, Gila Woodpeckers, and Brown-crested Flycatchers, to name a few.

The best introduction to the region is the Arizona-Sonora Desert Museum just west of the city. It is an outdoor "museum," providing outstanding interpretive displays of the desert plants and animals. Serious birders avoid museums on the assumption, usually true, that the bird list won't be dented. This one is different. Representative birds of the Sonoran are found in a pleasant aviary and are a good introduction for the first-time visitor. Other local birds freely come and go, partaking of the free feed. (See Chapter 2 for which birds are "countable.")

Birders visit southeastern Arizona from all over North America and often from Britain too, looking for Mexican species that regularly reside or rest here. The Rose-throated Becard, Elegant Trogon, Painted Redstart, Red-faced Warbler, and up to a dozen species of hummingbirds are among the many jewels found only here.

California offered a boon for birders in the fall of 1984. Rarity seekers trekked to Santa Barbara County to see the Little Curlew, an Asian stray making its first appearance in North America.

California is a remarkable birding state. From the open sea, with its migration lane for pelagic birds, to coastal sea cliffs, sea beaches, lagoons, river estuaries, tidal flats, salt and freshwater marshes, chaparral, grasslands, woodlands, deserts, and mountains—California seems to have it all. The attendant diversity of plant life adds to the attractiveness of this state to both birds and birders. Both animals and people enjoy the bristlecone pine trees, more than 4,000 years old; the great redwood forests; tall ponderosa pines; citrus trees; and cacti.

According to the American Birding Association, California ranks second only to Texas in number of bird species. At this writing, it probably has lost one, the California Condor. Birders flocked to California in the summer of 1985 for perhaps their last opportunity to see them in the wild.

There were only seven left that August. The mountain lookout at Los Padres National Forest, north of Ventura, was perhaps the most poignant of all birding "hot spots."

Benton Basham, left, talks with friend about plight of the California Condors

One of the best birding areas lies north of San Francisco up the coast to Point Reyes National Seashore. On the way is Bolinas Bay, a great gathering place for shorebirds, and the adjacent Audubon Canyon Ranch with its mountain grandstand looking down on the high evergreens capped with Great Blue Heron nests. Head up there after your convention in San Francisco.

The Pacific Northwest, with its spectacular scenery, is full of excitement. From rocky mountains to rocky coastlines, traveler and birder will find endless fascination. Take the great ferry to Vancouver Island with its very British city of Victoria and see, perchance, poet Shelley's "blithe Spirit," the Eurasian Skylark. In coastal areas, Tufted Puffins, Rhinoceros Auklets, Harlequin Ducks, Arctic Loons, Surfbirds, and Black Turnstones will eagerly be added to your life list.

Gray Jays and Clark's Nutcrackers are common in mountain forests; watch for them in the Canadian Rockies. Pine Grosbeaks, Rosy Finches, Bohemian Waxwings, White-tailed Ptarmigans, Black Swift, and Blue and Spruce Grouse are here in the great Northwest.

Spectacular scenery and beautiful birds are not the only reasons to visit the Pacific Northwest. Watch for the golden-mantled ground squirrels, moose, black bear, and elk, and with sharp eyes you may spot bighorn sheep and mountain goats.

"***Alaska*** is the most interesting birding place in the United States," according to Ben King in a *Birding* magazine interview. King is one of the country's best-known bird tour leaders and author of *A Field Guide to the Birds of South-East Asia.* He is credited with the discovery of three new species for North America.

Many Alaska first-timers marvel, as I did, at their first sighting of puffins in Glacier Bay. If you fly out to the Pribilof Islands you will see thousands of nesting birds precariously perched on high cliffs, dropping sharply down into the gray Bering Sea: Horned and Tufted Puffins, Black-legged and the local Red-legged Kittiwakes, Common and Thick-billed Murres (rhymes with what cats do), Fulmars, and Pelagic and Red-faced Cormorants, to name a few.

Birds are not the only attraction of the Pribilof Islands. I'm not sure which most stimulated my travel glands: the puffins and other cliff birds, or the Northern Fur Seals. I did want to see what a million fur seals looked like. They were wall-to-wall; hardly a square foot of beach was visible. Certainly you can't avoid them anywhere on St. Paul Island. They're noisy, sounding like a million men all gargling at once.

Attu Island, way out at the end of the Aleutian Island chain, is probably the coldest "hot spot" in North America, one so cherished by the real hot shot birders that they make repeat trips. Larry Balch, one-time president of the American Birding Association, has been leading groups to that lonely, stormy outpost for a number of years. The targets are Siberian strays. A substantial number of the serious birders' most wanted birds, particularly if they are in the 600 to 700 range, can only be found on Attu. They'll look for Siberian Rubythroats, Whiskered Auklets, Eyebrowed-Thrush, Wood Sandpiper, Oriental Greenfinch, Hawfinch, Orange-flanked Bush-Robin, and other birds with exotic names. You might even see some of Santa's reindeer.

Churchill, located on the western shore of the Hudson Bay in Manitoba, packs a "double whammy" for the adventurous traveler. Few people would ever see this place, in the cold vastness of northern Canada were it not for polar bears and birds. Wildlife programs on television have publicized this remote place, and many travelers go just to ride in the huge, tanklike "bear buggies" to see the magnificent king of the northland.

Here you can watch millions of shorebirds in breeding plumage. You could see the Great Gray Owl if you're very lucky. Three-toed Woodpeckers, Smith's Longspur, lots of breeding warblers, Bald Eagles, Tundra Swans, and Ross' Gulls can be seen, along with many other birds hard to find except in such an unlikely place. Unfortunately the breeding birds haven't coordinated with the polar bears, and they are not likely to both be seen on the same trip.

Maine to Newfoundland is a tourist and birding corridor worthy of exploration. It's a land of rocky coasts, islands, waterways, and whales. Directly across the North Atlantic, as the Northern Fulmar flies, is England. The corridor runs from northern Maine up to Nova Scotia,

New Brunswick, the Gaspé Peninsula, to Newfoundland with the French outposts of St. Pierre and Miquelon islands off the southern coast.

You'll see tens of thousands of seabirds at Bonaventure on the Gaspé Peninsula, Northern Gannets, Common Murres, even Razorbills. High cliff areas are nesting sites for great colonies of these and other pelagic birds that must come to the coastal shore to breed and raise their young. You'll find Atlantic Puffins in coastal areas from northern Maine to as far north as you're likely to go. Machias Seal Island, involved in a minor border dispute between the United States and Canada, is good for puffins. For the best birding, be there in the nesting season, July.

Point Pelee, during spring or fall migration, is one of the most famous of the migrant "traps," as birds approaching or flying across Lake Erie flap down on that point of Ontario soil, southeast of Detroit. A good place for cobweb-clearing after a boring business convention in that city. Most eastern warblers, vireos, tanagers, grosbeaks, buntings, and their friends can be spotted here—by the hundreds and thousands. You'll have plenty of company. Birders from all over the world will be there with you. Good birding news travels fast and far. In spring, some birders will go on from here to the jack pine forests of north-central Michigan to try to find the endangered Kirtland's Warbler.

Hawk Mountain, which overlooks the Kittattiny Mountain Ridge of the Appalachian Mountains in eastern Pennsylvania, is a hawk "hot spot" where thousands of birders gather in September and October to watch the southward movement of anywhere from dozens to thousands of hawks. Sitting on the crown of the mountain, hundreds of birders will be found each day. Often with picnic lunches, they peer through binoculars at the horizon watching the tiny dark dots in the sky appear over the ridge become a few of the 20,000 raptors that pass by the Hawk Mountain Sanctuary each year. September 13, 1984, was a good day: 3,109 Broad-winged Hawks. That fall, forty-one Bald Eagles were spotted.

Many birders regularly set up hawk watches along the eastern United States to tally the number of each species. In 1984, in Westchester, New York, birders counted a whopping 7,403 Broad-winged Hawks over Mount Aspetong, and down at Cape May, New Jersey, 9,259 American Kestrels were counted. (Totals courtesy of *American Birds,* which records this kind of information.)

Plum Island and the Parker River National Wildlife Refuge is a favorite migratory bird "hot spot" just thirty-five miles north of Boston and adjacent to the delightful town of Newburyport. The barrier island provides good diversity of habitat: ocean beach, dunes, salt marsh, brackish wetlands, and good upland growth that attracts a variety of coastal, marsh, and land birds. Tie in a visit to Plum Island with your business meeting in Boston, but go early in the day as the number of automobiles allowed in the refuge is limited. Peter Alden points out that Newburyport

Harbor is superb for water birds and shorebirds. He reminds us that it was here in the 1970's that the famous Ross' Gull was found, making *Time* and CBS' *60 Minutes.*

Cape May, New Jersey, where the Delaware Bay joins the Atlantic Ocean, is another wonderful place for birders to be in the fall. Hawks and great numbers of migrants, both land and shorebirds, gather here before taking off across the bay for their southbound coastal journey. The last weekend in September and early October is usually the peak time for fall migrants.

AND NEXT THE WORLD

These brief "hot spot" descriptions are meant to tantalize, not to take the place of more detailed information available in the publications listed in Part III.

Know the birds of North America, and it will be easier to identify birds wherever you go in the world. One could of course make the birding jump from the backyard in Teaneck to Tanzania, or from Pittsburgh to Peru, but it's easier and better to bird America first.

World birders encounter many birds they already know. The Osprey and the Common Moorhen are the same wherever they are encountered around the world. We may have seen more American Coots, *Fulica americana,* than we want, but coots look like coots from Norwalk to Norway, and it won't be terribly difficult to identify others of the nine to ten species.

Black Skimmers, *Rynchops niger,* sipping the surface of North American coastal waters are the same ones we see along South American coasts. The one flying over the Ganges (that's how you know) is the Indian Skimmer, *Rynchops albicollis,* and the one flying over the Uaso Nyiro River in Kenya is the African Skimmer, *Rynchops flavirostris.*

Oystercatchers with their plastic-looking, fire engine red bills are unmistakable on beaches throughout the world. Once you learn the American Oystercatcher, the others fall into place: the Black Oystercatcher one might see at Glacier Bay in Alaska, the Blackish on the Falkland Islands, or the Sooty in Australia. So distinct are they as a group that they are in a family of their own, Haematopodidae.

Even with very different families in the New and Old Worlds we will recognize that two different families or even orders will occupy the same environmental niche. New World hummingbirds (family, Trochilidae) for example, are replaced in the Old World by sunbirds (family, Nectariniidae.) Hummingbirds are found in the order Apodiformes, which also includes swifts. Sunbirds are one of many families in the order Passeriformes, the perching birds. Both groups are easily spotted as they work the flowers in the garden. From your garden, the world beckons.

⪻ *Six* ⪼

Tropical Treats: Birding Mexico and Central and South America

Many North American travelers learn about the tropics while visiting Mexico or Central America. Birders, though, can actually begin a tropical bird list without a tourist card or passport. Tropical species cross the border regularly each year into southern Texas and southeastern Arizona. Tropical travelers like the Elegant Trogan and the Rose-throated Becard take up regular residence in *El Norte*. Although some are common south of the Rio Grande, visiting rarities often create intense excitement among ardent North American listers.

In April 1984, a vireo spotted near Galveston was later identified as a visitor, the Yucatán Vireo, setting off a buzz in the birder and scientific community. Ultimately 1,000 eager birders saw this small, brownish bird. The excitement of a new find keeps birders' adrenaline flowing.

Tropical birds are among the most colorful, most spectacularly beautiful in the world. Who wouldn't want to see a Resplendent Quetzal, a bright red-orange male Andean Cock-of-the-Rock, or a pair of Scarlet Macaws against a clear blue sky? A purplish bird with the turquoise crown and plastic-looking red legs, the Red-legged Honeycreeper, must be seen to be believed.

No other continent has the diversity of bird life found in South America. It blows the mind to contemplate the numbers of species found in just one country. Mexico—over 1,000; tiny Panama, nearly 900—more than on the entire North American continent north of the Mexican border. Upward of 1,700 species have occurred in Peru, 1,300 in Venezuala, 1,400 in Ecuador, and 1,600 in both Brazil and Colombia.

Ornithologists estimate that nearly 3,000 species of birds are found in South America, one-third of the world's total!

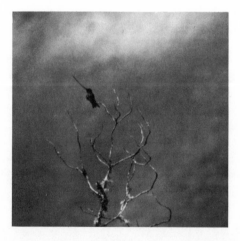

With a third of the world's species of birds, South America's birdlife reflects tremendous diversity shown here by the Sword-billed Hummingbird, whose bill is longer than its body, that can be found in the Andes Mountains

The Magellanic Penguin is found by the tens of thousands in Patagonia

The tropics, home to the largest number of species in the world, seem to many North Americans to be distant, mysterious, maybe dangerous, exotic, remote, and romantic. Tropical countries often live up to these impressions. Frequently, travel within them is difficult. Beyond the big cities are one-lane dirt or gravel roads—if there are roads. Even in tourist areas, directional signs are often inadequate or nonexistent. Rivers often are the only connection between one village and another.

Although causing the birding traveler major inconvenience, accessible areas harboring intact bird populations are still to be found. In some remote areas, particularly in the eastern Andes of Peru, birds new to science are still being found. Such may not be the case for long. Peruvian bird expert Ted Parker (whom you will meet very shortly) in the summer of 1986 participated in an expedition funded by the National Geographic Society in northern Bolivia. They found fifty-one species new for Bolivia, "surely the last time so many species will be added to a country list," Ted wrote to me.

Tropical forests are disappearing around the world at a catastrophic rate. When a forest disappears, it takes a tremendous toll on the great diversity of life within the forest, from fungi to animals. So protective is the forest of the many forms of life within it that scientists will be discovering the hidden secrets of the forest for many years to come—if the forest survives. At the present rate of destruction, in a very few years, some of the ferns, trees, spiders, butterflies, and birds that have lived there for millennia may disappear without our knowing they ever lived.

Most North American travelers seek not forest but city. Thousands of North Americans visit Mexico without remembering a tree or a single bird. Yet over 1,000 birds have been identified in that country.

Pursuing a world birding hobby guarantees that you will see much more of the world than the capital cities. Typically, the tourist traveling to Peru flies into Lima, goes to Cusco for a day or two, takes the early morning train down the beautiful Urubamba River valley to Machu Picchu, spends a few hours touring the ruins, takes the afternoon train back to Cusco for a flight to Lima, and leaves Peru. Maybe there will be a short jungle cruise with a stopover at a jungle camp, a sampling of the riches beyond.

Such quickie trips reveal little of the beauty and diversity of a country like Peru. Birders will see all the above but will also walk down forest paths in the deep jungle, hear the chatter of monkeys high in the trees, watch a coatimundi family cross the path ahead. They will hike in the puna, high grasslands of the Andes, and observe the way of life of remote Quechua Indians in the highlands. They will visit offshore islands, washed by the Humboldt Current, famous in years past for their guano treasure. With all this sightseeing, birders will see incredible numbers of birds to delight the eye and to satisfy the listing lust, best slaked in tropical America.

When North American birders go beyond Mexico City to the far corners of our neighbor country, they may not speak the language but they will recognize many familiar birds—the vireos, warblers, tanagers. These birds come north to breed but fly south for the winter. Some species are endemic to Mexico—they are found nowhere else. Other birds in Mexico are in the northern part of their range and really belong in Central or South America. Birders visiting Mexico and Central American countries will see both temples and toucans.

PENGUINS AND PARROTS

A look at topographic maps of the Western Hemisphere shows clearly the dominance of the great mountain chain that extends down the western borders of both continents from the Arctic to Antarctic. Mountains and seas interact to affect the nature of plant and animal life.

In South America, it is the long Andean chain that is one of the major influences on life. The added influence of the frigid Humboldt Current, flowing north from Antarctica, bathing the Andes on the west, brings penguins to the tropics. Offshore from Peru, it is the Humboldt Penguin. Offshore from Ecuador, in the Galápagos Islands, it is the Galápagos Penguin.

Across the Andes is another great geographic influence: the Amazon Basin. The Amazon River is the largest river system on earth. With its thousand tributaries, it drains the largest and widest part of South America, 40 percent of the entire continent. This mighty river system drains nearly three million square miles of the continent into the Atlantic Ocean. Most of Amazonia is tropical rainforest, providing home to a vast variety of plant and animal life, a variety so great that all the scientists who have ever visted there still have not uncovered all its treasures.

Parrots are here in profusion in the low-elevation, moist, forested areas, particularly in Amazonia. Seventy of the world's 332 species of parrot have been found in Brazil; forty-one in Peru. In the tropical and sub-tropical zones in Venezuela forty-eight species of parrot have been identi-fied; in Colombia, forty-nine.

South America and Africa both have extremely large land areas lying between the Tropic of Capricorn and the Tropic of Cancer, that area north and south of the equator where the sun, at some time of day, at some time of year, is shining directly overhead. That sun begins the life cycle that provides such wonders at the other end of your binoculars.

TRINIDAD TREATS

The world birding gurus you met in Chapter 1 proposed that the place to begin world birding was Trinidad. It has a wide variety of tropical birds, once having been a part of the Venezuelan mainland; it's readily accessi-ble by air from New York and Miami; and there is a good field guide for the area.

Here, where a drawing of the Scarlet Ibis is on the scarlet Trinidad dollar bill, you surely will take the boat trip at sunset into the Caroni Swamp. As daylight fades, anywhere from hundreds to thousands of Scarlet Ibis, with color suggesting the most intense of passions, fly in, circle a few times, then festoon themselves against dark green mangroves. The mystery of this daily phenomenon and the silence of the swamp is broken only by the slap of the water against the boats and hushed murmurs of the waiting birders.

Birders likely will stay at the Asa Wright Nature Center, a cool moun-tain oasis, or at the Guest House of Mount St. Benedict Monastery, lower down the mountain. Trips around the island, led by knowledgeable local guides, are readily available.

The nature center, catering to birders and photographers, is on a love-ly hill, surrounded by a small, tropical farming plot (lots of bananas and citrus). Sugar-water feeders around the main house attract hummingbirds. Fruit feeders attract tanagers, sunbirds, and honeycreepers.

Crested Oropendolas crisscross the front garden. Yellow Orioles fly from tree to tree. A Common Black Hawk hangs overhead in the morn-ing. A Chestnut Woodpecker may be pecking at a grapefruit not yet ripe, a White-tailed Trogon stays close, and Smooth-billed Anis constantly con-verse. Mixed-feeding flocks, such as you will encounter throughout South America, move from tree canopy to tree canopy: Turquoise and Bay-headed Tanagers, Blue Dacnis, Violaceous Euphonias, Purple and Red-legged Honeycreepers.

Down the hill from the main house, you may see your first lek, a gathering place for male birds to display themselves to visiting females. This one is a White-bearded Manakin lek, under the trees down a wooded hillside. It is a small circular area on the forest floor, cleared of leaves and other debris, where the fat little black-and-white birds prance about. Later in the day, if you are lucky, you may see one of the elusive Little Tinamous, whose melancholy whistle you've been hearing every afternoon. And overhead, the splashy Squirrel Cuckoo jumps from limb to limb.

One of the highlights of a birding trip to Trinidad will be seeing the strange, cave-dwelling Oilbirds, which aren't closely related to any other birds. They are in the monotypic family Steatornithidae but are now thought to be cuckoos. There are not many of them, but they are often seen in a dark cave reached by hiking down a steep hill from the nature center.

SOUTH OF THE BORDER

Birding in Mexico and Central America is a good introduction to the birds of tropical America. Good areas in Mexico are the central and western coastal areas from Mazatlán through San Blas, to the very "birdy" state of Colima; the Catemaco area of southern Veracruz; Oaxaca southeast of Mexico City; and the Yucatán. If you're an archaelogical buff, you'll love the Mayan ruins in the Yucatán and nearby areas: Palenque, Chichén Itzá, Uxmal, Tulum, and Cobá.

If you're a buff of another kind, take your binoculars with your bikini to the Club Med at Cancun. Cancun and the neighboring island of Cozumel have become tourist meccas, particularly for North Americans seeking respite from frigid winters. This area on the east coast of the Yucatán offers a great combination of diving and snorkeling, ruin exploring, and birding. Partially cleared archaeological sites are particularly good places to see birds. Staying at a "camptel" like KaiLuum offers birding opportunities from the moment you emerge from your tent (to visit the facilities) until early evening sunset.

Birds will include some North American familiars down for the winter and a good collection of tropical birds, such as the Tropical Mockingbird, Black Catbird, Aztec Parakeet, Melodious Blackbird, and perhaps Flamingos. Look for the endemics: the Yucatán Woodpecker, Jay, and perhaps Parrot. On Cozumel Island, a few minutes flight from the mainland, look for the Cozumel Thrasher and Vireo. Don't laugh, but watch in the dead treetops as you drive along the roads for the Laughing Falcon, a creamy white hawk with black-mask and back.

"Ruin-ed" birders will also do well to visit in Guatemala the magnificent ruins of Tikal, perhaps the most impressive of the Mayan ruins. Impressive too are the birds to be seen in the jungle surrounding and protecting the ruins. Birds are so important in Guatemala's history that its unit of currency is the Quetzal, named for the Resplendent Quetzal.

Tikal is the best place in the world to see the improbably festooned Oscellated Turkeys, the only close relative of our Wild Turkey. Yellow-backed, Black-cowled, and "our own" Northern Oriole, Pale-billed and Lineated Woodpeckers, look-alikes to our Pileated Woodpecker, sit together in the same tree. Keel-billed Toucans, Collared Aracaris, Emerald Toucanets, and Collared, Citreoline, and Violaceus Trogons seem to be all over. Crested Guans perch in the tree over your head. The object of many a birder's visit to Tikal is the Orange-breasted Falcon, found right there in the Central Plaza.

A one-day fly-in is not for the birder. A week is none too long for both exploring the vast ruins and seeing the large numbers of tropical birds and some of the animals. Spider and Howler Monkeys frolic in the leafy branches over the jungle paths. At night, birders spot the red eyes of the Pauraque sitting quietly in the grass beside the airstrip, the Vermiculated Screech-Owl responding to a call, or a Cacomistle, cousin of our ring-tailed cat, in the nearby forest.

Costa Rica is another beautiful country of mountains, rainforests, coastal marshes, shores, and jungles, where wild and beautiful ferns, orchids, and bromeliads delight the nature lover. This is a popular tropical birding destination because of its stable political climate and friendly people. Accommodations generally are pleasant, but the roads are not only long but bumpy. Birders, in order to be close to the good birding in lowland jungles, stay in less than luxurious surroundings.

Listen to that soft gurgle that sounds like a running stream; it's a Montezuma Oropendola. You'll see their great pendulous nests hanging from tree branches all over the place. Flashes of red on a black bird flying in the clearing could be a Crimson-collared or a Scarlet-rumped Tanager. The emerald and scarlet bird flying through the Monteverde cloud forest must be the Resplendent Quetzal.

Panama, that bridge between the Americas, smaller than the state of South Carolina, probably has more birds per square inch than any place else. Its mountains, humid, lowland rainforest, dry Pacific savannah, and geographical location make this tiny country a migration "hot spot."

Getting about is quick and easy. Forested hills are visible from the airport in Panama City. In the company of a local birder, even a few hours layover between planes could be memorable. You'll see manakins, toucanets, aracaris, barbets—a variety that will dazzle you if this is your first tropical birding experience. On a two-week trip with competent guides, it is easy to see over 400 species.

SOUTH OF SOUTH: WHERE TO GO IN SOUTH AMERICA

Caracas, Rio de Janeiro, São Paulo, Buenos Aires? Or perhaps a flying tour of a dozen capital cities? South America's cities are well known but little visited by North American travelers. Unsettled political conditions in some countries have raised caution flags. Poverty and its handmaiden, crime, abound. Yet the seasoned traveler will find much fascination with the cultural tapestry of its many countries, the sophistication of its great cities, the magnificence of its scenery, its vacation variety from the ski slopes of Chile to the beaches of Rio. Discretion and caution will guide the traveler, as they should anyplace in the world.

Although the best birding in South America, as is usually the case, is found far from the great cities, even the business traveler who wants to sample tropical birding can do so in or near most of the cities. Try the Botanical Gardens in Rio. Take a boat trip from Valparaiso, Santiago's port city, for a collection of pelagic species. Visit Cabo San Antonio on the coast, south of Buenos Aires.

A birding tour to a South American country may be the ideal way to experience more of the country than the capital city, overcome any language barrier, and—through seasoned guides totally familiar with the country—tour in safety. Victor Emanuel, who has run countless tours to South America, suggests Peru, Southeast Brazil, and Venezuela as among the best birding areas, with Argentina added because of both birds and spectacular scenery.

Ecuador is popular with travelers, and then out to the Galápagos Islands. You will enjoy visiting the colonial capital of Quito, sitting at 9,000 feet, improbably located within sight of the snowcapped volcano Cotapaxi, 19,300 feet high. Now those are real "highs." If you can, get out of the city and learn the birds beyond the hotel gardens and city parks. Although a small country, the great variation of terrain and habitat provides marvelous birding. Sitting astride the equator, Ecuador provides a range of elevation from coastal beaches and marshes to the high Andes at 21,000 feet. A good introduction to Amazon birding is available using the *Flotel Orellana,* operated by Metropolitan Touring.

Caracas, Venezuela, a short flight from Miami, is the starting point for birding this country capping the northern coast of South America. If you're familiar with the language, you may want to bird on your own. Roads and accommodations are good, and there's an excellent bird guide covering the country's 1,296 species, forty-six of which are endemic. Most world birders will probably opt for an organized birding tour, which will hit the birding highlights. One of the best sites is the Henri Pittier National Park, boasting over 500 species.

Colombia, gateway between Central and South America, is both readily accessible from North America and popular with birders. With shores bathed by the Caribbean and the Pacific Ocean, it ranges from high Andes to vast low-lying Amazonia. Like the other countries of tropical South America, it is a country of birds nearly matching the number of species in Peru.

Argentina, its northern border touching the Tropic of Capricorn, its southernmost point once linked with Antarctica, hosts fantastic bird life, matched by dramatic scenery. From the Cordillera, rimming the country on the west at elevations over 16,000 feet, to the subtropical forest whose great rivers flow into the Atlantic, the birding traveler will find much to delight. Ever heard of the Toco Toucan? Bet you didn't see it when you visited Iguassu Falls. It is the largest of the world's toucans and worth the trip. Also making a birding trip worthwhile would be seeing the endangered Black-fronted Piping Guan. The Chaco Chachalaca may make you chuckle, as you surely will when you tote up your Argentine trip list.

A major South American tourist attraction, Iguassu Falls, is not only a spectacular falls—higher than Victoria Falls—it is a good birding area. Although your traveling friends probably raved only about the falls, you might see a Red-breasted Toucan, Blond-crested Woodpecker, the common Red-rumped Cacique, and maybe a Red-ruffed Fruitcrow along nearby forest roads.

Penguins too. The New York Zoological Society regularly inveigles volunteers to band the Magellanic Penguins at their breeding colony at Punta Tombo, a remote, windswept beach on the coast, south of Buenos Aires.

One of the volunteers, Vermonter Maida Hodges, writes, "Our group of nineteen pitched tents and set up a campfire behind a ridge—well away from active penguin burrows. There was a constant din of braying penguins, relentlessly blowing cold wind and roaring surf; all-in-all the most unlikely spot imaginable for one's winter vacation. . . . In the morning we discovered a Magellanic Penguin had begun burrowing under the corner of our tent."

After doing that labor of love (?), the rest of Patagonia, the area of Argentina south of the Rio Colorado, beckons the birder seeking birds yet unfound, places yet unexplored; a great fascination for adventurous travelers seeking our vanishing wildlife.

On the Peninsula Valdes there are also colonies of sea lions and elephant seals on cliff rocks. Perhaps birders will pass through desert brush, where they will see the Guanacos, cousins of camels, and the Elegant Crested Tinamou. Then on to Glacier National Park with its spectacular scenery.

Brazil, larger than our forty-eight states and site of a conservation battle of epic proportions as environmentalists attempt to stem the deforestation tide, is a favorite destination for world birders. Knowing that the birds disappear when the forest disappears, many birders have a sense of urgency about visiting this vast country. They most want to see the Hyacinth Macaw, the world's largest parrot. And for collectors of odd names, it may be the Firewood-Gatherer, a member of the Ovenbird family (not related to our Ovenbird).

The Ovenbird family seems to have more than its share of unbelievable names, many of them found in Brazil: Straight-billed Reedhaunter and Larklike Bushrunner are other examples. Their close cousins, the Band-tailed Earthcreeper and Spectacled Prickletail, will be found in Argentina and Colombia respectively. Try them on your friends back home.

Your first trip to Brazil may be a business or vacation trip to Rio de Janeiro. There are places like the Botanical Gardens near Ipanema Beach that can be readily reached and where birding may be good. Several national parks, particularly Itatiaia, offer good birding and can be reached by the birder-traveler from Rio. Brazil is so vast, the habitat so varied, that choices will have to be made on where best to concentrate. Central Brazil, with its vast but dwindling open woodlands and high plateau grasslands, is a favorite of many birders.

With nearly one-fifth of the world's bird species, Peru may be the epitome of South American birding. Rich avifauna and diverse habitats make Peru one of the finest places in the world for the birder to visit. From the barren Atacama desert coast to tropical forests to the snow-mantled Andes, it is a country full of wonder.

Nearly 1,700 birds have been sighted in this small country where valleys not yet described and remote mountains beckon the scientist to discover new plants and animals. Ted Parker says that more than thirty species have been discovered there during the last quarter century.

Peru provides a synthesis of tropical bird life in the New World. Not only is the country host to 110 endemic species, it is a passageway or resting place for migrants from as far south as Argentina and even Antarctica; from Central America, Mexico, and North America as well. The tremendous diversity of trees, bushes, vines, and ferns, with their berries, fruits, and flowers, combined with gradations of terrain, ranging from sea level up to the high puna of 16,000 feet, provide a constant source of nurturing food for birds of different appetites and styles of living.

Yet the destruction of that habitat is one of the most searing impressions I gained on my July 1985 birding trip to Peru. Arranged by Victor Emanuel Nature Tours, our birding group consisted of twelve birders. Theodore A. Parker III, coauthor of the soon-to-be-published landmark book *A Guide to the Birds of Peru,* headed our team of leaders.

Birding with Ted is an unusual treat. His easy-going personality belies his tremendous knowledge of the birds of Peru. He's seen most of them, described for science some of them. Ted "reads" the forest with his ears, so familiar is he with the songs of hundreds of birds. In a letter, Ted once wrote: "With regard to the importance of hearing vs. seeing in the tropical forest (or any forest for that matter), one must remember that the most common species are usually the most visible, and that their movements are a great distraction to anyone who seeks the rarer, more reclusive species. When I walk along a forest path in search of "special" birds of the latter kind I often keep my head down so as not to be distracted by something large and common moving through the foliage above me, and concentrate on listening for the often faint and distant call of a sought-after species. One could easily spend an entire morning being drawn to the motion of one common bird after another, and in the end miss dozens of lesser known and exciting varieties that were perching motionless just a few yards away. In a tropical rainforest, where as many as 500 species might live within an area of a few square miles, it could take months or years for an inexperienced birder to find the majority of species present. In contrast, one who has a good knowledge of avian vocalizations can find 300 + species in a day, and well over 400 in a week or two! The importance of knowing calls and songs cannot be overstated."

Our team of leaders is completed with Victor Emanuel and Tony Meyer, medical doctor turned naturalist. As we traveled up or downriver toward remote locations, we witnessed more clearing and planting, more erosion, more pollution, and inevitably, fewer animals. Many birds and mammals have retreated even farther into the dense jungle than we were privileged to go. But the message was clear: the rainforest, home to incredible numbers of living things, is fast disappearing.

So it was with some sense of urgency that I had decided to bird in Peru. As in so many undeveloped countries, habitat destruction is combined with political instability, putting them on an "endangered country" list. Catch the flavor of Neotropical birding in Peru in these excerpts from the journal of that trip.

ONE BIRDER'S PERUVIAN ADVENTURE
BIRDING PERU: EXCERPTS FROM A DIARY

Amazonia

We leave Lima's cool grayness July 4 to fly over the sharp spine of the Andes and the broadly meandering rivers in lush green valleys, to land at Iquitos, a city of two million people situated on the edge of the Amazon. A Gray-breasted Martin greets our plane, poking at the wingtip once the engines quieted. A life bird for some. Familiar Black Vultures soar overhead and wire-perching Tropical Kingbirds line the road into the city. Smooth-billed Anis perch precariously on road-edge reeds and bushes.

Our bus, soon to reach retirement age, delivers us to riverside, and we clamber aboard a motorized thatch-covered riverboat. Quickly, we begin learning the birds of this milk-chocolate river. First downriver, then up the Napo, one of the larger tributaries of the Amazon. Kingfishers bearing the river's name, Yellow-billed and Large-billed Terns, a familiar Black Skimmer (but of the South American race), Osprey, familiar everywhere in the world, searching fish from aloft, Pied Lapwings, Collard Plovers and Sand-colored Nighthawks on a sandbar, Yellow-headed Caracara, White-winged Swallows swooping low over the water.

Four hours from Iquitos we arrive at a place called Yanamono, meaning "black monkey." Here is Explorama, a complex of simple wooden-stilt structures with thatched roofs. Our rooms are narrow, opening onto a walkway the length of the dormitory building, outfitted with mosquito-net-covered beds and a washstand with enamel bowl and pitcher. Used wash water is simply poured over the open railing. Privies and showers are down wooden walkways, at forest edge. Meals are buffet style; food is plentiful and good.

Following our briefing in one of the buildings where soft drinks, beer, and limited alcoholic beverages are available, we lunch and then head down the trail—for some, a first experience in tropical birding. Within minutes we spot on the muddy path in front of us one of the highlights of the trip, a Sunbittern. Related to cranes and rails, the Sunbittern is the sole member of the family Eurypygidae. Its foot-and-a-half long body has a long, thin neck. Body resting solidly on moderately-long legs, it sort of looks like a long-necked Dachshund on stilts.

The afternoon's bird list strains the imagination: Chestnut-eared Aracari, Social and Boat-billed Flycatchers, Roadside Hawks copulating, White-throated Kingbird, Russet-backed Oropendola, Speckled Spinetail, Fork-tailed Palm Swift, White-eyed Parakeet, Buff-breasted Wren, Dusky-headed Parakeet, Chestnut Jacamar, Scarlet-crowned Barbet, Dark-billed Cuckoo, Red-eyed Vireo, one of "our" North American birds, Tui Parakeet, Lineated Woodpecker, reminding us of our Pileated, Glittering-throated Emerald (hummingbirds have such exotic names), Spot-breasted Woodpecker, Yellow-crowned Tyrannulet, Orange-fronted Plushcrown, Guira Tanager, Short-crested Flycatcher, Red-capped Cardinal, Bare-necked Fruitcrow, Black-throated Mango, Southern Roughwinged Swallow, Yellow-rumped Cacique, Thick-billed Euphonia, Chestnut-bellied Seed-eater, Yellow-browed Sparrow, Short-tailed Parrot, Yellow-tufted Wood-pecker, Blue-winged Parrotlet, Wattled Jacana, Lesser Kiskadee, Striated Heron, Palm Tanager, Straight-billed Woodcreeper, Black-capped Mocking-thrush (which probably is a wren!), Masked Crimson Tanager. Whew!

Each of the three lodges we were to visit had its own "pet" birds. At Explorama they were colorful Scarlet and Blue-and-Yellow Macaws. We were later to see macaws flying in the wild. During a brief rainstorm they had an instant bath, turning their faces and wings upward to catch as much rain as possible.

With eyes barely open our first morning in the jungle, a visit to the privies produces the first of many Black-fronted Nunbirds, perched on a slender sapling. The list would grow substantially by mid-morning. Plain-breasted Piculet, Tropical Screech Owl (it enjoyed early evenings under the thatched roof in full view of some beds), Solitary Black Cacique, Spotted Tody Flycatcher, Large Elaenia, Greater Manakin, White-winged Becard, Plumbeous Kite, Black-banded Crake (a rare bird of the under-growth persuaded with a tape recording of its voice to cross the path in front of us), a pair of Pale-legged Horneros, Gray-crowned Flycatcher, Yel-low-breasted Flycatcher, Hooded Tanager, Grayish Saltator, White-eyed Parrot. And it isn't even lunchtime!

Ted Parker speaks always of "learning" the birds, not just seeing them. The river we travel must be learned too, for it is ever changing, spawning sandbars and new islands that have a life of their own, support-ing successive populations of bird life. As sandbars grow up to be islands they are first covered with grasses providing food and shelter for a few seed-eating birds. As the island "grows," tessaria bushes become rooted, followed by willows and cecropia trees.

Later, Mimosa and the flowering Inga trees create a more complex environment, crowding out the early shrubs and grasses but providing a "living room" for a different group of birds that need a more complex plant world. Finally, the island matures and becomes "old" with an even greater mix of trees: the Ficus, or fig tree, Erythrina, Bombax, Ceiba, or kapok tree. Now an even larger number of bird species can be found. Sometimes this growing complexity of island life can be observed on a single island, showing a progression of complexity from the lower end to the upper end.

At Sucasari, farther up on the Napo River, the Explornapo camp has no electricity or running water. Sleeping quarters consist of a wing of an I-shaped structure built on stilts with thatched roof. We are warned that "the walls are very thin" as we approach mattresses on the floor, each with a mosquito-net hood. The netting provided a small degree of privacy but, at the time we were there, it wasn't really needed for mosquito protection.

We quickly encounter Explornapo's pets. Most engaging were the pair of Gray-winged Trumpeters, chickenlike birds with long necks and longish legs. They squawk like chickens but have an engaging "purr," a low, rumbling sound that seems to arise from deep in the belly. Running down the porch to greet our group, the trumpeters stir up the pet dogs, and once we are welcomed, trumpeters and dogs engage in a game of "chase." The trumpeters want very much to join us on birding trips and always must be shooed back to camp, only to greet us again when we return. A baby Kinkajou, brought to the camp when it was abandoned by its mother, completes the delightful collection of pets.

We bird nearby riverine islands reached by boat. We hike on muddy trails through the dense forest. From the boat dock Ted points out a bird he discovered, not yet officially described to science, the Orange-eyed Flycatcher.

Our early Explornapo list includes many new birds: Leaden Antwren, Blue-headed Parrot, Speckled Chachalaca, Pale-vented Pigeon, Orange-winged Parrot, Bat Falcon (chasing a bat), Striped and Straight-billed Woodcreepers, Silvered Antbird, Short-billed Antwren, Buff-breasted Wren, Coraya Wren, Amazonian Antshrikes, Yellow-bellied Dacnics, Castelnau's and Barred Antshrikes, Pale-billed Hornero, White-winged Becard, Fork-tailed Woodnymph, Blackish Antbird, Short-crested Flycatcher, Blue-chinned Sapphire, Crimson-crested Woodpecker, Sooty Antbird, Golden-crowned Manakin, Short-tailed Nighthawk, Phyrattic Flycatcher, Slender-footed Tryannulet, White-chinned Jacamar, Pygmy Antwren.

Birds in the forest's deep recesses are called into view by playing tapes of their calls. Often Ted would predict just where the bird would appear to investigate the apparent intruder: "Watch in that little clearing to the left of the big tree trunk; it will probably hop onto the dead log."

These are the antbirds, the antwrens, the antshrikes, small dark birds hiding in the dark forest's undergrowth—scores of different species, each distinguished from the other by slightly different markings, size and shape, or height at which they are found.

An expert in identifying these birds, by shape, size, call in particular, and activity, Ted concentrated on helping us learn them. In one morning in these deep woods, we find more than can be imagined, including the rare Slate-colored Antbird. Small birds are food for the Lined Forest Falcon, whose screams overhead suddenly quiet the forest. A Ruddy Quail-dove nervously flies off as we approach, its nest filled with hatchlings.

We visit Llachapa Island to explore its young-island marshy habitat. Purple Gallinule, Rufescent Tiger-Heron, River Tyrannulet, Black-and-white Antbird, White-bellied and Dark-breasted Spinetails, Little Cuckoo, Bicolored Conebill, Troupial, Lesser Hornero, Orange-headed Tanager, Lesser Wagtail Tyrant, Swallow Tanager, Blue-headed Parrots (with their deep wing-beats), and Lesser Yellow-headed Vulture perched on a treetop.

Birders are always looking. They see birds, of course, but they see many other things. At night, it may be the shadowy shape of an owl or a flitting bat, or just a jet black sky filled with shining stars. Binoculars pick up a tiny, shining prism—a droplet at the end of a leaf, an encapsulated rainbow.

And over there in the crotch of a tree sleeps a three-toed sloth. A rustle in the bushes attracts our attention: a mother Coatimundi, followed by three babies. Crashing sounds, or silent movement in the tops of the trees, direct our eyes to Squirrel Monkeys and Brown Capuchins. A look just in time prevents one birder from stepping on a Fer-de-lance!

Before leaving Explornapo we add many new birds to our lists, including the handsome Plum-throated Cotinga, Pheasant Cuckoo, several species of Trogons, and the very rare Pearly-breasted Conebill we find on our second visit to one of the special "young" islands.

Back down the Napo, we pass an occasional simply built stilt house with standard thatched roof, clothes spread on grass to dry, an Indian family in a dugout canoe; a school of Sotalia Porpoises plays nearby.

We are now accustomed to hot, humid Amazonia, mud-slogging in high boots, sudden showers, and bright sunshine. More new birds are added on our return to Explorama. Black-spotted Bare-eye, Cinnamon-rumped Foliage-gleaner, Green-and-Gold, Bay-headed, Opal-crowned, and Flame-crested Tanagers, Green and Purple Honeycreepers, Pink-throated Becard, and Ochre-bellied, Yellow-margined, and Ruddy-tailed Flycatchers. These are birds of canopy flocks, feeding together as they move through the high trees.

Flocks containing various combinations of birds are often seen at various levels—canopy, mid-story, understory—providing birders with a hasty look at up to twenty different species within the flocks. Pairs of different species live with these flocks all their lives, except at breeding time when they spend most of their time about the nest. Banded together as protection from predatory hawks, flocks are efficiently organized to spot danger. Each species picks off the kind of insects each species needs. Some are "dead leaf specialists," others forage on live leafs, some on small twigs, others in vine tangles. Once they tire of a particular tree or group of trees, the flock flies on to another part of the forest.

Our return to Iquitos jars us out of our primeval reverie. A mean look about this unattractive city proves more than a look; Victor's briefcase is stolen from beneath our feet as we pause on a restaurant veranda to view this busy Amazon port and to have a snack before returning to Lima. The worst of the adventure was the hassle later in obtaining a new passport.

"Civilization" is not without interest: ocean-going freighters mingle with crude dugout canoes, riverboat life bustles below us, cute pygmy marmosets scamper along our arms as we wait for our soup. Iguanas sleep in a tree outside the restaurant; and we later see a monkey exploring the kitchen of the airport restaurant, where a plane delay dictates another meal.

Coastal Peru

A greater contrast than between Amazonia and coastal Peru can hardly be imagined. Although most coastlines around the world are well vegetated, the circumstances of Peru's coast has created long stretches of stark landscape devoid of all but the most minute plant life. Dingy, dilapidated towns mirror the barren hills and sandy plains. A few small rivers bringing life-giving water out of the Andes create a few scattered marshy areas where bird life abounds.

Starting down the coast from Lima, we see the common Blue-and-White Swallow, the equally common White-winged Dove, and the doubly common House Sparrow. In a swampy area south of the city, steadily being encroached upon by minimum-standard housing, we see a surprising number of birds. Cattle Egret, Groove-billed Ani (the Smooth-billed is found on the other side of the Andes), Plumbeous Rail, Least Bittern (a different race from the one found in North America), Shiny Cowbird, Many-colored Rush-tyrant, Wrenlike Rushbird, Cave Swallow (Peruvian race), Yellowish Pipit, Blue-black Grassquit, and the familiar Common Moorhen, Vermilion Flycatcher, Rock Dove, and Killdeer.

Stopping occasionally in a suitable habitat along the Pan American Highway, we add new species to our bird list and our first ruins to our "ruins list." Pachacamac, one of the largest ruins in Peru, dates from A.D. 45. All we see from the highway is the dark brown wall shielding ancient history. Many of us add a new family to our list with the Least Seedsnipe, smallest of four members of the family, related to sandpipers, stilts, and gulls. Later on, I spot another relative, a pair of Peruvian Thick-knees close by our bus—as our leaders search far fields for this interesting bird.

As we approach Pachacamac beach, we stop to eat our box lunches. We see our first Peruvian Boobies, Kelp and Gray Gulls, and porpoises porpoising. Proceeding south through tan sand dunes sprinkled with dilapidated shacks and abandoned roadside stands, we see many birds of the dry desert. Some of the vast desert has been snatched from aridity since the 1968 agrarian revolution, which provided irrigation from the Andes for corn and other crops.

Paracas

Passing through Pisco (from whence comes the delightful Pisco Sour we later enjoyed before dinner), we arrive at one of Peru's seaside resorts, the pleasant Hotel Paracas. A late-afternoon bus journey brings us to the high cliffs on the south side of Paracas Bay. We wait for the flight of the Condor over the barren cliffs and blue Pacific, but settle for a steady stream of Turkey Vultures, Cormorants, Boobies, and roaring sea lions, way below us at the water's edge.

An early morning boat-ride across the coastal Pacific brings us to the Ballestas and Chinchas Islands. These islands were once covered with huge deposits of guano, known as a potent fertilizer and mined by the early Indians. Remnants of guano factories can be seen on the major islands, but today's "take" is limited to the annual production of "guano birds," the boobies and pelicans that roost there by the hundreds of thousands. The Humboldt and Peruvian Penguin were once there in great numbers too, building their burrows in the thick guano. We see only a pair here and there, half-hidden in rocky caves ringing the islands.

Here was our chance to add seabirds to our list, many of them up from Antarctic breeding areas, following the cold Humboldt Current just off the Peruvian coast. Giant Fulmars, a couple of Slender-billed Prions (a small but exciting bird in these waters), Sooty Shearwater, Wilson's Phalarope, White-vented, Sooty, and Ringed Storm-Petrels, Peruvian Diving-Petrel, familiar Brown and much larger Peruvian Pelican, Peruvian Boobies by the thousands, Blue-footed Boobies, Neotropic and Red-legged Cormorants along with the Guanay (or guano) Cormorant, Red Phalarope, five species of gull, including the striking Swallow-tailed Gull, and the stunning Inca Terns.

Our early objective for the following morning's birding is the rare Slender-billed Finch; we track it down in a brown field with clumps of acacia bushes. Quarry found, we head for a long stretch of beach south of the hotel to find the Puna Plover mixed in with bunches of familiar shorebirds.

High Andes

Contrasting to sea-level birding is high-altitude birding from Cusco to the puna, the dry grassland of the altiplano reaching up to 13,000 feet at Abra Malaga pass. Immediately following our flight across the Andes from Lima to Cusco, we board our minibus for a gradual descent from 11,000 feet to 9,000 feet to the valley of the Urubamba River, the "Sacred Valley" of the Incas. Birding along the way, we stop for specialties south of the colonial capital.

Relaxed birding in consideration of the high altitude produced different birds on rocky slopes and reedy meadow ponds: Cinereous Conebill, Rusty-fronted Canastero, Streak-fronted Thornbird, Rufous-naped and Spot-billed Ground Tyrant, our first of numerous Andean Lapwings, Andean Coot along with the familiar American Coot and Common Moorhen, Yellow-billed and Speckled Teal, White-tufted Grebe, Puna Ibis, Yellow-winged Blackbird, Plumbeous Rail, Andean Gull, Ash-breasted Sierra-Finch,

Chiguanco Thrush, Rufous-backed Negrito (a tiny flycatcher), Bare-eyed Ground Dove, and Andean Ruddy Duck.

Continuing on a dirt road following the falling Urubamba River, we stop frequently to spot river-loving birds: White-winged Cinclodes, White-capped Dipper, a single Torrent Duck placidly drifting downstream, Andean Swifts and Brown-bellied Swallows swooping between the canyon walls, a Bearded Mountaineer (not the human type but a large humming-bird), Rusty Flowerpiercer, Black-backed Grosbeak, and Golden-billed Saltator.

Two days in the high country produce exciting birding in clear, cold air in full view of spectacular, snow-covered Veronica Peak. In the early morning hours at sunrise we appreciate our long underwear and down jackets. One of our first triumphs at the Abra Malaga was finding the Inca Wren with its streaked breast and cheerful song, not yet officially described to science—a write-in on our list. This bird is another Parker achievement; he is an official codiscoverer.

We spot other birds so fast we can hardly record them in our note-books: Chestnut-bellied Mountain Tanager, Spectacled Redstart, Puna Thistletail, Red-crested Cotinga, Superciliaried, Parodi's, Drab, and Black-capped Hemispingus, Pale-footed Swallow, Sapphire-vented Puffleg, the Great Sapphirewing (second-largest hummingbird), Mountain Caracara, White-throated and Puna Hawks, our first Andean Condor way up high, White-winged Diuca-Finch, Rusty-fronted Canastero, Plain-capped and Puna Ground-Tyrants, Bright-rumped and Greenish Yellow-Finches, Marcapata Spinetails, Mustached and Masked Flower-piercers, White-rumped Hawk, Blue-backed Conebill, Andean Flicker, Plumbeous Sierra-Finch, Black-chested Buzzard-Eagle, Great Horned Owl, Pearled Treerunner, Brown-breasted Swallow, Cinereous Conebill, Unstreaked Tit-Tyrant (which really has some streaking), Amethyst-throated Sunangel and Long-tailed Sylph (two beautiful hummingbirds!), Andean Guan, Scarlet-bellied Tanager, Mountain Wren, a perched Swordbilled Hummingbird (whose bill is longer than its body), Paramo Seedeater, Green and Sparkling Violetears, Collared Inca (the southern race), Blue-and-black Tanager, Slaty-backed Chat-Tyrant, Capped Conebill, and Hooded Mountain Tanager. Who could ask for more?

Machu Picchu

Of course you'll visit Machu Picchu, one of the historic highlights of South America. Ruin viewing, however, does not preclude bird viewing. Most visitors to Machu Picchu would say they don't remember any birds there; certainly they are not obvious around the ruins themselves. But they are there. There is likely to be a pair of Kestrels easily spotted; perhaps an Andean Condor high over the cone-shaped Andes.

Walking a short distance down the road, down one of the paths below the hotel, or climbing above the ruins towards the Inca Trail over which backpackers travel to the ruins, produces bounty for birders. The familiar Hepatic Tanager flits about the hotel gardens and several varieties of hummingbirds are readily seen. Black Phoebe, White-winged Black Tyrant, Highland Elaenia, Great Thrush, and Rusty Flower-piercer are nearby.

Staying overnight at the Hotel de Turistas greatly enhances our opportunity to explore and photograph the ruins as well as to see a good variety of birds. Two major birding achievements add excitement: seeing the Giant Hummingbird, the largest hummingbird in the world, perched on a slender branch over the road as our bus begins its final descent to the train station; and seeing the Andean Cock-of-the-Rock down by the river.

Few persons travel to Peru without visiting Machu Picchu, a half-hour's drive up the steep mountain-side etched by a sharp, hair-pin turn road. Birders will later bird along the riverside shown in the lower right corner of the photograph

In the vicinity of even such a great attraction as Machu Picchu, the active birder will make arrangements to bird nearby, in this case down in the valley on the banks of the Urubamba River. In fact, the birder will be birding out the window of the train that winds along the river from Cusco. Several of our group spot the beautiful Golden-headed Quetzal from the train. Views out the large windows are spectacular, birds or no birds. High above the valley for most of the way are the snow-capped mountain peaks of the Vilcanota range.

In all, our group sees seventy species in this visit to one of the most famous tourist attractions in the world. Our Machu Picchu trip list is completed in Urubamba on our bus ride back to the Inn when we stop suddenly in the middle of the road to scramble out for a great view of the Black-chested Buzzard-Eagle.

Dinner this evening is topped off with a sampling of a questionable local delicacy, roast guinea pig. Andean music by a local group completes the scene, with John Ribble's birthday being celebrated with a cake and "Happy Birthday to You," Andean version.

Puerto Maldonado

Early next morning we fly to Puerto Maldonado in southeast Peru. The terrain below changes dramatically from sere brown Andean valleys to lush green jungle stretching west as far as one could see. Surely this is the "Green Mansion."

Waiting in the typical outback airport for our baggage (priority unloading is supplies of every sort for this frontier community), we walk outside to scan for birds. I spot one of the trip highlights atop an antenna tower, a Pearl Kite. Quickly two scopes are set up in the parking lot and, taking turns guarding the baggage, the whole group has good views. Life birds can be found in all kinds of places.

A rickety bus drives us through a rickety town with one paved street. We enjoy watching the frenzy of fixing up and painting the rickety storefronts. At the spotting of a Black Hawk-Eagle flying low and close to the bus, we lurch to a stop and the birders scramble out for good views.

At the river we clamber down the muddy bank to our roofed riverboat, which takes us on the four-hour ride up the Rio Tambopato to Explorer's Inn at the confluence of the Rio de la Torre. Here one will find the largest number of bird species of any single locality in the world.

For nearly a week we will enjoy being part of a near-virgin rainforest, watching a great variety of birds calling at the clearing, walking the main trail five kilometers to the oxbow lake, walking other trails that fan out from the complex of cottages and dining hall/research center.

On arrival at Explorer's Inn, scopes are quickly set up in the clearing. In quick succession we see Spix's Guan, Cuvier's Toucan, whose yelping calls become familiar to all of us, Speckled Chachalaca, a tree-full of tanagers, Black-spotted Barbet, and a colony of Yellow-rumped Caciques busily and noisily building their pendulous nests in a small tree next to the main path.

We are comfortable here in stilt cottages, four to a unit, backing up to the forest. The dining hall/research center is a round building in the center of the dormitories with a second-story library and workroom used by the many visiting scientists. *Cerveza* and soft drinks are always available, and sometimes fried banana slices for snacks.

The numbers of species of birds, trees, bushes, ferns, orchids, and butterflies is mind-stretching; the greatest variety of any place in the world. Animals are there too. But even in that tropical paradise, they are very wary. Some of the group saw a tapir, to the great despair of those of us who missed it. We all see the Giant Otter, one of the rarest animals on earth. It was first seen crunching on a large fish, but on seeing us, it abandons the meal, and chases us away across the lake, barking all the while.

Brown Capuchin and Squirrel Monkeys silently scurry through the treetops; Agouti slink through the forest, and a magnificent Red-tailed Squirrel. One day there was excitement outside the next cabin because a small boa constrictor was found in a tight ball, trying to slither into the cabin but prevented in the attempt by the protuberance caused by something recently eaten.

My Explorer's Inn bird list is diverse and overwhelming: White-necked Heron, Reddish Hermit (in a screaming lek), Screaming Pihas (in an even more screaming lek), Collared and Violaceous Trogons, Ringed Woodpecker (one of the most spectacular), Spix's Woodcreeper, Bluish-slaty Antshrike, White-eyed, Plain-throated, and Iherings (one of the rarest) Antwrens, White-browed, White-lined, and Striated Antbirds, Great, Fasciated, and Bamboo Antshrikes (only recently described to science), Red-bellied Macaw, Cinereous and Undulated Tinamous, Gray-fronted Dove, Large-headed and Dusky-tailed Flatbills (another rarity), and Thrush-like Wren, which looks like its cousin the Cactus Wren. (Pause for breath.)

Begin again. Sapphire-spangled Emerald, Blue-crowned Trogon, Gray-cheeked Nunlet, Blue-black Grosbeak, Red-billed Scythebill, Lemon-throated Barbet, Great Antshrike, Short-crested, Ruddy-tailed, and Brown-crested Flycatchers, Blue-headed and White-eyed Parrots, Shiny Cowbird, Yellow-browed Sparrow, Bat Falcon, Sirystes (a flycatcher), Masked Yellowthroat, Plain-capped Spinetail, Hoatzin (that improbably scruffy throwback), Horned Screamer, Olivaceous Woodcreeper, Wing-barred Manakin, Paradise, Violet, White-shouldered, Flame-crested, and Green-and-Gold Tanagers, Golden-bellied Euphonia, Long-winged and Gray Antwrens, Goeldi's, Bluish-fronted and Warbling Antbirds, White-necked Puffbird, Dusky-capped Greenlet, Swallow-tailed Kite, Masked Crimson Tanager, Bran-colored, Yellow-margined, Sulphury, and Euler's Flycatchers, Blue-and-Yellow Macaws, Mealy and Black-headed Parrots, Bluish-fronted Jacamar, Yellow-browed Tyrant, White-cheeked Tody Flycatcher (new to science in 1959), Peruvian Recurvebill, Chestnut-winged Hookbill, Crimson-crested Woodpecker, Nightingale Wren (with its seemingly unending song), Musician Wren (lovely of song but plain of body), Mustached Wren, Needle-billed Hermit, Grayish Mourner, White-eyed Tody Tyrant, Bar-breasted Piculet, Golden-crowned Spadebill, Black-capped Becard, Lawrence's Thrush, Chestnut-bellied Macaw, Double-toothed Kite, Zone-tailed, Slate-colored, and Great Black Hawks, Crested and Olive Oropendolas. To mention but a few!

Our last day we take our second hike to the oxbow lake early in the morning; the first hike had ended in a flashlight "death march." Right off the bat we spot the elusive Sungrebe (relative of the Sun Bittern) and pursue it by canoe along the shore. Simultaneously we have our only glimpse of a Green Ibis. Red-and-Green Macaws fly overhead, and an Epaulet Oriole sits on a branch over the water.

Walking back, we stop at the little pond to rest. Wonderful views of the Band-tailed Antbird, Euler's Flycatcher, and Pygmy, Green, and Rufous Kingfishers. Later at the small oxbow lake we watched in vain for Piping Guans but were satisfied with a raggedy Crane Hawk and macaws flying overhead.

In all, our group sees 256 species at Explorer's Inn, roughly half the birds that have been seen there. The 256th, and the last bird on our trip list, is a Capped Heron, spotted from the boat as we go down the river in the early dawn to catch the plane to Lima. Our final count for the group is in the neighborhood of 700.

A fitting end to this superb experience is our flight from Cusco. We are treated to a nostalgic panoramic view, as the pilot flies low from Cusco down the Incas' Sacred Valley to Machu Picchu, following the snaking Urubamba River; past the hairpin-turn road up to the Abra Malaga, the shining, snowcapped Veronica Peak, and the tremendous Andean range.

≾ *Seven* ≿

Chaffinches and Churches:
Birding Europe

"Europe has it all," Wendy said. The continent is often the first destination for overseas travelers. We've heard from childhood about all the famous places: Big Ben and Stonehenge, the Arc de Triomphe and Nôtre Dame, the Prado and the bullring, St. Peter's Square and the Vatican, Shakespeare's Stratford-upon-Avon and Dutch windmills. Storks on chimneys.

"Rich and I love birding, but he'd never been to Europe, so we decided to go. We love the museums, all the castles and cathedrals. But we love to bird too."

"Joe's never been to Europe, and as soon as he retires we're going to spend a couple of months over there."

"I grew up birding in England, but as soon as I could afford it, I went to the continent—France first—the Camargue."

Europe doesn't have a whole lot of species of birds. Its total of 635 species (Peterson) isn't very impressive in the birding world—fewer than any other continent (except Antarctica).

We want to visit Europe to learn something about the cultural heritage common to many of us. Perhaps we're searching for our roots. North Americans may head for England first—no language problem there—well, hardly any.

For the British, traveling to Paris or to most other places in Europe is as simple as it is for New Yorkers to visit Miami. The mainland of Europe is right at hand, just across the English Channel. Would you believe, there's even talk of a tunnel, already dubbed the "Chunnel"? After searching the mainland for its special birds, British and other European birders may stretch their wings to experience great adventures in North America, a place they know well, thanks to Hollywood.

"The British are really *up* on birds," commented Wendy Wallace, board member of the Tropical Audubon Society, on her return to Miami. "If you have binoculars around your neck when you're walking around, the British will stop you and ask what you've seen." With more nature education than in America, they will probably know the species too.

Travelers becoming interested in birds will find wonderful opportunities in Europe to combine Chaffinches and churches, Rooks and ruins, and wagtails and waterfalls. Mary and Tom Wood, devotees of abbeys and castles, set out for Fountains Abbey in North Yorkshire, considered the most beautiful twelfth- or thirteenth-century Cistercian Abbey in England. While admiring the ruins, they watched a Eurasian Nuthatch climbing the walls. Their photographs are full of cathedrals, their walls are hung with their brass rubbings, and their notebooks are full of bird sightings.

Often castles, churches, and other architectural wonders are surrounded by fine ancient trees and park areas. Adjacent to Fountains Abbey is Studley Royal Country Park, where, in addition to many woodland birds, you may see up to eight species of deer grazing on the lawn. For the birds, particularly the tits, have some crackers in your pocket; a few crumbs on the ground will bring them to your feet. Watch for the Tree Creeper spiraling up a tree trunk, woodpeckers tapping above, warblers in spring and summer, and the very shy Hawfinch with huge bill in winter.

FAMILIAR FEATHERS

Many of Europe's birds already will be familiar to North American birders. Gannets, shearwaters, Herring Gulls, Kittiwakes, Atlantic Puffins, terns and other seabirds, and ducks are common to both North American and European waters. The Kentish Plover will be recognized as the Snowy Plover of North American beaches, and the Grey Plover as the Black-bellied Plover. The Swallow swooping over the fields clearly is the Barn Swallow. Some birds of prey will be readily recognized. Black-billed Magpies are as common and as easily found in Britain and Europe as they are in many parts of the American West. The House Sparrow and the European Starling will be especially familiar.

Many birds will look familiar but in reality may be different species. Nuthatches are on both continents. Thrushes, flycatchers, buntings, redpolls, crows, and crossbills may be the same species; some are close relatives. The cheerful tits are mostly in the same genus (*Parus*) as North American chickadees.

British birders are especially fond of rarities reaching their shores, many blown across the Atlantic from North America. In recent years, numerous vagrants have caused the twitchers to twitch overtime: the American Robin, Yellow-billed and Black-billed Cuckoos, Black-and-white Warblers, Red-eyed Vireos, a Tennessee Warbler, Northern Waterthrush, Gray-cheeked Thrush, Yellow-rumped and Blackpoll Warblers, and American Redstarts—for starters. Prevailing westerlies bring more American birds east, than European birds west. The Collins bird guide lists sixty North American species as accidentals in Britain and Europe.

Atlantic Puffins are highlights of any visit to their northern breeding cliffs on both sides of the Atlantic Ocean

Europe, diverse in its history and culture, is also geographically diverse. Running down the western border, it includes Iceland, the British Isles, Spain, and Portugal. On the east it includes that part of the Soviet Union west of the Ural Mountains and the countries on the western border of the Black Sea, including the bit of Turkey west of the Bosphorus. On the south is the Mediterranean Sea; on the north, the countries of Scandanavia push toward the Arctic Circle.

From the geographer's point of view, the boundaries are fairly straightforward. From the birder's viewpoint, things aren't that simple. Some European bird guides are limited to the geography of Europe proper. Others encompass the Middle East and North Africa in order to include the entire Western Palearctic faunal region. You'll hear your English birder friends refer frequently to the birds of the Western Palearctic. (North American birders seldom refer to North America as the Nearctic.)

Europe is the least southerly continent. Cities like Athens, Rome, and Madrid are located at the latitude of Philadelphia and New York. Finland and Sweden share the latitude of Hudson Bay in Canada. London is as far north of the equator as the Falkland Islands are south. Without the warming Gulf Stream, latitudes in Europe would be far colder.

TITS ON THE TEMPLE TRAIL

The North American birder often lands in Europe with the dual objectives of seeing tits on the temple trail, Nightingales and Nôtre Dame, Linnets and the Louvre. Europe probably is the best place in the world to indulge an interest in birding together with an interest in art, architecture, archaeology, music, mountain climbing, and beautiful scenery.

Visiting the ancient ruins of Greece, the Acropolis, Soúnion, and Delphi in the mountains may easily bring you good views of Serin, Blackcap, and Sardinian Warblers. A Rufous Bush-Robin may be singing in a nearby, you guessed it, bush. Watch for the Rock Nuthatch as you climb the ancient steps of the Temple of Apollo. High in the cliffs you may see Griffon, Egyptian, and the rare Black Vultures (a different family from the Black Vulture of North America). If you're *very* lucky, a Lammergeier with its distinctive wedge-shaped tail may soar overhead.

The bird-wary tourist *will* find birds at popular tourist attractions, but on the typical tour, you'll have time for only quick glimpses. Tour bus drivers are not notably bird-wise—"All aboard!"

Wherever the tourist trail leads, you will see birds. Cheery Chaffinches are likely at fairy-tale Heidelberg Castle on the Neckar River in West Germany or nearly anyplace else. You will quickly learn that a bird easy to see, and insistently vocal, is likely a Chaffinch. A first-timer in Europe saw her first Greenfinch in tiny Liechtenstein, and Pied Wagtails in the charming ancient city of Maulbronn in West Germany.

The Chaffinch will be recognized by its cheery song and will be found sitting atop a wall, low tree branch, or scrabbling for crumbs on the ground

Visit Knossos, the partially restored palace of the legendary monarch Minos. The capital of Minoan Crete nearly four thousands years ago, the ruins today provide a fascinating glimpse of an ancient time, complete with plumbing as modern as exists in much of the world today. Don't miss the ruins of Malia on the crumbling steps, of which you might see a small yellowish bird with a black head, the Black-headed (you guessed it) Bunting.

It's possible but difficult to miss the tits on your European trip. The Great Tit probably will be around, hanging upside down on the tip of a tree branch. Blue Tits flit about in temple trees, and in nearly every public park and private garden. Visiting in Salzburg, you could see the Willow Tit, as close a relative of the Black-capped Chickadee as you could find.

As Europe is a mix of human cultures stirred into a savory stew over the centuries, so is it also a rich mix of avian life. Some birds "belong" in Europe. You must go to specific places to see them. Mountain climbers in the Pyrenees, the Alps, and other high mountain ranges of the Western Palearctic will be rewarded with the Alpine Accentor, related to the familiar Dunnock, and the Citril Finch. Visit the island of Corsica to see the Corsican Nuthatch. The Ural Owl can be found in the great mountain forests of northern Europe.

Where to see birds in Europe? Where to find new birds? Travelers will see birds everywhere they *look* for them. Initially, they'll be found on the beaten path. The lovely lake in the heart of Geneva yields the Little Grebe. A visit to the Staines Reservoir on a short layover in London adds the Great Crested Grebe and the Shelduck to the list.

Looking out your hotel window near Heathrow Airport, watch the "real" Blackbird *(Turdus Merula)*, the black bird with orange bill and eyering, and the Redwing, not our Redwing Blackbird but a small, common thrush *(Turdus iliacus)*. The London airport area is surprisingly good for birds, including Pied Wagtails, Carrion Crows, Eurasian Kestrels, Common Moorhens, and great flocks of magpies.

Don't complain about the forced layover. Instead, wander through Hyde Park, Richmond Park, and maybe Kew Gardens. "Pick up" the Tufted Duck in one of the ponds. Walk through fields and historic neighborhoods. Exercise your legs and eyes. If the weather is bad, watch one of the superb nature programs on the telly to appreciate how important they have been in turning England into a nation of bird watchers.

Vienna, another favorite destination for travelers, is a marvelous city, filled with cathedrals and palaces, music and May wine. When you visit Schönbrunn, the summer palace of Emperor Franz Joseph and Maria Theresa, take time to visit the park and the zoo, the oldest in Europe. Like so many zoos, it attracts a variety of wild birds. Sipping coffee, watch woodpeckers just a few feet from your table.

Although Vienna Woods conveys images of waltzes and warblers, it is not particularly noted these days for bird life. Better is a walk through the Bois de Boulogne during your springtime in Paris. You may find more lovers there than bird lovers, but it's a welcome bit of green.

If you have an extra day in Paris, go out to the Forest of Fontainebleau. You may see woodpeckers, including the Eurasian Wryneck, Crested Tits, a Hobby (a falcon, not a pastime), Common Redstarts, Nightingales, and Cuckoos. The latter two respond best to tapes. If you're looking for a Short-toed Tree Creeper, this is a good place.

Walk around Lake Geneva in between winter conferences in that international city, and watch the Mandarin Ducks, natives of China, favorites of zoos, and now breeding in a few selected areas in Europe. Red Pochard, many familiar ducks, and Mute Swans will be hard to miss on lakes in Geneva and Zurich. In springtime, listen for Linnets singing from a nearby hedge.

Another wonderful winter attraction is Sir Peter Scott's Slimbridge Wildlife Reserve in England. It contains the largest collection of ducks and geese in the world. Wintering waterbirds find it a safe haven. There may be upward of 5,000 White-fronted Geese. Take your scope out to the new grounds to watch the wild birds.

Wandering around the charming village of Zermatt, don't be so dazzled by the Matterhorn that you miss your first Black Redstart. It's not related to the American Redstart (a Wood Warbler) but is a small thrush, or chat, as the British call it. Take the cable car up to the Schwarzsee for lunch. The scenery is awe-inspiring, and the Snow Finch scrabbling on the ground is fun to watch.

Wendy and Rich camped on the eastern shore of Lake Constance, at the border of Switzerland and Austria, near Bregenz. It's a bird reserve with reedy shores, open waters, and nearby woods. They particularly remember the Wheatear and the Woodchat Shrike, a "smart" bird, and were pleased to have their sighting of a Chiffchaff, one of those confusing *Phylloscopus* warblers, confirmed by other birding campers who pointed out its distinctive song. Their favorite birding spot in Europe was the Zwin reserve in Belgium, bordering the Netherlands, famous for its impressive aviary, a favorite with children.

On your way through Holland, don't miss the miniature city of Madurodam, complete with tiny automobiles traveling down ribbon-sized highways, and toy airplanes taxiing at a minuscule Schiphol Airport. The crow picking up crumbs at your feet probably will be a Jackdaw. Holland provides good birding, so keep your eyes open for both windmills and wooden shoes, woodpeckers and warblers.

Try the islands of Texel and Vlieland, washed by the North Sea, north of Amsterdam. If you've never seen Black-tailed Godwits, there are gobs of them. Though a relatively small island, there are nineteen bird reserves to be explored on Texel.

Pigeons and doves "coo" throughout most of the world. A stroll through Regent Park on your first visit to London most likely will produce fat Wood Pigeons; walking up to the Parthenon in Athens, watch for familiar Turtle and Collared Turtle Doves. Look for Blue Rock Thrushes, mildly like their cousin, the American Robin; and Lesser Gray Shrikes, unmistakably shrikes.

Emily's brief weekend visit to friends in Stocksund outside of Stockholm was notable for an alfresco picnic complete with smoked reindeer that she ate and a handsome Green Woodpecker that she watched. She was surprised to see a coot, so familiar in her Florida home. But on checking its Latin name, she discovered that it was *Fulica atra*, not *Fulica americana*. Chalk one up to loving Latin.

MIGRATORY MILLIONS

Much of Europe is a migrant funnel, accounting for a good bit of birding excitement. Birds seen on their northern breeding grounds wing through Europe on annual spring and autumn journeys. If you're enraptured by raptors, particularly in enormous numbers, hot-foot it to the migration "hot spots." In spring and fall, visit those points of land with the shortest water crossing to the birds' destinations.

Southern Spain, and Gibraltar on either side of the Strait, is great. Gibraltar is a bit of a tacky town, but it's redeemed by its spectacular wildflowers. The town of Tarifa, but sixteen miles from the African coast, is a good vantage point.

"It is a sight of a lifetime to be able to see raptors and hawks circling over the Atlas Mountains in Africa and then drift over the Strait of Gibraltar toward you," writes Peter Carlton. "I had 16,000 Honey Buzzards in one day, plus several thousands of White Storks and many other birds of prey such as Ospreys, Black Kites, Short-toed Eagles (500 in one day), Griffons.

The rocky shore along the coast is home to the beautiful Black and Black-eared Wheatears, Blue Rock Thrush and nearby Europe's only breeding White-rumped Swifts. The Strait is also good for seabirds passing through."

Istanbul, on the Bosporus, is the Eastern European bottleneck where tremendous "kettles," circular swirls of raptors riding the thermals, can be seen in the fall. Birds that have bred in eastern and northern Europe in summer concentrate there for the short crossing to the Middle East and down into Africa for a warm winter. Even casual birders are thrilled by this spectacle, as raptors, storks, and many other birds wing across the narrow Bosporus. In nonmigratory periods, there still are good birds to see. Sail to Byzantium and see the birds in the trees: Palm Doves in old streets, or Syrian Woodpeckers in city parks and wooded areas.

The best place in northern Europe to watch the great migration is Sweden's Falsterbo peninsula, jutting down toward Denmark. It provides marvelous opportunities for birds of passage from June through November. Visiting birders will have good company here, for there are lots of great Swedish birders.

Migrating birds also fly down the narrow boot of Italy, bringing them close to their North African objective. In Italy, birders need to exercise caution. While you are training your binoculars on the birds, Italian hunters are training their guns. A reported million and a half hunters annually kill some 200 million birds, half of which are using the Italian "boot" as a migratory freeway. To be fair, the Italians are not the only ones who like lark pie. The French and the Spanish are also known to be more interested in shooting Wood Pigeons *(Columba palumbus)* than clay pigeons. Fortunately, growing numbers of birders and conservationists are having a positive impact on changing local attitudes.

AFTER BASILICAS, BIRDS

Climbing the steps of one more castle, cathedral, basilica, temple, palace, or museum at some point may lead the tired tourist to quote the raven, "Nevermore." Birders will long for cool forests, sparkling lakes, reedy shores, rocky coastlines—the "other" Europe. They will seek out the bird reserves, parks, and birding "hot spots."

Impressive as is the Hofburg and St. Stephans Cathedral, the birder will want to follow Alden and Gooders' advice and visit Lake Neusiedl, southeast of Vienna. One of Europe's birding "hot spots," this series of large, shallow lakes is particularly noted for its large colonies of Great Egrets and White Spoonbills.

Birding tours to the good birding areas of Europe are somewhat less common and not as accessible than tours to some other parts of the world. Some areas such as Lapland, above the Arctic Circle, where specialized birds are difficult to find, and where climate and terrain may cause difficulties, are best approached with a competent birding tour leader.

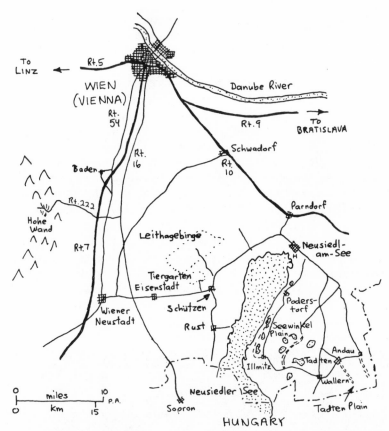

To LINZ ← Rt.5

WIEN (VIENNA)
Rt. 54
Rt. 16

Danube River

Rt.9   TO BRATISLAVA

Schwadorf
Rt. 10

Baden

Rt.222

Hohe Wand

Rt.7

Parndorf

Leithagebirge

Neusiedl-am-See

Tiergarten
Eisenstadt

Wiener Neustadt

Schützen

Poders-torf

Rust

Seewinkel Plain

Andau

Illmitz

Tadten

Wallern

miles   10
P.A.

km   15

Neusiedler See

Sopron

Tadten Plain

HUNGARY

Ways to get off the beaten track are mapped in the Alden/Gooders' *Finding Birds Around the World*

Doing it alone in most of Europe is nearly as easy as it is in the United States, although many reserves are highly restricted to protect them from egg collectors and falconers. Where-to-find guides exist for several countries. The Gooders *Where to Watch Birds in Europe* and *Where to Watch Birds* [in Britain] have guided many hundreds of birders over and beyond the temple trail. Ten of Europe's hot birding spots are also covered in the Alden/Gooders *Finding Birds Around the World.*

Peter Carlton, lifetime English birder, suggests, as one might guess, that Britain, Europe's largest island, is a truly great place for seabirds. His favorite birding areas are in Norfolk and Suffolk in East Anglia, that "bump" of England northeast of London. Cley, on the north coast of Norfolk, is probably the best-known birding area in England. The coastal area west to Titchwell and south to Minsmere attracts hordes of birds and birders, along with that uniquely British "twitcher" who is visibly aflutter at spotting a real "crippler."

The North Norfolk coast boasts the largest number of species in Britain. Coastal reserves, as well as many others, are well supplied with comfortable hides (Americans call them "blinds," but we don't have very many). They can't be beat for the best views and photographs. It's a great way to see Ruffs (a large shorebird with a great feathery neck ruff marking its breeding plumage). At Minsmere, nearby woodlands and heath attract land birds. It's an unbeatable combination of habitats. Many bird reserves in Europe require a permit and fee to enter. Generally reserve headquarters will be obvious. If not, seek out the local pub and ask.

During migration, nearly everyone in Norfolk is watching the sky for the Bewick's and Whooper Swans to swoop in. Peter was one of the birders at Minsmere the day of the whopper fallout: 10,000 Redstarts, 7,000 Wheatears, 500 Garden Warblers, 25 Bluethroats, 20 Wrynecks, 250 Curlew Sandpipers, and 1,000 Black Terns, to account for just a few.

Though the fens were filled in many years ago, and marshlands are rapidly disappearing, bird-cliffs around the coast of Britain, particularly in the north and west, remain indestructible. Two dozen species of seabirds create precarious nurseries on sheer cliffs, bringing them alive with winged comings and goings. Readily accessible are the Bempton Cliffs in Yorkshire, where you will see breeding Atlantic Puffins, guillemots (Murres), Razorbills, and Fulmars; it is the only place on the British mainland where Northern Gannets breed.

Guillemots (Common Murres) breed in densely packed colonies on northern coastal cliffs and islands

A Guillemot pair thinking it over

For closer encounters, of the head-pecking kind, take the boat trip to the Farne Islands. During breeding season, the parent terns are fierce protectors of their nests, often right on the paths crisscrossing the island. The Farnes are full of history, as is Bamburgh Castle, guarding the sandy headland nearby. Off the coast of Scotland, visit the out-islands for nesting specialities: tiny Fair Isle between the Orkney and Shetland Islands, and St. Kilda in the Outer Hebrides for huge colonies of gannets, Atlantic Puffins, petrels, and other marine birds.

The Scilly Isles in the far southwest are a rapturous dream for fervent British birders, and you will find there that most British birders appear to be afflicted with advanced cases of fervency, a seemingly incurable disease. The Isles, offshore from Land's End, attract scads of stray migrants from the continents and from North America. Exploring the unbeaten paths can be enriching for the traveler and a bonanza for birders.

If you must go "down to the seas again, to the lonely sea and the sky," along with poet John Masefield, try also the coast of Norway for alcids, auks, jaegers, and the beautiful White-tailed Eagle. Go all the way to the North Cape at the tip-top of the country, and while basking in the midnight sun, you'll have some pretty exciting birding. At Spitsbergen, watch for the lovely Ivory Gull, the Iceland Gull, and with luck—Ross' Gull.

Staying in England, take a few of the hundreds of wonderful country walks, so popular with both Americans and the English. Just follow the "Public Footpath" signs or check with the Automobile Association or local bookstore for maps showing paths, points of interest, and even guides to wildflowers and birds. In early morning or evening, you might spot a Little Owl sitting on a bus stop or fence post. It will remind you of the Burrowing Owl in North America (same genus). Wandering will bring you Winchats, Whitethroats, Willow Warblers, Wheatears, woodpeckers, warblers, goldfinches, Greenfinches, Chaffinches, Bullfinches, and buntings. Try to learn their songs.

Take the high road in Scotland and visit the Cairngorms for a touch of Arctic atmosphere. Although only 3,600 feet high, you will find alpine flowers on the screes. Climbers will often be rewarded by good views of the Dotterel, with its lovely chestnut belly and beady eye, walking ahead and then stopping for you, so you can get a good photograph. Watch carefully for the Rock Ptarmigan. Overhead soaring Peregrine Falcons, Goshawks, Golden Eagles, or Ospreys may attract your attention. Loons on the lakes ("divers" to the British) may include both the Black-throated and Red-throated Divers.

In old pine forests near Aviemore, look high in the trees for the extremely localized Scottish Crossbill, the only species of bird restricted to the British Isles, and in that small patch of Scotland to boot. Herds of Red Deer may be cooling off in patches of snow in early summer or leading young through the forests.

The Osprey is so famous and sought-after in northern Scotland that there are signs pointing to where it can be sighted

One of the best reasons Britain is known for excellent birding is the Royal Society for the Protection of Birds (RSPB). This large membership organization (425,000 members) acquires land for bird reserves, manages over 100 open to the public; engages in scientific research, and publishes a fine magazine, *Birds*. Join and support their cause, and you'll have free admission to most reserves.

A priority objective for many birders visiting the continent for the first time is the Carmargue in the south of France, near Arles. A French National Reserve at the delta of the Rhône River as it washes into the Mediterranean Sea, the enormous Reserve encompasses reedy marshland, including fresh, brackish, and salt water, prairies, agricultural lands, rice fields, and woods. The area is famous for gypsies, cowboys, wonderful white horses, and black bulls, as well as hundreds of birds attracted by the varied habitat. It is also a favorite of European tourists seeking its warm sunshine. The most famous of the birds here are great flocks of Greater Flamingos picking their way gracefully through the mud of the many shallow *étangs* (lakes), but you'll see birds of prey high in the sky, tiny but noisy warblers like Cetti's warbler hidden in the thick grasses, lots and lots of water birds, and the familiar Cattle Egret surveying the grasshoppers from the rump of a white horse.

After birding the reserve, wander around nearby Arles to enjoy the scenes painted by Van Gogh. In the fall, great fields of sunflowers throughout Provence will remind you of the famous painter. Don't miss Les Baux, an ancient town perched incongruously atop a rocky road, a favorite area for the Alpine Swift. Just beyond are the ruins of the even more ancient Roman town of Glanum. After absorbing the ruins, explore the woods, fields, and olive groves that surround the site, and listen for the lovely song of the Orphean Warbler. Watch for the Hoopoe here and for another handsome bird, the Woodchat Shrike. In the springtime the warblers will be warbling their little hearts out. At other times, birding is more of a challenge, which makes the sighting of a Sardinian Warbler even more satisfying.

Every area of Europe has its special birds. Peter Carlton recommends Spain and Yugoslavia. After you've "done" Madrid, walked through the gloomy art in the Prado, visited the churches and museums in Toledo, and the walled city of Avila, head south to Sevilla in Andulasia. Another great nature preserve is on the coast not far away, the Coto Doñana National Park, a wetlands preserve at the Rio Guadalquivir delta. You may see flamingos, but surely Rainbow-hued Bee-eaters will delight you. Along with the white-shouldered Imperial Eagle, you might see upward of forty species of raptors. Lesser Kestrels will be flying in great flocks over town and field, often in the company of the Eurasian or Common Kestrel. Both look much like the American Kestrel. Watch also for the Red Kite with its deeply forked tail; watch out for herds of wild boar.

North Americans may be stunned to see here a giant Purple Gallinule. It is also known as the Purple Swamphen, to distinguish it from the Purple Gallinule of the New World, a close cousin. If you don't want to visit China, watch here for the Azure-winged Magpies ("Azzies" if you want to be one-up) flocking through piney woods. Pratincoles and many ducks and waders are in the vast marismas (marshes), but you'll have to get there with a group in a four-wheel drive. Nearby is the famous bridge at El Rocio, the most famous Roman Catholic shrine in Spain. You may think you're back in some Arizona ranch town.

For a change of pace, go to the opposite end of Spain and climb in the Pyrenees at the French border. You will love the mountain scenery, as the eagles love the mountain updrafts. You'll see Golden Eagles, Bonelli's and Booted Eagles, Short-toed Eagles (the toes are *not* a field mark). Both Red-billed and Yellow-billed Choughs (rhymes with "huffs") are there but chancy to see.

You may not be able to resist driving through the tiny country of Andorra, where the birding is best in the mountain areas rather than in the valleys. Head for Ordessa National Park, with smashing views of the Pyrenees capped by Monte Perdido. The park, with its many mountain trails, is a favorite of Spanish backpackers. The birders you meet are likely to be British birders looking for the Wall Creeper, an elusive but spectacular member of the nuthatch family. Constantly scan the high cliffs for its flash of bright red wing-patches.

The Camargue and Coto Doñana National Park are hardly off the European beaten path and are well-known places even to the nonbirder. You may get a ho-hum from your birder friends if you tell them about these places, but try the Obedska Bara Reserve in Yugoslavia on them. Some good birding habitats, less known than the Camargue, may be a bit more difficult to reach.

Breeding White-tailed Sea Eagles will be a highlight of Obedska Bara. Yugoslavia is ideally located for both eastern and western species. Babuna Gorge, in southern Yugoslavia near the town of Titov Veles, is famous for raptors: Lanner Falcons, Lammergeiers, Egyptian Vultures, Bonelli's and Imperial Eagles. Owls and woodpeckers are in the nearby forests. The mountains of Yugoslavia and the Pyrenees of Spain are good places for the elusive Wallcreeper.

One doesn't necessarily think of Poland for pigeons or other birds, but birders think highly of Bialowieska National Park east of Warsaw, on the Russian border. A beautiful remnant of the primeval forest that once blanketed Central Europe, it is known for special birds like the noisy Capercaillie, a very large grouse, and the Lesser Spotted Eagle. As a bonus, the visitor will be watching for the famous bison, the last remaining herd in Europe. The Pripit marshes on the Polish/Russian border constitute one of the Old World's greatest wilderness areas.

Poland has several other "greats" worth going for: the stately Great Bustard, standing over three feet high, the elusive Great Snipe, the Great Gray Owl, and the Great Gray Shrike, one of four shrikes commonly found there.

Scandinavia, close to the top of many a tourist list, is not often thought of as a birding mecca. It is the beautiful fjords rather than flycatchers that lure the traveler to this northland of the midnight sun. Snowcapped mountains, alpine lakes, dramatic waterfalls, and northern forests provide a scenic feast.

Include Lake Vattern in central Sweden on your spring itinerary, and see the spectacular aggregation of 50,000 Common Cranes feasting in old potato fields. Lorimer Moe, whose birding zeal never flagged during a seven-year stint as press attaché at the U.S. Embassy in Stockholm, recalls that "the narrow, ninety-mile strip of Oland along the Baltic coast is truly a birder's mecca, boasting such Mediterranean species as the Hoopoe as well as ancient Viking ruins."

Forested areas in the middle of the peninsula have many woodpeckers, of course. Crossbills, including the Parrot Crossbills, can be found. Hazel and Black Grouse are good finds. Look in the many lakes for the Smew, often called the world's most beautiful duck.

At the far end of the great Scandinavian peninsula is the only accessible Arctic region in mainland Europe, Lapland. It's tough to get to, tough to bird, but worth the effort. Best to go on an organized birding trip with knowledgeable leaders, for you wouldn't want to go so far and miss the Lapland and Rustic Buntings, Bluethroats, Shore Larks, and Red-flanked Bluetails, not to mention the many species of breeding owls.

Copenhagen is an ideal blend for sightseeing and birding. After visiting the famous Tivoli Gardens, walk through the city parks and surrounding area and sample a wealth of bird life. An island link between Scandinavia and mainland Europe, Copenhagen is predictably a good place to be during migration, but good birds can be found at any time.

Iceland, easily reachable by air on flights between New York and Luxembourg, will please the bird-alert traveler. A stopover in Reykjavik provides the opportunity to sample some of the island country's 260 species. On a lake right in the heart of the city, watch for Red-necked Phalarope. Seabirds, of course, proliferate. If you missed the Gyrfalcon, try for it in Iceland.

More travelers visit Russia for ballet than for birds. Visitors to Leningrad and Moscow are not likely to be impressed with the bird life. You'll see a few Common Rose Finches and Yellow-breasted Buntings, otherwise mostly the same species found elsewhere in Europe. Near Moscow is the Archangelski Forest, and Lenin Hills may be good for Crested and Long-tailed Tits, Golden Orioles, breeding Fieldfares and Redwings, and a good selection of warblers.

Independent traveler/birders find it difficult, even impossible, to go traipsing about the Soviet countryside, as they do in so many other places in the world. Russian authorities take a dim view of that sort of thing. They are nervous about indiscriminate use of cameras and binoculars and like it best when they know exactly when you are going to be where, and what you are going to be doing.

Now, how can a birder predict where the best birds will be at any given moment? Best to join an organized group familiar with both birds and local rules and regulations. You'll get to the good birding areas with a minimum of red tape (no political aspersions intended).

Europe has been rewarding travelers for centuries. Fortunately, most countries have maintained and nurtured fine wildlife preserves. Visiting the wilder areas of the continent will provide both traveler and birder an extra dimension in experiencing the continent that "has it all."

🐦 *Eight* 🐦

Peacocks and Pheasants: Birding Asia

Who has not been mesmerized by the sight? A male peacock trails its gorgeous feathered train across some lawn or zoological garden, then turns and fans that tail in a many-eyed arc of feathers for the admiring glances of peahen and people alike. Who has not been startled at the iridescent beauty of the Golden Pheasant seen in an aviary? These creatures are more beautiful than life; they seem otherworldly. They must belong, we think, in fairy-tale settings created just for them, not just a forest with ordinary trees.

Yes, they will be found living in ordinary forests in Asia. Exotic Asia. Startled, a Common Peacock flies up to perch on a tree branch in a forest in southern India or Sri Lanka. Its long tail waving in the breezes, he screams to let the peahens know where he is. In the mountain province of Szechwan in northwest China, the Golden Pheasant catches a momentary ray of sunlight on its gold and red adornment, and we are dazzled.

The vast continent of Asia is home to some of the most colorful birds in the world, and some of the most drab. Its contrasts range from arctic to tropical, from deserts to swamps, from the highest places on earth to the lowest. It ranges from places that have been home to millions of people for thousands of years, to areas rarely seen by human eyes, where it is still possible to discover new plants and animals.

No one knows how many species we might find in Asia. The continent is like Africa and South America, so vast and so diverse that embracing the idea of "birding Asia" may be impossible. There are no field guides to the birds of Asia, as there are for North America, Europe, and Australia. Asia is just too vast an area to cover successfully in one volume.

North Americans are less sophisticated in their knowledge of Asia than their European contemporaries. Historically there have been many ties between Europe and the rest of the Eurasian continent. Still, our knowledge is quite recent. Interestingly, the Alden/Gooders guide for world birders published in 1981 draws on pre-1945 material for the birds of Shanghai, and on the World War I era for information on Beijing (Peking), as it was written just before the great opening to tourists. Fortunately, the gaps in our knowledge are being filled rapidly with the publication of several new books about birding in Asian countries.

Asia is a continent of superlatives: biggest, highest, lowest, deepest, richest, poorest. Some of the highest places on earth are found in Asia, the highest point being Mount Everest at 29,028 feet above sea level. Some of the lowest places on earth are in Asia, the lowest place on earth being the Dead Sea at 1,292 feet below sea level. Lake Baikal in Russia is over a mile deep.

Northern Asia shares the Palearctic faunal region with Europe and North Africa. The Oriental faunal region includes the Indian subcontinent, the southeastern quadrant of the continent including the southern part of China roughly south of the Yangtze, Taiwan, most of Indonesia, and the Philippines. Although we tend to think of Japan as being "Oriental," of the East, it lies in the Eastern Palearctic, along with northern China and Mongolia.

Until quite recently, birding in Asia has been for the stouthearted and most dedicated of birders. With the publication in recent years of field guides for Japan, China, Russia, Southeast Asia, India, Nepal, Sri Lanka, and Borneo, birding Asia is now much easier than it was a decade or more ago.

For world birders, Asian birds have always held a great fascination, but not until recently are birders beginning to appreciate the wealth of bird life in Asia. Some of the fascination for birders is the same as that for sophisticated travelers who have been sampling Asian history and culture and its exotic traditions, exotic birds.

Some of the exotic birds of Asia have become domesticated. Red

Birding group watches both Buddhas and birds, a common combination in Thailand

Junglefowl (no reflection of the bird's politics), seen in India, Thailand, and other parts of Southeast Asia, are the progenitors of domestic chickens throughout the world. The Ring-necked Pheasant in North America was introduced from Asia. The beautiful and familiar peacock with long trailing tail is the Common Peafowl, *Pavo cristatus,* of India.

To find any of the species of pheasants and peafowls in their native setting, one must travel to Asia. (The one exception is the Congo Peacock, an endangered species of the Zairian rainforest.) To see any of the members of the family Panuridae, the parrotbills, with the exception of the Bearded Tit (how did *it* get that name?), you will need to go to Asia. "Falling leaf birds" may be a joke for some of us, but we hope, while birding in Asia, not to see a member of the family Irenidae, mostly bright green leafbirds, fall from its perch. The four members of the family Hemiprocnidae, handsome treeswifts, can only be found in Asia and the Pacific. Marvelously colored minivets are special Asian delights.

Although Asian birds are among the most exotic in the world, not all birds seen in an Asian country will be unfamiliar to the western birder. The Black-crowned Night Heron, Cattle Egret, many shorebirds, gulls, terns, doves, and of course the House Sparrow will be familiar to both North American and European birders.

BUSINESS AND BULBULS

Perhaps most travelers' first Asian encounter is at one of the great stopover cities of Hong Kong or Singapore. Besides being famous commercial and tourist centers, both can provide avian rewards to the traveling birder with a few extra hours or days to spend there.

Hong Kong, still a British Crown Colony, is located off the southern coast of China. According to Alden and Gooders, it is the only part of the Chinese region where the birder can wander at will. Bird records are so complete that the new guide to the birds of China contains separate notations for birds found in Hong Kong. The colony is also included in the bird guide for Southeast Asia. Eager birders will be looking for the Chinese Egret or the Asiatic Dowitcher.

Like the Hialeah Race track in Florida, famous for its flamingos, the Hong Kong race track is a good place to comb the gardens for birds. Look for Light-vented and Sooty-headed Bulbuls. Typically, Hong Kong is a good place to be during spring migration. If you go out to the Mai Po Marshes in spring, you might even pick up a couple of Spoon-billed Sandpipers. Some birders claim they would "kill" to see one. As always in this part of the world, make local inquiries before bashing through the local paddies.

Singapore, the island country off the southern tip of Malaysia, is another place to combine business and birding, or to bird seriously after you buy out the duty-free shops at the end of your vacation. The Botanical Gardens and several nature reserves are convenient for the visitor and should be investigated. You will admire both orchids and sunbirds.

In most of Asia, travelers are not free to wander about the countryside, binoculars swinging around their necks, scopes in hand, and cameras ready. Roads are often inadequate, accommodations for the traveler are limited, and the local militia is often nervous about all that hardware. Directions in a local dialect may be unintelligible. In order to get to the best places for finding birds in a particular area, birders are better off joining organized tours.

Business or vacation trips to the cities where one can expect some measure of decent accommodations, and guided tours to the local sights in English, is more the norm. Here is where hotel garden birding can be most productive. Pull the curtains back and look out the windows. Wander through the gardens. Take your binoculars—don't leave your room without them.

A Red-vented Bulbul is often the first bird spotted at your hotel in Delhi, followed up quickly by Rose-ringed Parakeets. John saw an Azure-winged Magpie and a Green Pheasant at the Imperial Hotel in Tokyo. Peter watched a Thrush Nightingale while he was breakfasting in a hotel in Alanya, Turkey, and an Eleneora's Falcon on his hotel balcony while doing the same thing in Istanbul. David spotted a White-breasted Wood Swallow in the hotel gardens on a business trip to Jakarta. (His bird-sharp eyes even spotted a Water Rail outside his sixth-floor office window of the Bank of England in London.)

Birding expeditions often begin in the hotel gardens. At the Rama Gardens Hotel in Bangkok there were Eurasian Tree Sparrows speckling the lawn, Streak-eared Bulbuls conversing in pairs in the bougainvillaea, and a Magpie-Robin on a wire. The Birdquest group (a British birding tour organization), quickly scanning the gardens of the Royal Garden Resort Hotel in Hua Hin on the Thailand peninsula, spotted Common and Pied Mynas, Plain-backed Sparrows, an Olive-backed Sunbird in a tree on the pool deck, Black Drongos, and familiar Barn Swallows overhead. After a day's exhausting birding, some of the group relaxed at beach-edge by scoping Crested Terns swinging back and forth over the Gulf of Siam. Sitting every afternoon on the blue-tile roof of the Orchid Hotel in Chiang Mai, Thailand, was a Blue Rock Thrush.

In Eilat, Israel, the Ladbroke hotels' Red Sea Resort advertises that it is cooperating with the Society for the Protection of Nature in Israel to promote bird-watching vacations. (Perhaps other hotels, particularly those located in birding "hot spots," as this one is, should get the word out that birders are welcome. Birders make great guests: they appreciate hotel gardens; they're gone most of the day so they save on wear and tear of hotel facilities; and they go to bed early in the evening, so they don't annoy the guests with late night carousing. The hotel's only minor inconvenience would be getting the cook up early enough to fix a pre-dawn breakfast.)

Israel and the other eastern Mediterranean countries attract both tourists with wide-ranging interests and birders fascinated by the huge numbers of Palearctic birds flowing up and down the eastern edge of the sea in the spring and fall. Over one million birds of prey are known to overfly Israel on migration paths, spiraling up to the top of one thermal and gliding down to the bottom of the next, as they roller-coaster their way along.

The New York Times reported in September 1985 that Israel's bird-watchers have worked closely with the Air Force to identify times and routes of the migrations, to protect both pilots and birds. Working together, military personnel and birders have identified and protected 475 species of birds that fly today over that ancient land. They have done so since before the prophet Jeremiah, an early birder observed, "The kite in the air hath known her time: the turtle, and the swallow, and the stork have observed the time of their coming. . ."

Tiny Tiran, an island at the mouth of the Gulf of Aqaba, may even have benefited from the shooting—between Egypt and Israel. A "no-man's-island" as a result of the hostilities, it is now known for its rare breeding grounds for the Osprey, White-eyed Gull, Sooty Falcon, and other birds needing protected environments.

Asian Turkey also beckons the adventurous traveler and birder. Aside from being a fine place during migration, it provides a satisfying diversity and an element of the unknown that appeal to the inveterate wanderer. Lake Tuz, Turkey's great salt lake, may produce Bimaculated and Calandra Larks; on the southern coast near Antalya, Desert Larks. Down in the Taurus Mountains you might stay at Adana to pursue the Caspian Snowcock; toward the Syrian border, watch for the Bald Ibis and the See-see Partridge ("Sammy, see the Partridge; see the Partridge, Sammy.")

TIGER AND TAJ

Birders around the world seek birds, but most seekers are also fascinated by the other animals encountered, especially the big ones. To see a python curled up on the bank of an Indian river, sunning itself, or a small herd of Asian elephants silhouetted against the trees under a full moon in Thailand, or a lone male elephant crashing across a forest trail in Corbett National Park, or a herd of swamp deer nervously grazing in tiger country is to store up a cache of priceless memories.

In Asia, it is the tiger that thrills and excites. A birding trip would not be worth its stripes if, when in tiger country, a major effort were not made to see this magnificent beast. Such was the effort made by Birdquest on our trip to India in March 1985.

There were elephant rides to look for tigers every day we were in Dudwa National Park on the eastern border of India, and at the famous Corbett National Park, northeast of Delhi. Although all but the last ride on the last day were tigerless, they were far from a total loss, for we found ourselves face to face with owls and other birds perched on low branches. Then at the end of that last ride, the lead elephant nearly stepped on the tiger's prey. There was a low growl, the elephants quivered, the tiger looked at us for a moment, then became but a blur in the tall grass, quickly lost to sight.

Mention is made of the trip date because it is famous in both bird and tiger history. Balram Singh, brother of Arjan (Billy) Singh, well-known Indian naturalist, gives his guests some insight. The Singh home and sanctuary, Tiger Haven, is at the edge of Dudwa National Park, home to sixty or so tigers. Balram sketched the conflict between humans and tigers. Nearby were sugarcane fields, evidence of the human need for food. Such fields give the big cat ideal cover, and there have been numerous encounters between humans and tigers in which the humans have lost.

"When humans and tiger conflict, the humans are always at fault," Singh said.

David Hunt, well-known expert on the birds of England's Isles of Scilly and accomplished birding tour leader was fatally at fault in 1985, just days before our group arrived in India. At Corbett, leading a group of birders, he violated his own rule to "stay together in the forest." Thinking he heard a different owl, he left the group and disappeared into the dark forest. Later, when the film in his camera was developed, the last picture was of a tiger leaping forward.

Hunt's death was a tragedy in the birding world, but a lesson on the dangers ever present when human beings invade the territory of wild creatures.

Although subdued by the news, which permeated the birding community in India, our visit to northern India was an outstanding success. We saw the Great Indian Bustard, the "GIB" in the "GID," the Great Indian Desert. Nesting Lagger Falcons, Cream-colored Courser, Chestnut-bellied Sandgrouse, Stoliczka's Bush Chat, and a rare Graceful Warbler were among the birds of this dry, dry land.

Some birding tour organizations almost ignore the tourist highlights of a country, and some birders so intensely pursue their hobby that they have little time to assess such famous marvels. The Taj Mahal is an exception. It is the reason many travelers visit India. Of course, tens of thousands of people each year are overwhelmed with the beauty and perfection of this monument, without remembering a single feather. Not true of birders. Yellow-legged Green Pigeons and Laughing Doves in the trees lining the pathways of the lovely gardens, Dusky Crag Martins over the river, Spur-winged or River Lapwings, Black-winged Stilt, familiar shorebirds, and gulls and terns are seen down by the placid Yamuna River at the back of the Taj.

Wetlands are magnets for birders everywhere around the world. Bharatpur sanctuary in India is one of the best, although there are fine Indian wetlands at Sultanpur Jheel, just outside Delhi. Bharatpur, created as a hunting preserve for Lord Curzon and others of the British ruling class, is famous worldwide. In the area now officially the Keoladeo National Park, birders can see nearly as many species in a day as the early hunters bagged.

Three endangered Siberian White Cranes (referred to irreverently by Birdquest leaders Steve Madge and David Bishop as "Sibes") were still wintering there in mid-March. Seeing them, even at a distance, was one of the trip's highlights. Nearby were their cousins the Sarus Cranes. We had seen Common (not uncommon in much of Europe) and Demoiselle Cranes earlier.

On our first day there, with the help of Steve, David, and Raj Singh, our noted Indian naturalist-guide, I was able to see·113 species. Highlights included Painted, Open-billed, and Wooly-necked Storks, Painted Snipe, Pallas's Fishing Eagle, Pheasant-tailed and Bronze-winged Jacanas, three species of owls, Yellow-fronted Pied Woodpecker, Rose-colored Starling (a beautiful bird), and my first Scarlet Minivet.

Some sightings on birding trips are worthy of reporting to the scientific world, and the Indian trip was no exception. Steve reported the Plain Leaf Warbler, which some of us thought was, well, plain. Most of the *Phylloscopus* warblers are. Equally dull visually, but important to the ornithologists, was the Smoky Warbler, a real "LBJ." Steve and a few hard-core birders saw it while most of us were spotting the tiger.

THAILAND AND TAILORBIRDS

Some of the 400-plus birds seen by the group in India would be seen again during another Birdquest trip to Thailand a year later.

Birding tour groups typically spend most of their time in national parks and nature reserves even in countries not known to the outside world as being conservation-conscious. Thailand was no exception. Silently walking the many paths through the great, unspoiled, evergreen forest at the Khao Yai National Park was an almost mystical experience. Suddenly there would be the sound of huge wings flapping, and through the tall treetops black specters flew—Great Hornbills.

Indian Pied Hornbills were seen by the dozens. A lone Mountain Hawk-Eagle surveyed the forest from a high treetop. A flock of beautiful Long-tailed Broadbills, and Green-billed Malkohas, with their lovely, long tails, brightened the forest canopy. Brown Hawk-Owls called each evening as we returned to our cabins. Brown Needletails, large swifts, sipped their evening cocktail from the lake. Huge Great Eared Nightjars, looking and flying like harriers, silently crisscrossed in front of our cabins each evening precisely at 6:20. Chestnut-headed Bee-eaters swarmed around the trees in open fields, and Scarlet Minivets flashed their scarlet feathers in the clear sunshine. These are some of the birding memories of this mountain forest.

Squeezing in a quick walk before dinner our first evening at Khao Yai, the intrepid group watched a troup of Pigtail Macaques. On our last night, a night game run produced many Sambar deer grazing in the moonlight and seven Indian elephants, but not the sought-after tiger. In the chilly early mornings, Gibbons chorused in the nearby woods. Birders see and hear more than birds.

Shouting "Quile," Australian John flushed a pair of Barred Button-quail as we went "paddy bashing" across a typical soggy rice-field. We bashed quite a few paddies here and in the rice fields outside of Bangkok and Chiang Mai, Thailand's northernmost city.

From sea level, we bussed, in chilly predawn mornings, out of Chiang Mai into the mountains up to 8,000 feet, where we were glad of down jackets. Box breakfasts along a mountain stream always produced a new bird or two as we warmed our insides with coffee from a huge thermos. Later, up at a mountain camp near the Burma border, sleeping bags were welcome.

Many species of bulbuls live in the mountains. Bulbuls are in a family of their own, Pycnonotidae. Many bulbuls are found in Asia, some of which are endemic to very narrow ranges. The Red-whiskered Bulbul, an escapee that is thriving south of Miami, and that North American birders are eager to see, is one of the more common bulbuls in mountain areas. Although rather dull, the Flavescent Bulbul always aroused smiles as we dubbed it the "florescent" bulbul. We "ticked off" six species of Drongo, another common bird, mostly found in forests, belonging to a separate family, Dicruridae. Typically, the group dubbed the Spangled Drongo the "strangled" drongo.

Many birds of the mountain forests are small and drab. Shyly, they hide in dense canopy or thick bushes. Patience and a passion for togetherness is certainly necessary when trying to lure the Mountain Tailor-bird out of a dark hiding place. Often in the forest, viewing areas are minuscule and birders must pack themselves together, gently jostling for space, for *both* feet, elbows, and binoculars, virtually breathing in and out in unison. Although we did this repeatedly one afternoon, only a couple of the group members were situated at just the right spot when the bird flashed between one dense thicket and another.

Not all birds cause such a buildup of anticipation as did that elusive species. Many openly flaunt their beautiful colors for all to see. The Gould's Sunbird with its scarlet breast, yellow belly, and long, azure tail flitted frequently to the outer branches for all to see. As flycatchers often do, the Verditer Flycatcher, sun shining on its iridescent blue-green feathers, sat on a bare branch long enough to be studied thoroughly. A Daurian Redstart with black face and throat and bright rufous breast, what Peter would call a "smart" bird, perched quietly on a fence post in full view of fifteen birders.

Birding tour participants typically receive a list of birds seen on previous trips. One of the most satisfactory accomplishments is to find additional species to write in. Write-ins on the Thailand list that were life birds for me reflect the marvelous diversity of birds. They included Asian Barred and Spotted Owlets, White-browed Shortwing (a thrush), and

Chestnut-headed Tesia, a tiny Old World warbler, picking its way along a tiny pond as we hid quietly in the nearby woods. Dusky Broadbill, one of the trip's "best" birds, White-rumped Falconet, Yellow-breasted, Chestnut-eared, and Little Buntings, Brown-breasted Bulbul and another bulbul, the Crested Finchbill, Lesser Whitethroat, a fairly common Old World warbler, and the White-browed Laughingthrush were added. We also saw, with some effort, White-crested, White-necked, and Chestnut-crowned Laughingthrushes, laughing loudly in the deep forest at some avian comedy.

India and Thailand provide a good overview of oriental birding. Both countries are relatively well attuned to essentials for sophisticated travelers willing to cope with box lunches and toilet facilities that range from non-existent to "intriguing" (but, especially in Thailand, clean!).

Thai people are friendly, seem totally unconcerned when a small army of binocular-armed people, swinging scopes on tripods, descends on their rice paddies or hike the dikes where they are fishing. Birding on one's own in that country would seem to pose few problems, provided one had some sense of where to go. Roads are generally good, but signs are in Thai.

Birding in other countries in Southeast Asia is equally rewarding although some countries provide easier access than do others. Malaysia offers great opportunities to see many of the birds found in Thailand plus some, like the Malaysian Eared Nightjar, that just don't get that far north on the peninsula. The Taman Negara National Park with its huge, virgin rainforest is known worldwide as a place that welcomes sophisticated travelers willing to be transported in dugout canoes.

Birdquest birding tour group "paddy bashing" near Chaing Mai, Thailand, walks on tiny dikes to keep shoes dry

BIRDING FRONTIERS

Birding tours to China, Russia, and Japan are of recent vintage. Bird guides to the three countries are now available. Casual birding beyond the hotel garden in China and Russia ranges from impossible to politically dangerous. The Chinese, and the Russians particularly, want their tourists, especially those with binoculars around their necks, to be in tightly organized tour groups. Birding tours are now being offered to these countries and are by far the best way to go, unless you are a scientist with special privileges.

For the British birder, Russia has a special allure as it is the home for so many of those long-sought rarities that turn up in Britain, the world's capital for rarity-seekers. The Soviet Union, within its wide borders, mirrors all the habitats of the continent, except for the tropical areas of Southeast Asia. Birds reflect that diversity of habitat.

Many of Russia's birds are difficult to find and see; some are drab. The Azure Tit, though, is sure to dazzle you. Thrushes and larks will be singing. Over the taiga, the vast northern coniferous forests of Siberia, you'll see the Crested Honey Buzzard or a Hazel Grouse in the woodlands, and a Swinhoe's Snipe with its amazing song, sounding like a plane rushing past. At Lake Baikal, the deepest lake on earth, the birding may be limited but can still be rewarding with good views of Siberian Blue Robins and Thrushes, Red-flanked Bluetails, and Citrine Wagtails. If you're lucky you'll get a glimpse of the Gray's Grasshopper Warbler and hear its distinctive song. Not singing, but still of interest to the visitor, will be the Baikal seal along the lakeshore.

Tashkent will be warmer, good for buntings like the Red-headed and Grey-necked. Each part of the Soviet Union will have its own specialties and will warrant careful study of your tour operator's itinerary.

Although the new bird guide to China identifies 1,200 species, many will be familiar to world birders of some experience, or even to the casual traveler. There are always Cattle Egrets, Mallards, Northern Harriers, Rock Doves (the "park pigeons"), Barn Swallows, House Sparrows, European Starlings, and Ravens, flapping and chirping in Chinese, reminding you of home.

Even some of the more exotic species in China, such as the Golden Pheasant and Mandarin Duck, are well-known residents of zoos around the world. However, many of China's birds, representative of eighty-eight different families, are *really* China's birds. One needs to travel to some of the most remote places on earth in order to see them.

A birding tour will likely aim for the Szechwan province in mountainous western China, forbidden territory for so long. Here in the Wolong Reserve is the home of the Giant Panda, one of the highest lights of any birding trip! Fifty-two species of the Phasianidae family are found in China: pheasants, partridges, and quail. See the Chinese Bamboo Partridge, Verreaux's Monal Partridge, Blue-eared, Blood, and Lady Amherst's Pheasants, the worldwide common Ring-necked Pheasant, Temminck's Tragopan, and the gorgeous Golden Pheasants on their home territory. Szechwan Grey Jay, Przevalski's Rosefinch, Golden and Crested Parrotbills, the lovely Verditer Flycatcher, and the Fukien Slaty Bunting will be worth looking for. Beautiful and intriguing though they are, birds don't come easy in China.

If you get to Hainan, you'll be looking for the island's only endemic, the White-eared or Hainan Partridge. Birders going to Taiwan should look for the Mikado and Swinhoe's Pheasant.

Japan in recent years has become an object for both business and pleasure travel. It is known as a "foreigner-friendly" country. Perhaps it is the Japanese passion for cameras and other high-tech equipment, and their own passion for traveling the world, that encourages a laid-back attitude toward birders not equaled in China or the Soviet Union. There is even a guide to finding birds in Japan, so don't hide your binoculars the next time you are there.

Even if your trip to Tokyo is a quick one, don't miss the Meiji Shrine and its extensive gardens for an assortment of tits, crows, greenfinches, thrushes, bulbuls, starlings, and the Azure-winged Magpie. Japan is a good place to mingle artistic and cultural interests with birding some unusual habitats.

One need not visit Japan, however, to know that among the best birds of that country will be the beautiful cranes. So much Japanese art for many centuries has glorified these magnificent birds. The endangered Japanese Crane is resident on Hokkaido.

Hooded and White-naped Cranes winter in the south. Another beautiful white bird, near extinction, is the Japanese Crested Ibis. It has been the subject of a last-ditch effort to breed them in captivity. Its last small colony has been discovered in mainland China.

"Made in Japan" has had a familiar ring about it for a long time. Looking at a list of birds one might see on a birding trip, it would appear that many birds must be "made in Japan." So many species are called "Japanese." In addition to the Japanese Cranes, there are Japanese Cormorants, Murrelets, Wood Pigeons, Green Woodpeckers, Pygmy Woodpeckers, Bush Warblers, Accentors, Wagtails, Waxwings, White-eyes, grosbeaks, and perhaps more.

These are but a smidgen of the 530 species known to the Japanese archipelago. Many will be familiar to western birders such as the Common Buzzard, Northern Goshawk, Eurasian Jay, Nuthatch, Brown Creeper, Tree Sparrow, Northern or Winter Wren, and even Bohemian Waxwings.

Although casual birding in this country is relatively easy to accomplish, serious birders are likely to make their visit to Japan a group trip. Leaders of group trips will have already visited the country and perhaps will be local experts, who know just where to go to see particular birds. A variety of habitats will be visited, and therefore a good variety of species will be seen. Green and Copper Pheasants, Amami Woodcock, and the endemic Lidth's Jay are possibilities.

Asia is a massive continent trailed by a string of island nations appearing as a comet's tail (some of which will be covered briefly in Chapter 12). It is full of mystery, wonder, the exotic, and the erotic. It is known for its crowded cities. It has unknown, unexplored, and untold wilderness areas. The world birder's sense of adventure can be heightened here when finding birds depends as much on native knowledge and ingenuity as on a fine-tuned ear and quick eye. One lifetime would not be long enough to explore and absorb even this one continent.

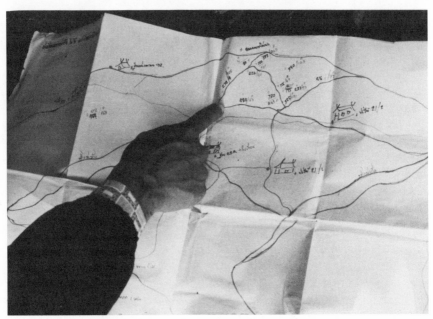

Primitive map helps birding group in Thailand hike little explored area

⤶ *Nine* ⤷

In to Africa: Birding Africa

Africa. Great herds of wild animals on the Serengeti Plain. The Congo. Dark, secretive jungles full of distrust. Memories of childhood wonder with old *National Geographic* magazines. (Where else were we to see bare bosoms?)

The alluring images of the exotic Casbah of Morocco and the awe-inspiring pyramids and temples of ancient Egypt. Safari! Our soul's eye sees giraffes, zebras, rhinos, lions, wildebeests, gazelles, baboons, elephants, and the rest of the Ark's animals.

Africa is a marvelous place to combine bird watching with mammal watching. On safari, it's hard to ignore the birds. They are present everywhere there are animals. Hard though it may be, some members of a safari manage to do so. Most safarists are so overwhelmed with the animal spectacle, they hardly see the birds. They will use their binoculars for distant views of shy rhinos that the guide points out. When you go on safari in Africa, take the next step; scan for birds too.

Nearly 1,200 species of birds are known in Kenya alone; over 900 in southern Africa; nearly 1,100 in West Africa. In recent years, birding tour operators have been conducting birding trips in many different countries: Egypt, Ethiopia, Kenya, Tanzania, South Africa, Namibia, Botswana, Senegal, Rwanda, Natal, Ivory Coast, the Canary Islands, Morocco, Madagascar, Zimbabwe, Zambia, and Zaire. Other countries are being scouted for new birding possibilities.

Modern-day safaris are not yesteryear's lengthy treks with native bearers carrying folded tents and guns. Rather, they are comfortable travels by minibus to national parks where modern accommodations and good food are standard. "Game-runs" to view and photograph, rather than shoot and bag, the animals are the order of nearly every day.

A few countries such as Kenya, South Africa, Egypt, and Morocco have long been well-equipped for tourists. Other countries may just now be appreciating the need to satisfy the sophisticated traveler's thirst for new lands to conquer, with camera and binoculars. Often it is at the outposts of what we understand as "civilization" that the wildlife excitement begins.

For some, that excitement is just being close enough to the wildlife to "see the whites of their eyes." For others, like the naturalist, it's finding a new bird. The more remote areas of Africa, like many other remote areas around the world, still offer opportunities for scientific discovery. Recently new mammal species have been discovered in Tanzania's Mwanihana Forest and a new bird too, the Rufous-winged Sunbird.

From time to time, political unrest in a particular country may interrupt one's travel plans. For some travelers, this may now be the case in South Africa. Different people have different tolerances for what they perceive as danger. Remember that South Africa is a country; Southern Africa, like East Africa, refers to a region.

The sophisticated traveler will not write off a whole continent because of trouble in one country. That traveler may not even avoid visiting a country just because it is the object of scare headlines. Top United States woman birder Phoebe Snetsinger raved about the beauty of South Africa and of its birds after her visit there in 1985. Racial tensions are localized, and birders would not be near the source of such trouble. Tour operators are cautious; their reputation hinges on getting travelers into and out of any place in one piece.

You won't need binoculars to see the pyramids or the Sphinx, or the Aswân High Dam; but while there, you wouldn't want to miss the Nile Valley Sunbird. During your visit to the Valley of the Kings to contemplate the glory of ancient Egypt, you can also wonder at the living jewel perched on the tree branch, the Little Green Bee-eater.

You won't need binoculars to see an antelope or a giraffe, but what is that small creature climbing up its long neck like a woodpecker? Binoculars to the eyes; you recognize a bird, an oxpecker. If it has a red bill, it's a Red-billed Oxpecker busy picking off the ticks from the animal's hide. Take your binoculars; don't go to Africa without them.

As with the Americas and Asia, Africa is particularly rich in bird life because of its tremendous range of life zones, and therefore its tremendous contrasts of habitat. It ranges from the dryest of deserts to humid jungles, from salty seas to the perpetually snowcapped mountains, Mount Kilimanjaro and Mount Kenya.

The Congo River system, second in the world only to the great Amazon, dominates a great portion of Central Africa. The Nile, the world's longest river, dominates East Africa. Like mountains and plains and deserts, great rivers create special habitats in which special animals occur.

Africa, the second largest continent, is a remarkable mix of tropics and desert. From the Sahara north to the Mediterranean, where it reaches the latitude of Washington and Philadelphia, it shares the Palearctic faunal zone with the Eurasian continent. From the great desert south, two-thirds of the continent lies in the Ethiopian faunal zone. Its greatest landmass is tropical, located between the tropic of Cancer and the tropic of Capricorn. Tropical rainforests once dominated Central and West Africa; only remnants remain.

On the west, Africa is bathed by the Atlantic Ocean. On the east, it is the Indian Ocean. On the south, it is the vast stretch of water known as the "Southern Ocean" which both separates and links the continent to Antarctica, the core of the ancient landmass, Gondwanaland, of which Africa, South America, Australia, and India were once a part.

The continent's topography is peculiarly balanced by the Atlas Mountains on the north and the Drakensberg escarpment on the southeast. Equatorial rainforests are bordered on the north by the Sahara and on the south by the Kalahari Desert. Separating deserts from mountains are bands of bushland and semiarid habitats.

In East Africa, it is the Great Rift Valley, one of the most remarkable geographic features on earth, that dominates, serving to separate some species. Beginning in Turkey, this rift in the earth's surface formed the Dead Sea, then proceeded south from Ethiopia through Kenya and Tanzania, petering out in Mozambique.

With its alkaline and freshwater lakes, the valley provides some of the finest birding in Africa. Huge flocks of flamingos are famous in the brackish lakes of Ethiopia, Kenya, and Tanzania. The largest colony of Goliath Herons, their size matching their name, and the Hemprich's Hornbill are specialties at Lake Baringo. You'll find a wonderful assortment of water birds at beautiful Lake Naivasha, much favored by safari tours.

CRADLE OF THE ARK

The region of East Africa is a magnet for modern-day photographic safarists, as in the early part of the century it was a magnet for the "Great White Hunter." This area includes Kenya, Tanzania, and Uganda. It ranges from Arctic habitats near the top of Mount Kilimanjaro and Mount Kenya, virtually on the equator; to the great grasslands of Kenya and Tanzania, home to the largest concentrations of wild animals anywhere on earth; to the seashore of the Indian Ocean.

It is here on the Serengeti Plain where thousands of tourists every year witness the most spectacular movement of animals on earth, the migration of the wildebeests. Northward through the millennia they have moved by the millions, every spring and summer, seeking water and grasses. Slowly moving from Tanzania to the northern limits of the Serengeti in the Masai Mara National Reserve in Kenya, they cross the Mara River and turn back south again. In fall and winter they return to the Serengeti to breed, and so begin again the cycle.

To watch hundreds of these ungainly antelope (which remind us more of bison) milling around at the edge of the Mara, then suddenly, as though on signal, plunge down the steep banks to fight the current and reach the opposite bank, is one of the most unforgettable experiences of a lifetime.

Some of the wildebeests just aren't strong enough to make the crossing. Crocodiles are waiting for a good meal. Others drown and pile up against the bank, where great vultures know they will feed. The stench of these beasts is also unforgettable.

Like the mixed feeding flocks of birds moving through the tropical forest, each foraging on different insects in different parts of the trees, the wildebeests are part of the mixed-feeding herds of animals. In this version of the Peaceable Kingdom, the zebras move into the grasses first, eating the tender tops. Leaves and stems now exposed are the food of the wildebeests. Next follows the gazelle, which nibbles at the roots.

With so much meat on the hoof, lions and other carnivores eat too, leaving carcasses for jackals and vultures. Rains wash the natural residue of these millions of animals into the earth, and in another season the grasses grow again and the cycle repeats itself.

Wildebeests, zebras, and other animals caught up in this great undulating movement are more numerous than they were twenty years ago, but other mammals such as rhinos and cheetahs are scarce. In much of Africa, mammal populations have declined due to human depredation. Although natural forces have regulated animal populations throughout the earth, humans in most of the world have not regulated *their* populations. Africa's animals were decimated by trophy-seeking hunters of the early twentieth century, but today humankind's desire for agricultural lands will have a much more devastating effect on the survival of Africa's wildlife in the future than did all the guns in the past.

Still, one sees animals, large and small. Colobus Monkeys swing high in the treetops. Dwarf Mongoose peek out of a termite hill. Heavy-lidded hippopotamus eyes break through the surface of the muddy Mara River. Olive Baboons rove in large packs, and Vervet Monkeys sit ready to steal a banana. Sinuous Cheetahs crouch for the kill, as Spotted Hyaenas circle the arena. The Large-spotted Genet, a catlike creature with a long, ringed tail, sleeps high in the tree. Adorable warthog families are forever running away, their tails raised high like bicycle warning flags. Cuddly Rock Hyraxes scamper over a rock wall; elephants trumpet a warning at the minibus, approaching too close; and graceful giraffes run across the grasslands as smoothly as if they were an ocean's wave.

On the vast, golden plains, antelope are everywhere, singly or in great herds. There are hartebeest, known as kongoni in East Africa, and topi with striking, black markings on rich, red-brown bodies. Lovely, warm brown impalas are in the company of the Grant's Gazelle and Thomson's Gazelle, "Swara Tomi," the little tail-waving "Tommie." The long-necked Gerenuk, known in Swahili as "Swara Twiga" (little giraffe), will be standing on hind legs, stretching long necks up into the bushes, to nibble on succulent leaves. Common and Defassa Waterbuck and Bushbuck are there. A tiny dik-dik will be seen slipping quickly into shadow. A herd of Beisa Oryx with their long, straight horns and striking face pattern will raise their collective heads to watch you.

Africa's bird life astounds and abounds. Birds range all the way from Ostriches and penguins, to canaries and finches—the farthest reaches of the bird kingdom. In East Africa, a magnet for wildlife watchers, birding is truly rewarding. There are some birds that even the nonbirder can't miss. Who cannot exclaim over seeing an Ostrich, our largest bird, flightless though it is? Its impact, when seen on the wild plain, certainly ranks it with lions and giraffes and zebras. And then there's the Secretary Bird, walking with stately hauteur across the plain. Nor will you ignore your first sighting of the regal Crowned Crane, or the three-foot-tall Kori Bustard.

Africa's Secretary Birds, only species in the family, Sagittariidae, need only
bow and arrow to measure up to their Latin name suggesting an archer

Birds of prey and vultures will be circling overhead, often on the
ground, cleaning up the remains of a "kill." Sometimes they sit on a tree
branch, waiting patiently for death to come to a Cape Buffalo, ravaged
by a lion. Africa's vultures are modified eagles, not a distinct family such
as those found in North America.

Arriving in Africa, eager birders will begin to spot birds as soon as
customs are cleared. There's an African Pied Wagtail on the airport roof.
All will be confusing and exciting, but surely that black-and-white bird
is crowlike. It is indeed the Pied Crow. A life bird, and you're not even
checked into your Nairobi hotel. Look around your hotel; it will probably
have a garden. And where there is a garden, there will be birds. You'll
begin to see some of the common birds, be ready to become familiar with
a whole new population. The Yellow-vented Bulbul may be one of your
first new birds in Nairobi; in Darkar it will be called Common Garden
Bulbul.

Commonly seen in hotel gardens will be starlings. Don't summarily
dismiss the idea of starlings. The African varieties would certainly put our
European or Common Starling to shame in a beauty contest. They are all
in the same family but are in different genera from our *Sturnus vulgaris*.
You will see the Superb Starling nearly everywhere, its iridescent blue-
black head and back with orange breast topped with a white necklace,
as superb as a starling can get.

On safari in East Africa, you'll see as many new birds as you're willing to look for. You'll see an exciting array of "smart" birds in gardens
around game lodges, in the Masai Mara, in trees everywhere, in the brushy
edges of the lawn, in the treetops at the "treetop" lodges, along the Uaso
Nyiro River at Samburu Lodge, along the edge of the golf course at Mount
Kenya Safari Club. Game-runs will also be bird-runs, even though in most
reserves you will not be allowed out of your vehicle.

Around the lodges, birders usually are free to walk. It pays to be prudent. Once, binoculars to my eyes, I was walking at forest edge near one of the lodges, moving toward the trees, looking up at a little kingfisher. When it flew, I lowered my binoculars to find myself face to face with a Cape Buffalo watching warily. Slowly, I stepped backward, not wanting him to get the idea that chasing me might be fun. Warning: they are very dangerous animals.

Minibus drivers will be good at spotting the mammals and will probably identify the more common, larger birds. Bustards are easy to see; you could see Kori, Black-bellied, and White-bellied Bustards from your minibus. The driver will also point out an African Ground Hornbill, a large, black bird looking something like a turkey but with a long, heavy downcurved bill. The much smaller Red-billed and Yellow-billed Hornbills are visible, perched in trees or sitting along the roadside. Some hornbills, like the Silvery-cheeked Hornbill, with its enormous white casque on top of its bill, has to be seen to be believed.

A satisfying sighting is the African Ground Hornbill, easy to see from minibus distance

FAMILIAR FLAMINGOS

You'll need no help identifying some birds. If you visit Lake Nakuru or one of the other alkaline lakes in the Great Rift Valley, you will spot familiar flamingos. You may need help to distinguish between the Greater Flamingo and the Lesser Flamingo. Both species are here.

Anytime you see elephants, you are likely to see the familiar Cattle Egret, that emigrant from Africa to the New World. Don't be surprised if someone dubs it the Elephant Egret, or even the Rhino Egret.

Cattle Egrets, which originated in Africa, are often dubbed "Rhino Egrets"

Everyone recognizes pelicans. Near interior water areas throughout Africa you'll see the Eastern White Pelican, close cousin of the American White Pelican that you may have seen in Yellowstone National Park in the summertime or in the Everglades National Park in the wintertime. If you see a smaller pelican, it's likely to be a different species, the Pink-backed Pelican, but the pink is hard to see. Pelicans are all in one family, Pelecanidae, and share the order Pelecaniformes with the ABC's: anhingas (or darters), boobies, and cormorants.

Other birds you will recognize quickly are herons, egrets, ibis, storks, and spoonbills. Most will be different species from those familiar to North American birders, though some regularly occur in Europe. The Black-crowned Night Heron, however, is the *Nycticorax nycticorax* virtually worldwide. You'll prize your view of a Saddlebill Stork with its absolutely improbable black-and-white bill with a little Yellow Saddle perched like a gun-sight right in front of the bird's eyes.

A little world travel can give you a good handle on egrets and herons. Look carefully at those you see in Africa. The Grey Heron, *Ardea cinerea,* looks much like our Great Blue Heron, *Ardea herodias*, and the Little Egret, *Egretta garzetta,* with its golden slippers looks like our Snowy Egret, *Egretta thula*. This is when you learn to love Latin a little. The Squacco Heron will be common in watery habitats. It's in the same genus but is much buffier than the Cattle Egret. In African coastal waters you'll see the Western Reef Heron.

One of the more interesting of such birds is the monotypic Hammerkop, the only species in its family. It's a dusky, brown bird with a laid-back head, and you'll find it methodically plodding through shallow ponds searching for frogs.

Kestrels in Africa are kissin' cousins of the American Kestrel. The Peregrine Falcon will be the same (*Falco peregrinus*) as it peregrinates around the world. Some birds of prey will be difficult to identify without assistance, but others will quickly become familiar. The Black Kite frequently will be seen soaring over African cities.

WEAVERS AND ROLLERS

Lots of birds in Africa will be new. Immediately, you'll notice the large numbers of eagles and other birds of prey soaring overhead, some of them with stunning wing patterns. The Bateleur is an almost tailless eagle with wide white underwings tipped with black. The Long-crested Eagle, a large, black eagle has, of course, a handsome crest. Sitting on the bank of the Uaso Nyiro River will be an eagle that looks much like the Bald Eagle, the regal African Fish Eagle. In western Africa there is another bird that looks a bit like it, the fairly common Palm Nut Vulture.

Many birds of Africa don't fly so much as they scurry across the ground. Some, like the francolins, spur-fowl, and sandgrouse, look like large versions of our quail. Even easier to see are guineafowl. Listers can count them in Africa, although not their cousins, which have been domesticated in North America. Other common birds seen mostly on the gound will be noisy lapwings and plovers, larger and more dramatically marked than the more familiar little plovers, common at shore and pond edge.

"Whoopee—a hoopoe!" Or words to that effect. Often a picture of a bird in a book stimulates a desire to see it "in person." Thus I was delighted to meet this unusual cinnamony bird with the rufous and black crest and dramatic black and white wings. The hoopoe, *Upupa epops*, is the only member of the family Upupidae. How's that for a family name? Climbing up a tree trunk, rather than scuffling along the dusty path, there will be another bird called a Green Woodhoopoe, *Phoeniculus purpureus*, belonging to a closely related family. It has glossy, greenish-black feathers and a red scimitarlike bill.

Often it seems as though every bird is going away from us. It's very frustrating. Well, in Africa there are birds called "go-away" birds. You are likely to see the White-bellied and the Bare-faced Go-away Bird on your African safari, and they won't "go away" from you as quickly as some birds do. Actually they're a turaco, sometimes known as a plantain-eater. Other turacos are much more colorful, bright green and blue, with wings that flash red in flight. You could see a Hartlaub's Turaco, shiny green with a black cap. If you were very lucky, you would see the largest turaco (thirty inches), bright blue with a stunning crest, known as the Great Blue

Turaco in East Africa and as the Blue Plantain-Eater of West Africa (same species, *Corythaeola cristata*).

One of the most satisfying birds is the Lilac-breasted Roller, cousin of kingfishers and hoopoes. It is large enough to see without binoculars (better with). It perches quietly in very visible places, like a low tree branch outside your room at one of the lodges, or on telephone wires easily seen out your minibus window, as if inviting you to admire its beautiful colors and long tail-streamers. Almost as beautiful is the Abyssinian Roller in West and Central Africa. Other rollers are found in other places in Africa.

With luck and sharp eyes, you'll see a parrot or two, or Fisher's Lovebirds moving from tree to ground like a swarm of big bees. In West Africa, it may be the Yellow-bellied Parrot or the common Rose-ringed Parakeet shrieking to attract attention.

Colorful kingfishers and Bee-eaters will delight you almost anywhere in Africa. With the exception of the common black-and-white Pied Kingfishers, most of the others have beautiful ultramarine backs, and long red, daggerlike bills and are much more colorful than the Belted Kingfisher of North America. Some, like the Pygmy and Dwarf Kingfishers, are true to their names. They're about the size of chickadees, with dark blue backs, rufous red breasts, and those long red bills, striking in every sense.

Bee-eaters and their cousins are also brightly colored, easily seen birds. They are mostly green-backed, and several, like the Cinnamon-chested Bee-eater, have distinctive yellow throats bordered by a black collar. The White-throated Bee-eater obviously doesn't have a yellow throat, but it does have lovely, long blue tail feathers. The Little Bee-eater, the littlest one, is widespread in eastern Africa south to South Africa. You'll also encounter these beautiful birds in India and in other parts of Asia.

Sunbirds may remind you a little of the Bee-eaters, but they behave more like our hummingbirds. Their lovely iridescent colors and typical nectar-seeking flight patterns will instantly identify them. Some, like the Malachite, Bronze, and Tacazze Sunbirds, have long streamer-tails.

Barbets will be a new group of birds if this is your first birding outside of North America or Europe. Mostly small, dumpy birds with short tails and thick bills, they are related to woodpeckers. You'd never guess it but, like woodpeckers, their first and fourth toes aim backward. Chances are you never noticed that about woodpeckers! Some barbets and tinkerbirds, a kind of barbet, are brightly colored; often they have red faces.

Anywhere there are woodlands, look for woodpeckers. They act like woodpeckers anywhere. They tend to be smallish in Africa and often have greenish backs and red on the tops of their heads. Missing will be the large ones like the Pileated Woodpecker of North America or the Black Woodpecker of much of Europe.

As in most places in the world, passerines, those small, sparrowlike birds, are numerous, diverse, often brightly colored, and sometimes marvelously shaped. Some look like birds we see in North America or

Europe though they belong to different families. The Yellow-throated Longclaws look for all the world like our meadowlarks but have evolved in different families. Our meadowlarks belong to the same family as orioles and blackbirds, Icteridae. The African longclaws are in the same family as wagtails and pipits, Motacillidae.

Swallows and swifts swirl around in Africa, just as members of their families do "at home." There are lots and lots of babblers (birds, not loquacious people) around the world, a few of which can be seen in Africa. They're rather inconspicuous, gray-brown birds for the most part, but they have a chattering, babbling call that may attract your attention.

If you see a bird you'd almost swear was an American Robin, it probably is an Olive Thrush. The White-browed Robin-Chat looks like the thrush it is, but will have a distinct white line over the eye.

One of the more spectacular birds in Africa is the male Paradise Flycatcher, a rusty red bird with a black, slightly crested head and blue eyering, and long, rusty red tail feathers. You'll be lucky to see the male. The female is nifty too, but has a short tail.

There are a lot of warblers in Africa, but they're known as Old World warblers (family, Sylviidae). The familiar Blue-gray Gnatcatcher of North America is an Old World Warbler, a different family from the more common American Wood warblers, Parulidae. Some of the warblers in Africa are not called "warblers" but apalis, eremomelas, camaropteras, cisticolas, crombecs, prinias. They're all small and relatively nondescript, typical LBJs (little brown jobs).

Some of the shrikes you will see will remind you strongly of Loggerhead and Northern Shrikes of North America. They are of the same genus. The Fiscal Shrike (not a notorious banker) will be among the most common and visible black-and-white birds; the Magpie and Long-tailed Shrikes are similar but have longer tails. Some shrikes will be called boubous, puffbacks, tchagras. Bush-shrikes are more colorful with greenish backs, yellow breasts, and red throats.

Among the most common and obvious small birds will be the weavers, a name derived from the Greek meaning exactly that. And weave their nests, they do. In fact, it may be those ball-shaped nests hanging from the branches of the acacia trees that you spot first. Once you see the nests, watch for the birds that, during breeding season, will be busily entering and leaving the nest through a small hole on the top, side, or bottom.

Common in many parts of Africa, weavers are predominantly yellow or yellow and black. It takes a good eye to spot differences between species. Most weavers are about the size of our orioles but one, which the driver is likely to point out, is bigger and fatter, the White-headed Buffalo Weaver. It has a white head and breast and a tomato-red rump that flashes when it flies.

Widowbirds are another kind of weaver. You'll get a birder's thrill when you see one of them, particularly the Long-tailed Widowbird with

Graceful Acacis trees, characteristic of the broad savannahs, are often festooned with weaver bird nests

its tail flowing like a bridal train. Widowbirds, appropriately, are attired in black.

Others of the weavers are whydahs. Long-tailed birds particularly attract our fancy, and the Pin-tailed and Straw-tailed Whydahs provide good birding stimulation. You would be fortunate indeed to see the Paradise Whydah with its long bustle-shaped tail feathers. These whydahs fly high in the air and indulge in daring displays like demented kites.

Another nice, familiar bird perched on a bare branch is the Fork-tailed Drongo, a rather quiet black bird with a red eye and a deeply forked tail. In forests, its brother will have a square tail and will be appropriately named. Scratching around the ground for food, you may be surprised to see some of the birds your friends keep in cages: the African Firefinch, Red-cheeked Cordon-Bleu, the Silverbill.

Many species we've talked about are found widely throughout Africa; others are endemic to particular areas. The Jackass Penguin (yes, that's what it's called) breeds on islands off Capetown, South Africa, and off the Namibian coast. As recently as the 1920's this penguin numbered 1,500,000 on Dassen Island alone. Oil spills and competition for food by commercial fishermen have reduced its numbers to a total of 100,000 throughout its limited range around Capetown. The Jackass is a close relative of the Magellanic Penguin found in Patagonia, at the southern tip of South America. Both are known for noises reminding one of a donkey's bray.

The penguin is not the only reminder that nothing separates Africa from Antarctica but a vast expanse of ocean. Actually, the great contrast between the mammal and bird life of tropical and subtropical Africa, with the petrels, prions, albatross, and skuas up from antarctic waters, is startling.

Southern Africa comprises the countries of Namibia, Botswana, Zimbabwe, Mozambique, Natal, Lesotho, Swaziland, and South Africa. Run for your map. In recent years, this African subcontinent has become increasingly popular with world birders.

No wonder. Over 900 species are found here, approximately 140 of which are endemic to the region, the highest number of endemics in Africa. They include three cormorants, the graceful Blue Crane, South Africa's national bird, four species of francolin, the Hartlaub's Gull for gull "collectors," the Bald Ibis, the African Black Oystercatcher, and the Cape Vulture, to mention but a few.

Speckled and Red-faced Mousebirds found in other parts of Africa will be found here along with the endemic White-backed. The Orange-throated Longclaw, a common endemic, looks a bit like the Yellow-throated Longclaw of East and Central Africa (the bird that looks like our Meadowlark). Both Red-billed and Yellow-billed Oxpeckers are found down here too.

Some species will have migrated to Southern Africa from Britain and Europe; the European Oystercatcher might be seen in coastal areas. Others will be perfectly familiar to the North American birder. Lo, the lowly House Sparrow; it is here too. The same Osprey, Black-crowned Night Heron, Cattle Egret, Caspian Tern, and a bunch of others will provide comfortable identifications.

Like most of the rest of Africa, Southern Africa has mammals as well as birds; some people of course would reverse the order. They are best seen in the game and nature reserves, and in the well-known Kruger National Park in the Eastern Transvaal bushveld. Numbers don't match those of East Africa, but the variety is enormous. At the Mkuzi Game Reserve the lovely forest antelopes, the Nyala and the Greater Kudu, can well be seen along with the largest number of bird species in Zululand.

Sometimes the name of the bird will give some indication of where it is found. The Karoo Lark and Karoo Eremomela are both endemic to the dry, flat plains of the Karoo, north of Cape Town. The Cape Bulbul, another endemic, is widespread in the Cape area. The Drakensberg Siskin is found in the Drakensberg mountains in Southern Africa.

Although a photo safari to Kenya will satisfy many travelers' yearning to see Africa's wildlife, other countries beckon those of us who long to return again and again. Perhaps we want to see the endangered Mountain Gorillas in Rwanda or Zaire. Human depredations are so heavily threatening this species that they may disappear completely in another decade or two. A tiny country, located on the western border of Tanzania, Rwanda offers an opportunity to sample much of the local culture of this part of Africa before too many tourists "discover" it.

Both countries offer a wealth of animal life. You might be looking for one of the strangest looking birds you'll ever see, the Whale-headed

Stork, or Shoebill, in another monotypic family. (There seems to be some disagreement whether its head looks like a whale or a shoe.) They're terribly difficult to see. Peering through papyrus swamps here, or in a few other places in central Africa, you will be lucky indeed to see this five-foot-tall bird.

Zaire, in addition to having great herds of elephants, buffalos, antelopes, lions, and other familiar animals of East Africa, has the largest known population of hippopotamuses. Eastern Zaire with its beautiful deep lake system, which separates the country from Tanzania, Rwanda, and Uganda on the east, is one of the most beautiful areas in Africa.

Head for Virunga National Park, created originally to protect the gorillas. The park offers birds, mammals, active volcanos, and an excellent trail system. Accommodations in the park are excellent, but it will help to know a little French.

Adventurous travelers may seek out Gabon, which typifies the image of "darkest Africa." It was here along the Ogooué River, they remember, where Dr. Albert Schweitzer built the hospital at Lambaréné. For some, this will be a pilgrimage in honor of a much revered doctor, philosopher, prolific writer, and organist. On a birding trip, birders will be looking for the rare Rosy Bee-eater or the Gray Parrot, too often found in cages but here flying free in the late afternoon.

Senegal and The Gambia in West Africa are easily reached by air from New York and are popular vacation spots for Europeans. Peter Alden writes of this area,

"Birds are surprisingly abundant and diverse in their mix of ocean shores, mangroves, bush, desert, and woodlands. While the animist religions of the formerly forested areas to the south from Sierra Leone to Togo, have massacred most birdlife, the Moslem peoples of the Sahel tend to ignore the birds. Each village here in the Sahel is rich in birdlife. To see 'jungle' birdlife with fine trails and hides, visit Abuko National Park near Banjul, the Gambia. Big game and rich birding are enjoyed at Niokolo-Koba National Park in eastern Senegal."

Because of its proximity to Spain and to North America, Morocco is more likely to lure the traveler than is Gabon. This country provides its own selection of birds for the sharp-eyed traveler, some familiar, some not.

The Cattle Egret will not be missed, nor the White Stork. Likely a Tawny Eagle and a Lanner Falcon will be flying overhead. The lovely Moussier's Redstart is often seen around towns. In desert areas it will be the Desert and Dupont's Lark, Fulvous Babbler, White-crowned Black and Red-rumped Wheatears, and many, many others. South of Agadir on the coast will be many water birds, gulls, terns, and long-legged waders, including the Purple Heron. Marrakech, below the High Atlas peak of Jebel Toubkal, will bring the birder to the Blue Rock Thrush, Alpine Chough, and Crimson-winged Finch, to say nothing of the sights and sounds of that fabled place.

When you get "into" Africa, you'll discover that it has many faces, that it is a vast continent of interest, excitement, and beauty. It is home to some of the most fascinating creatures in the world. Africa casts a mysterious spell on those who seek to know it. Part of the Mediterranean world, and part of ancient Antarctica, it is perhaps the birthplace of human-kind.

❦ *Ten* ❧

Overview of Down Under: Birding Australia, New Zealand, and New Guinea

KANGAROOS, KOALAS, AND KOOKABURRAS

"Wow! You should see the Sulphur-crested Cockatoos flying around in there. They're all *over* the place." Stinson had just emerged from a forest trail in Australia's "Top End."

Australia's birds and other wildlife truly are fantastic, much of it different from what you will find anyplace else on earth. Laughing Kookaburras cackle from the tree limb, raucous as drunken sailors telling bad jokes. Koalas curl up in the crotch of a high tree, snuggly as fur balls. Wallabies and 'Roos hop across the plain with the grace of ballet dancers.

Australia is more than Sydney and Melbourne, and the takeoff point for the great mountain scenery of New Zealand. Limiting your visit to such a standard itinerary would be like sunning in Miami and slumming in New Orleans and thinking you "know" the United States.

That geographic analogy is fairly accurate. Place the outline map of Australia over the lower forty-eight states. Brisbane roughly meets Washington, D.C. Sydney would be Charleston, South Carolina. The island of Tasmania fits neatly over South Florida, and Melbourne would be just west of Tampa, Florida. Perth would be about Los Angeles, and Darwin would be north of Montana.

In size, Australia may be comparable to the "lower forty-eight," but it doesn't have many people. Imagine all Texans spread across the United States, with most on the east coast, from the nation's capital to Florida. That should give you an idea of Australia's population.

Australia is a continent, the smallest. It is a nation, part of the British Commonwealth of Nations. Most important from a natural history viewpoint, it is an island, an island surrounded by immense oceans: the Indian Ocean, the Coral Sea stretching to the South Pacific Ocean, and a part of that Southern Ocean that encircles Antarctica. Only to the north are there close geographic relationships with other lands, particularly New Guinea, and the nation-archipelago Indonesia.

Of the 720 species of birds recorded in Australia, remarkably, nearly half, 329, are endemic. Like the survival and adaptation of the many species of marsupials, long after they became extinct elsewhere, the birds on this island-continent seemingly were there from the beginning.

Today's bird life reflects the continent's geologic ties with both Antarctica and Asia. However, its relative isolation from any other continent has been a remarkable factor in shaping the evolution of Australia's wildlife. New Guinea shares many of the continent's flora and fauna. New Zealand, once a part of the Australian landmass, is 1,200 miles to the southeast. Ancient geologic ties bind the three island groups into the unique Australasian faunal regions.

Except for Antarctica, Australia is the most difficult continent to see if you're looking at a globe. The way the globe sits on its axis, Australia is always "down under." Remember also, its seasons are topsy-turvy—winter is summer and spring is fall. Darwin on the north coast is in the tropics, hot and wet in December. Sydney in the south has snow-skiing up in the Blue Mountains in wintery July.

From a North American's perspective, the Australians drive on the "wrong" side of the road and walk on the "wrong" side of the sidewalk. Telephone dials are "backward," and the hot water faucet is frequently on the "wrong" side. Truly a topsy-turvy place.

Geologically, Australia is closely related to Antarctica. It is thought to be the last landmass to break away, a mere 60 million years ago, from that supercontinent we identify as Gondwanaland, from which South America and Africa had already separated. There is even a penguin in Australia, the Little Blue, or Fairy Penguin. Other penguins are found in New Zealand and on offshore islands. Nine species of albatross regularly fly up from southern oceans, and the Royal Albatross nests on the South Island of New Zealand.

The Emu, that ostrichlike bird, and after the Ostrich the second largest bird, is of such ancient origin that ornithologists believe it may date back to the old days of Gondwanaland, 165 million years ago. The kiwis of New Zealand are also believed to date from that ancient age.

GETTING ACQUAINTED

One of the best introductions to the wildlife of Australia is to visit the zoo or wildlife preserve near whatever city you are visiting. Most have excellent exhibits of native animals. If your visit to Australia is brief, this may be your only opportunity to see the Duck-billed Platypuses, wombats, capybaras, Spiny Anteaters, to say nothing of kangaroos, wallabies, and cuddly koalas.

You'll see the famous dingo, a tawny dog that you may even see in the wild if you get to where the wild is. Remember the popular rock group Three Dog Night? Reputedly, it was named for the way the Aborigines used the dingos to keep warm at night. A "three dog" night was a cold one indeed.

Don't miss the Royal Melbourne Zoo. It's small, but one of the best. It has excellent displays of native marsupials, and both common and uncommon birds. You'll see bowerbirds, the great architects and interior designers of the bird world, in settings so natural you'll wonder later whether the birds were confined, or whether they just wandered by.

Admire Rainbow Lorikeets, Emerald Doves, and Green Catbirds (really a bowerbird). Flying around the zoo grounds will be Spotted Turtle-Doves and smart-looking Crested Pigeons. You will be introduced to a Blue-faced Honeyeater, a Red-rumped Parrot, a Brolga, a Gang-gang Cockatoo, and a Cape Barren Goose.

Your visit to Philip Island, south of Melbourne, will be a stunning highlight. Each evening, Fairy Penguins (Little Blue Penguins) are washed up by the waves to a wobbly landing. After shuffling around a bit, they regroup into small pods and waddle up the beach to their burrows. A viewing stand and floodlit beach don't bother the penguins a bit. In fact, delighted tourists and penguins intersect on the walkway going back up to the bus. On signal, the tourists will pause and the penguins, after visibly screwing up their courage, will cross the path going between pairs of strange shoes. There are several nature reserves on the island, including the Oswin Roberts Reserve, where, if you have sharp eyes, you'll see koalas curled up at the tops of the eucalyptus trees—in the wild. If you have time, watch the sea crash against the high cliffs of the Nobbies. If you can hold your binoculars steady in the furious winds, you may be able to distinguish fur seals on the Seal Rocks.

Walk with wallabies at Healesville Sanctuary near Melbourne. Gentle creatures, they will nuzzle your hand looking for a handout. Emus will lead you down the road. Although they are widespread in Australia, they're not often seen in the wild. Healesville's aviaries are outstanding; you'll find out what a lyrebird is and what it sounds like (nearly anything).

Near Adelaide is another delightful wildlife reserve, the Cleland Wildlife Sanctuary. Kangaroos, wallabies, and people wander around together. There is a nice collection of water birds, including the Australian Pelican, like our White Pelican, and the Black-winged or Pied Stilt, a close cousin of our Black-necked Stilt. In nearby woods, watch for a splash of rainbow flying by; it's the Adelaide Rosella, a blue-red-yellow parrot found only in that Mount Lofty area.

For a close encounter of the koala kind, Cleland is a good place. Cradle the koala in your arm, stroke its incredibly soft fur, and of course, photograph it. A more famous place to see koalas is the Lone Pine Koala Sanctuary near Brisbane. You may also see them "in the wild" at Lamington National Park or in other places where there are eucalyptus trees, which nourish and lull them to nearly perpetual sleep.

Kangaroo Island, just a thirty-minute air-hop from Adelaide, is famous for you know what. Birders go there for both birds and beasts. It's a good place to see the Glossy Black Cockatoo, elegant rosellas, cockatoos, and even the blue-and-green Elegant Parrot. Some 200 species of birds have been spotted on the island. The Australian Sea Lion, maybe a few New Zealand Fur Seals, and a variety of marsupials may be glimpsed.

In Sydney, the Taronga Zoo will provide a wildlife preview for adventurous travelers and for the less adventurous perhaps the only view of Australia's amazing animals. The zoo is worth a visit just for the ferry-ride across the Sydney harbor. The stunning Opera House dominates the harbor and fairly begs you to take pictures of it. If you like cities, Sydney is certainly one of the finest in the world; it's a good city for walking, particularly in the Rocks section along the harbor. Wander through the

People and animals get acquainted in one of the fine wildlife sanctuaries in Australia

Royal Botanic Gardens and watch lots of local birds. Ask at the Visitor's Center for a bird checklist.

After being introduced at the nature reserves to Australia's wildlife, you'll particularly enjoy Lamington National Park, south of Brisbane. It is one of the best-known of many fine parks in Australia, most of them excellent places for birding. In the forests of the McPherson Ranges, the park overlooks, irrationally, a place called the Gold Coast (an echo of Miami Beach).

Lamington is a favorite of Australians who are eager to watch native wildlife in a cool, forested parkland. It may remind Americans of North Carolina mountains. The park has two very pleasant lodges and lots of Laughing Kookaburras. Bright green-and-red King Parrots sit overhead and preen.

Bowerbirds, master builders of the bird world, can be seen from the park's many hiking trails. Regent and Satin Bowerbirds are easy to see, but ask the naturalist for directions on where you can see the latter's nest. It's a dome-shaped affair constructed on the ground, strewn about outside its front door with bits and pieces of bright blue straws, blue flowers, and other odd bits of blue decorations. Satin Bowerbirds go bananas over blue.

If you hike through the forest, you could be lucky at Lamington and see the Prince Albert Lyrebird, one of two such species in its own strictly Australian family, Menuridae. Their lovely flowing feathered tails and fantastic mimicking ability make them one of visiting birders' most sought-after birds.

"What was that loud noise?" I asked the maid who was tidying up my room as I sat on the verandah looking out on the woods. It sounded like a sharp report of a whip being cracked.

"That's the Whipbird," she replied with the confidence of a native ornithologist. Unconvinced, I checked "'whipbirds" in the book. Unmistakably it was the Eastern Whipbird, more often heard than seen. It takes a bit of work to see this somewhat drab, greenish-brown bird in the dark forest undergrowth. Much easier to see are Brush-turkeys, second cousin (different family) to our Common Turkey. You won't have any trouble identifying it as some kind of turkey. Quickly you will learn to identify the Pied Currawong, a large black-and-white crowlike bird. The pretty little bird with the bright yellow breast is an Eastern Yellow Robin, no relative of the robin redbreast, but an Old World flycatcher.

Some birds are easily seen; some are secretive. Some, like the Tawny Frogmouth, think they're being secretive by pretending to be a part of a tree. Active at night (you might see one sitting on a fence post during a night walk), they "hide" out in the open during the daytime, camouflaged perfectly by their barklike coloration. They sit straight up, absolutely still, heads pointed skyward, certain they are invisible. They almost are.

Wallabies hop around the park along with a rabbit-sized marsupial, the pademelon, which feeds in small parties at dawn and dusk. The "action" in the evening at Binna Burra Lodge is at the kitchen window. Here the tiny sugar-gliders and Silver-tailed Possum, squirrellike marsupials, visit as dishes are being washed. Their reward, and our delight, was licking jelly (provided just for the purpose) from a fingertip. After breakfast, the window attracts rosellas, kookaburras, and currawongs begging to have their pictures taken.

The Great Barrier Reef, the largest living organism on earth, vies with kangaroos, koalas, and kookaburras as one of Australia's stellar attractions. Lying off the east coast, just a half-hour helicopter ride from Gladstone, the 1,240-mile-long reef is a worldwide mecca for divers, snorkelers, and sightseers.

"Come quickly—you have to see the rail. You know, that shy, secretive bird," Pat greeted me as I climbed out of the four-passenger helicopter that ferried our group in relays out to Heron Island. "They're all over the place!"

They certainly were. Banded Rails, related to moorhens, coots, and the like, were wandering around the lawn in front of the cottages as if they owned the place. Described in the bird guide as "shy, mostly keeps to cover . . . difficult to flush by day," they proved to be anything but shy. On Heron Island, they captivate guests by running around after them, hopping up the steps to their rooms, and with the slightest encouragement (a piece of bread from the breakfast table), will walk right in and make themselves at home.

Heron Island is an isolated forty-two-acre island right on top of the Great Barrier Reef. As a national park, Heron Island has a variety of accommodations for divers, snorkelers, birders, and just plain tourists. It has been called a "fantasy island" and well it is, particularly for birders. In addition to the "shy" rails exploring bedrooms, a couple of Eastern Reef Herons are equally at home in the dining room, begging for handouts. A life bird in the dining room! Australia *is* weird. The herons make themselves at home in restaurant and reef, flying up to roost on the roof when they tire of crumbs and crabs.

Picking up a "lifebird" in a dining room is a neat feat if you can do it

Sitting down to dinner, I looked over to a side table to see a small flock of little Grey-backed White-eyes sipping cream from pitchers. Another dining room lifer. The little birds, unique enough to have their own family, Zosteropidae, flitted in and out of the open-air dining room.

Naturally more at home are the Black Noddies, close relatives of terns, streaming across the reef toward the island in late afternoon. They roost by the hundreds, or maybe thousands, in messy nests in pisonia forests. You'll watch them fly in as you're walking across this multicolored fantasy reef world beneath but a few inches of water at low tide. Naturalist guides take visitors on a wet walk each day across the corals. Divers, snorkelers, and visitors who take the glass-bottom boats will see the great coral formations in deeper water.

Outback! Vast, lonely, mysterious, this remote heartland stirs the souls of the adventurous. Alice Springs, made famous by Nevil Shute's novel, *A Town Like Alice,* and the subsequent television series of the same name is the jumping-off point for excursions going in several directions. (Actually, the novel is not about Alice Springs at all, but about the place Miss Paget dreamed someday would be "like Alice.")

Although much of the Outback is flat, dry, relatively treeless, and characterized by red soil and red rock outcrops, the area east of Alice, along the MacDonnell Ranges, is more colorful. Intermittent water holes bring green life to many trees and bushes. High, jagged, red rock cliffs lend drama to the otherwise flat landscape. This was Aborigine country, and petroglyphs of their "dream people" can be found on these rocks.

The broad, flat valleys that lie in front of the Ranges, covered by gray-green scrub, are much like the desert lands of the Western United States. Where water is present, gum trees, eucalypts, abound; Red Gums along the little rivers and the streams, the Ghost Gum, with its startling white bark, on slightly higher ground. Mulga, an acacia, is the most common tree here.

A highlight in these parts for birders and nonbirders alike is the Galahs (rhymes with Ah-hah!), not so much for their rarity, for they are fairly common in the east and south, but for their beautiful rosy pink breast and pale pink crested head. The Galahs are members of the cockatoo family, for which Australia is famous. They festoon the trees like pink blossoms, screaming for admiring glances.

If you spend much time in the Northwest Territory, you'll see several other cockatoos. Pink Cockatoos, known as the Major Mitchell, lots of Little Corellas, handsome Red-tailed Black Cockatoos, and many others delight the observant birder.

In the other direction from Alice Springs, an hour's plane ride, is Ayers Rock, major tourist attraction of Australia's Red Center. The world's largest monolith, the Rock rises suddenly, out of the red, flat earth of central Australia. Uluru, as the Rock is known, has been sacred to Aborigines, a temple of their faith, for 15,000 years. Ayers Rock and the jumble of rocks known as Olgas, twenty miles away, constitute Uluru National Park.

You'll join the busloads of tourists at sunset and watch the Rock change colors as the sun's rays slant at an increasingly acute angle. If you're in good health and have been jogging around the neighborhood, go ahead and climb the "bloody" Rock. Your lungs may protest the climb up, and your leg muscles the climb down, but you'll have a great sense of achievement.

A magnificent new tourist complex has been built a few miles away, creating the new community of Yulara, with hotels, apartments, tourist facilities, shops, campgrounds, and housing for the small army of workers who must live here in the middle of the great Outback. You won't be roughing it.

The Top of "the Top" is where travelers and birders go to sample Australia's wild wildlife. Serious birders, having skipped the Rock, head for Darwin on the north coast. So remote and sparsely populated is the Top End that on some local maps, the major filling station/general store/rest room complex, the Bark Hut Inn, is identified as a real "place."

The first attraction for the birder will be the Fogg Dam wildlife sanctuary not far from Darwin. It has wetlands, savannah, and swampy woodlands. Palms, pandanus, and freshwater mangroves dominate the area.

The birder could easily spend a whole day here, or many. All manner of water birds can be seen: Pied Goose, Green Pygmy Goose (which is really a duck related to our American Wood Duck), White-headed Shelduck, Whiskered Tern, Royal Spoonbill, egrets, and herons. Two birds stand out, big and tall; the Black-necked Stork and the Brolga, or Australian Crane. They're hard to miss. A little bird with a funny name would be easy to miss as it skulks through the watery grasses. Haven't you wanted to see a pratincole?

"What the hell is a pratincole?" Lee exploded.

Patiently she had coped with friarbirds, wattlebirds, butcherbirds, and tiny pardalotes, but she thought we were just prattling when we pointed out the Australian Pratincole walking about in the wet grasses at Fogg Dam. Pratincoles are rather large ploverlike birds, different enough to have their own Old World pratincole family, Glareolidae.

Nearby is the small hamlet of Humpty Doo, a good place from which to mail postcards.

Many of these birds will also be seen at Yellow Waters, in Kakadu National Park, one of the world's largest wetlands areas. But do plan to be in this part of the country in the winter (our summer), as it is under several feet of water in the monsoon summer. Both fresh and saltwater crocodiles share the waterways with the birds. Peer into the bushes along the waterway to see the Pheasant Coucal, known locally as both "pheasant" and "cuckoo." (Let your imagination picture it.) It is a member of the cuckoo family. Comb-crested Jacanas, known in Australia as Lotusbirds, daintily walk on lily pads.

Darwin, almost surrounded by water, is a natural for sea birds. Offshore, there will be Masked and Brown Boobies, Wedge-tailed Shearwaters, gulls, terns, cormorants, tropic birds, and frigate birds. John McKean, well-known biologist, environmentalist, and wildlife tour leader, boasts of a "first record for Australia" right there over his own home in Darwin. It was the Christmas Frigatebird from Christmas Island in the Indian Ocean. Serious birders always hope to be credited with a "first record" for some bird, at some place, at some time.

Overhead, in the Top End, you are likely to see the White-breasted

Sea Eagle, Whistling and Fork-tailed Kites, and even a familiar Peregrine Falcon. Kingfishers abound: the Blue-winged Kookaburra, Forest, Azure, and Little Kingfishers, and perhaps others. You surely will encounter around some garden Australians' favorite bird, Willie Wagtail, a flycatcher with an engaging way of flicking its tail from side to side.

The more you travel beyond bright city lights, the more bright little birds you're likely to see. Fairy Wrens will surely light up the traveling birder's life. They're the little blue birds with *long* cocked-tails flitting around close to the ground. Males are all or partly blue, with the exception of the Red-backed Wren that has a black body. Females are generally brown. Actually, they're not wrens at all but Old World warblers.

Look for other interesting birds anywhere you see trees: Blue-faced Honeyeater, Silver-crowned Friarbird, cuckoo shrikes, and the Figbird, a colorful green-and-yellow member of the family Oriolidae (not, however, related to the orioles of North America). One of the most common birds in Australia is a ground-dwelling bird, the Magpie Lark, widely known as the Mudlark. It's a small black-and-white bird, smaller than any of the other black-and-white birds you're likely to see almost anywhere.

Australia has a great viariety of species of trees with nectar-producing flowers, a gastronomic boon for the honeyeaters. They fill the niche in nature filled by New World hummingbirds and by the sunbirds of Africa. Sleek, mostly yellowish-brown birds, generally with decurved bills, they are the most numerous of the passerines, and perhaps among the most difficult to identify. Go with an expert, and you might identify half a hundred species. It's a good place to build up your world bird list.

A birding "hot spot" during migration is the Broome area on the northwest coast, southwest of Darwin. Not an easy place to get to, it was little known as a migratory haven until a few years ago. The Eighty Mile Beach stretching from Broome down to Port Hedland is the winter home of a million shorebirds that migrate down from Siberia, Mongolia, and Alaska.

Tasmania, that broken-off tail of Australia, has its own special species, not the least of which is that animal more famous than the island itself, the fierce, almost legendary Tasmanian Devil. You are unlikely to see it outside the Tasmanian Devil Park, or zoos on the mainland.

KEAS, KAKAS, AND KAKAPOS

"Kea!"

There it was in the car-park at the head of the trail to the foot of the Franz Josef Glacier. The Kea nibbled on some crumbs, walked around, then hopped up to the top of a nearby car.

Keas, first species listed, *Nestor notabilis,* in the parrot family, are found only in the mountains on New Zealand's South Island. It is one of several endemics the birder absolutely must see. A dull-green parrot, it

New Zealand's signs really mean what they say; the Keas really do what the sign says they do

is widely known as a "cheeky" bird with a taste for the soft molding around car doors. If you do the Milford Track, you'll probably see several, and learn also to guard your luncheon sandwich.

New Zealand shares many birds with Australia. The Pied Fantail is the same as the Gray Fantail you saw in Australia (check the Latin name, *Rhipidura fuliginosa*). The little Silver-eye is the same species as the Gray-breasted White-eye, *Zosterops lateralis*, we saw in the Heron Island dining room. In Clements, it is identified as the Gray-backed White-eye (another good Latin lesson). You will see the Welcome Swallow, looking a little like the Barn Swallow in both countries. Many other species, as well, have flown across the Tasman Sea. Still, New Zealand has enough interesting species to warrant its own bird guide.

New Zealand's ties with Antarctica are also close. Many birds associated with the icy continent frequent New Zealand waters: penguins, petrels, prions, skuas, and albatross. It is from Christchurch that major Antarctic expeditions have been launched.

Travelers don't go to New Zealand for the native wildlife; there are no native mammals. They do go there for the magnificent scenery. It is the "Southern Alps" on South Island that lures thousands of skiers and tourists who marvel at the splendor of snowcapped mountains. Or perhaps it is the thrill of hiking the thirty-three-mile Milford Track, one of the most famous and beautiful walks in the world, that is the lure. Travelers go to sample the Maori culture on North Island, and wander around the bubbling hot springs in which Maoris still cook their food.

Although any visitor to any part of New Zealand will see 70 million sheep, give or take a million, birds generally are not easy to find. Few birds will be seen on the typical tourist fly-in that hits the high spots: Rotorua, Christchurch, Mount Cook, Te Anau Lake. Renting a car and really exploring the islands is better.

Likely the first bird you will see will be a House Sparrow, survivor of a shipment from England in the 1860's, or other introductions such as European Starling, Blackbird, Song Thrush, or Chaffiinch. Other familiar birds will include the Canada Goose, introduced from North America as game. Mallards were introduced from both Great Britain and North America. You may blink your eyes when you spot a California Quail, but it is really there, introduced and filling a niche left by the presumed demise of the New Zealand Quail back about 1875. Even the nonbirding tourist cannot help noticing the handsome Black Swans, introduced from Australia to ornament ponds and lakes.

Birders, of course, will want to see those birds that are endemic or are difficult to see elsewhere. Tuis, with their double neck-feathers looking like a white bow tie, and Bellbirds, both with lively voices, are fairly common. The New Zealand Bellbird is a member of the honeyeater family, very different from the bellbirds of Central and South America, members of the Cotinga family.

Handsome New Zealand Pigeons, and Pukekos, which look like overstuffed Purple Gallinules, are easy ones to add to your list. Whether the South Island Pied Oystercatcher is a separate species is a matter of some ornithological debate; put it down with a question mark. Unfortunately, you are probably too late to see the Kakapo, on the verge of extinction in the 1970's.

New Zealand, and particularly Stewart Island south of South Island, once was home to a variety of flightless birds that had adapted to their predator-free environment. Moas belonged to a family of large, flightless birds closely related to the Ostrich that were once thriving. Early Polynesians a thousand years ago were great hunters of Moas, and they have been extinct now for several hundred years.

Some flightless birds do still survive. The Kiwis, for whom New Zealanders named themselves, but which few have ever seen, can be found by the intrepid hiker on Stewart Island. Evolutionarily related to Moas, Ostriches, and Emus, Kiwis are chickenlike birds with a long, straight bill used to probe for insect larvae and worms in dense undergrowth. It requires considerable effort to see one in the wild, but several zoos in New Zealand have exhibits.

Penguins, most famous of the flightless birds, are also found on Stewart Island. The Yellow-eyed is there, and it also can be found at Dunedin on the east coast of South Island. The Fiordland Crested Penguin can be found with some difficulty. Others are far off the beaten track.

PARADISE: ITS BIRDS

Much closer to Australia than New Zealand, the enormous island of New Guinea appears on the map as a cap to that great island continent. After Australia, New Guinea is second in size only to Greenland among islands. Across the narrow Torres Strait, the tip-top of Australia's York Peninsula, it is perhaps but 100 miles, as the bowerbird flies, to New Guinea's shores. The shallow waters and many islands of the Strait indicate that this was once a land bridge connecting the two lands.

Politically, New Guinea is divided. Easterly is the independent country, Papua New Guinea, to which most references here refer. Irian Jaya, in the west, virtually unknown to the outside world and is part of the Republic of Indonesia.

Although it shares many species with its neighbor Australia, New Guinea has vast numbers of endemics, nearly half of the total 700 species found there. Even more remarkable, this island has nearly the same number of species as the entire Australian continent.

It is to New Guinea that the birder goes to see some of the strangest and most beautiful birds in the world, the birds of paradise. The story goes that skins of these birds with their fantastic feathers were presented to the King of Spain in the sixteenth century. They were so beautiful that the Spaniards declared that the birds must be from paradise. There are about forty species; most of them can only be found on New Guinea or on neighboring islands.

"It is a bird paradise," says ornithologist David Bishop, an authority on the birds in New Guinea.

"But not for long," says Ron Johnson, bird curator at Metrozoo in Miami.

The mountains of New Guinea, isolated from the world for so long, harbor a tremendous variety of birds in thick, primeval forests. They have been discovered by the lumber companies. Some of the finest timber left in the world is in New Guinea. It may well be one of the more recent additions to the birder's "endangered country list." When the forest is destroyed, or even tampered with, birds disappear.

Ron has collected birds in Papua New Guinea, the eastern half of the great island, for the fine Metrozoo aviary exhibit, "The Wings of Asia." One day, zoos may be the only places where some of New Guinea's birds will survive. One of the bird's greatest threats comes from the loggers. First they take just the biggest trees, the very ones the Papuan Hornbills need in order to dig out nesting holes large enough to accommodate their huge bodies. When the trees go, even selectively, Ron points out, the birds just disappear.

Several zoos in the United states have been cooperating to secure permission to get into the forests before logging operations begin. In one mountain area a few years ago, the zoo team collected in a five-day period fifty birds of paradise. The following year, in a different but similar habitat, natives had leased forestlands to a timber company that had embarked on a major clear-cutting operation. Only two birds of paradise could be found. Birds of paradise are not migratory. They have noplace to go when their particular forest is destroyed.

Adventurous travelers have been visiting Papua New Guinea for only a few decades, although missionaries and traders invaded the island a hundred years ago. Tourists have been eager to see a cannibal or a headhunter for real, or at least to see the tribespeople who used to engage in such practices. They want to get a glimpse into the ancient customs and cultures of peoples long hidden from the world. Along the way, they have been treated to the fantastic courting rituals of the birds of paradise and, with luck, have watched bowerbirds building and decorating their bower nests.

More recently, birding trips have been taking birders to the island. Not only does New Guinea have the richest variety of bird species of any island, it has the largest number of endemics. Enormous, flightless Cassowaries, as primitive a bird as the birds of paradise are advanced, will certainly impress anyone.

Birds of unbelievable beauty matched by unbelievable names will be seen by unbelieving eyes. What about the Glossy-mantled Manucode, one of the birds of paradise? Blue Jewel-Babbler? Fairy Gerygones? Hooded Pittas? Red-headed Myzomelas? Berrypeckers that are in the family of flowerpeckers?

It is the birds of paradise that are the principal object of the birder's attention. These birds are noted for their incredibly beautiful feathers, prized for centuries by the natives and known for some of the most spectacular courting rituals of any animal. There are approximately forty species, most of which are found only in New Guinea. If ever there was a place where an expert guide is needed, New Guinea is it.

For those who do manage to get to Port Moresby on their own, start birding right at the airport. At the end of the runway is a crocodile farm where it's easy to see, and hear, the Blue-winged Kookaburra. At your hotel you might see a beautiful Sacred Kingfisher and a friendly Willie Wagtail, both familiar Australian birds.

Birding in the nearby Bomana War Cemetery is pretty good. Upriver from the city, and accessible by road, is Variarata National Park, with many birds to add to the list: Count Raggi's Bird of Paradise, Yellow-faced Mynah, Crinkle-collared Manucode, Dollar Bird (really!), and beautiful little Bee-eaters.

Reachable by helicopter, the Ubaigubi Reserve, developed by the New York Zoological Society, has fourteen species of birds of paradise. Make your contacts before you go. There's a lodge there and blinds from which to watch and photograph the birds.

One of the most famous sanctuaries, and one easy to get to, is the Baiyer River Sanctuary, reached by plane to Mount Hagen and then by road. The Sanctuary has the largest collection of birds of paradise in the world. Three species can be seen in the wild along with other species of this mountain-forest paradise.

Birding down under is far from being a "downer." World birders put it up, perhaps at the top of the list.

◁ *Eleven* ▷

To the Ice: Birding Antarctica

Antarctica is an unlikely place to begin watching birds. Rather, it might be the ultimate place to go birding, and for some it is. For others it is the ultimate in travel experiences.

"I didn't know there were any birds besides penguins down there, or is it up there? Did you see polar bears and Eskimos?"

"No, there are no penguins at the North Pole. Nor are there polar bears or native people in Antarctica."

Information about the continent at the bottom of the world is so sketchy (some elementary geography books don't even provide a map of the continent) that many people confuse the Arctic and the Antarctic. You probably know more about the moon than about Antarctica.

It is ice and penguins that dominate the Antarctic vision. Could anyone go all the way down to Antarctica without having at least *some* interest in seeing penguins? Certainly not a birder. The thrill of seeing those Rockhopper Penguins, thousands of them, at our first landing on the Falkland Islands is an emotional high few people can ever forget. Not at all like the two at the zoo.

Birders and nonbirders alike share the excitement. For the nonbirders it may be the first time a bird has ever excited them. It may well be the first time they encounter people who are excited about *every* bird. The opportunities for birding in Antarctica are so limited, the species so special, that there will always be some birders on the few voyages that take tourists to that unknown continent.

An Antarctic expedition may be the first experience the traveler has with a real live ornithologist. Both the *Explorer* and the *Discoverer,* two tourist ships equipped for the Southern Ocean, have scientific lecturers aboard, one of which is an ornithologist. How lucky those passengers on the *Lindblad Explorer* were when the ornithologist was Roger Tory Peterson, Mr. Birdman himself. Likely he turned on many a sophisticated traveler to the delights and challenges of birding. Other noted ornithologists such as Arnold Small, introduced at the beginning of this book, have helped many an early birder become an enthusiastic world birder.

Ornithologists, and world birders who have seen thousands of species, sometimes generate excitement for birders and nonbirders alike. It is their enthusiasm, their unabashed enjoyment, and their eagerness to see each new species that ignites for many some inner light of discovery. After Antarctica, this birder was ready to explore the whole world.

Until the mid-1960's the idea of birding the Antarctic continent was pure fantasy. To be sure, ornithologist Robert Cushman Murphy, doing research on behalf of the American Museum of Natural History in 1912, sailed on a whaling boat to the Southern Ocean. He probably has the distinction of being the first birder to literally go to the end of the world to study birds. He didn't actually get to the continent, but he did get as far as South Georgia, the 100-mile-long island often visited by the Antarctic tourist ships. (Read Murphy's *Logbook for Grace* for an account of that voyage.)

Perhaps some of the explorers in the early 1900's were interested in the penguins and other birds for purposes other than food and fuel, but one gets the impression they had other priorities: survival, and reaching the Pole.

Then in the mid-1960's, along came Lars Eric Lindblad, a pioneer in adventure travel, to lead the first group of tourists to the Antarctic Peninsula. Since then, several hundred tourists each year have visited that vast, icy land, many specifically to see the penguins and other birds found in the southernmost latitudes. For a decade, the *Lindblad Explorer* provided birders and other sophisticated travelers with the only means of seeing this unique habitat.

Society Expeditions followed Lindblad's lead and launched the *World Discoverer* in Antarctic waters in the late 1970's. Passengers on both ships sailed from the southern tip of South America to the northern tip of Antarctica, often taking in the Falkland Islands and South Georgia, a mountainous, glacier-capped island. That was the scene of explorer Sir Ernest Shackleton's incredible rescue of his men in 1916 and is the location of his grave.

Take your globe off its axial spindle and turn it upside down. You've probably never really looked down there before. Interestingly, Antarctica is colored white. Maybe a white continent doesn't sound very interesting but, in fact, Antarctica is one of the most incredibly beautiful places imaginable. The whiteness comes in all manner of shapes; from sheetlike expanses to snowcapped mountains, as if the vistas of Wyoming's Teton Mountains were endless. Place that vision against a bright blue sky with brilliant sunshine sparkling on deep blue waters, splash some icebergs with a wash of translucent green or blue, and you have an unforgettable picture.

Covering 10 percent of the world's land area, the continent is about one and half times the size of Australia. Surprisingly, Antarctica is the highest continent. Not a surprise, it has the earth's coldest climate, although the part of the peninsula the tourists visit is known as the "banana belt."

Antarctica is the windiest place on earth, but great winds rarely are a major problem on the tourist trail during the austral summer. Within the ice cap and the magnificent icebergs is nine-tenths of the world's freshwater, locked up in the frigid grip of the cold for eons. (Small chunks of that eons-old freshwater occasionally cool the evening's Scotch and soda.)

It was not always thus, however. Scientists believe that Antarctica was once a part of the supercontinent known as Gondwanaland, from which what we know as Australia, India, Africa, and South America separated. At some point in the dark past, Antarctica was warm with luxuriant forests that in time produced coal and perhaps oil. Hard to imagine today.

South America, Australia, and New Zealand are the closest landmasses. It was from Christchurch, New Zealand, that the early explorers launched their daring voyages. Those fearless adventurers, Scott, Amundsen, Bird, Shackleton, and others, brought man's first real presence to our last continent. Incredible that it is within the memory of people living today!

As far as we know for sure, the first man who actually saw the continent arrived there in 1820. Both America and Russia claim to have been the first. From the reports brought back, the world had its first hard evidence that the land the early Greeks had called *terra incognita* really existed. Getting there in the eighteenth and nineteenth centuries was tortuous; only the whalers and sealers found it worth their while.

Our knowledge of wildlife on Antarctica comes mostly from this century. Particularly important was the International Geophysical Year, the IGY (1957-58), that gathered in the white wilderness scientists from twelve nations, some of which had lain claim to the still-nationless continent. It was an unprecedented international, cooperative program designed to explore the scientific mysteries of the continent. An outgrowth of that effort was the Antarctica Treaty of 1961, which specified that for a period of thirty years the continent "shall continue forever to be used exclusively for peaceful purposes." One of the by-products of a visit to Antarctica is the development of a real concern about its future once the treaty's thirty years are up.

When you looked at the bottom of the globe, you saw that virtually all Antarctica lies below the Antarctic Circle at 66 degrees 33 minutes south, although there are some islands just north of the Circle. From an ecological standpoint, however, the important dividing line is the Antarctic Convergence, an irregular line that demarcates the meeting of colder, less saline water and the warmer, saltier water to the north. This juncture is important for birders who discovered that some birds do not stray out of the warmer or the colder habitat.

Inside this "line" is what is known as the Southern Ocean, although it is rarely identified as such on maps. It entirely encircles the Antarctic continent; it provides a rich soup of nutrients and a unique ecosystem. Krill, a small shrimplike crustacean, is at the bottom of the food chain, either directly or indirectly, of every one of the millions of animals that inhabit those frigid waters: penguins, seals, whales, seabirds, fish, and squid. Billions of protein-rich krill are available for these animals and are supporting an infant, commercial krill-harvesting operation. No one yet knows what the effect of such activities will be on the animal population.

From the tourist's viewpoint, the Antarctic region also includes the Falkland Islands, lying due east of the tip of South America, and South Georgia, the desolate but beautiful mountain-island to the east and south. These islands, along with the South Sandwich, South Shetland, and South Orkney Islands (which may be tourist stops depending on the ice), and the islands just off the northern tip of the Antarctic Peninsula, are part of the Scotia Arc, which encloses the Scotia Sea. These land areas are evidence of the sub-marine range that links the Andes with Antarctica.

PENGUINS PLUS

Seabirds, of course, are the dominant birds. The Giant Petrel begins its lazy arc across the ship's wake as soon as there is a wake. It will stay with the ship for much of the journey. The bird every traveler will easily remember is the albatross. Who can go through school without reading Coleridge's lines:

> "God save thee, ancient Mariner!
> From the fiends, that plague thee thus!—
> Why look'st thou so?"—"With my cross-bow
> I shot the Albatross."

The first albatross we see is the Black-browed Albatross. It will be with the ship until it crosses the Antarctic Convergence. We'll see several species of albatross, and there may be a visit to a nesting site. Surely the most memorable is the Wandering Albatross, coursing the horizon and the ship's wake with effortless ease on its nearly twelve-foot wingspan.

The "wanderer," incidentally, is not believed to be the slain bird "that made the breeze to blow" and becalmed the Ancient Mariner and his crew. Rather it is believed to have been a Giant Petrel, or the Sooty Albatross. Travelers may see both of these, along with the Light-mantled Sooty Albatross, the Gray-headed Albatross, and possibly others.

The birding is almost always good on the aft deck. Soaring birds gracefully crisscross the wake as other small, swift birds sweep the surface of the waves. The birders will spend a lot of time on deck, bundled up in their red jackets and wool hats. Nonbirders will join them from time to time to relieve the monotony of sometimes-long sea passages. Nearly everyone will stop in the morning at the bulletin board to look at the list of birds seen the previous day.

Wilson's Storm Petrels, flashing their white rumps, will be fluttering and pattering along the water's surface. Thin-billed Prions, lovely, small gray birds, will be seen by the thousands. Petrels, other storm petrels and prions, diving petrels, skuas, and shearwaters are easy to see with binoculars.

For all passengers, it is the excitement of going ashore that later evokes the most vivid memories. Although wet landings in frigid waters may not appear to be your first choice, you did bring rubber boots and are not likely to get wet. Leaving the ship, everyone steps down into the yellow, inflated rubber boats or zodiacs, each holding about a dozen people. Powered with outboard motors, rubber boats ferry passengers from ship to shore. Close to the rocky shore, each person swings their legs over the side into a foot or so of water and splashes a short distance to dry land. Too brief a distance to get cold feet.

The landing may be on a deserted beach, or it may be at one of the scientific research stations. Often a reception committee welcomes you.

Neatly dressed penguins formally survey their guests. You almost try to shake their flippers and say, "How do you do?" Although their welcome is not exactly brimming with enthusiasm, their imperturbability leaves no doubt that you will be politely tolerated.

"Wet landings" via rubber boats are a major part of the excitement of an Antarctic voyage

On Salisbury Plain in South Georgia, our short swish through the icy water landed us in the midst of an enormous King Penguin colony, stretching farther than it was possible to see, even on a clear day. Adult Kings were coddling a single egg on their feet, covered over with a nice thick fold of belly skin. Adolescents from the previous year, clad in brown furry coats, some beginning to molt, were typically curious. Given the opportunity, they pecked at camera bags and gloved fingers, hoping, perhaps, they had found a new toy.

Penguins come to the ice-free beaches of the islands and the peninsula to breed, to build their scrabbly nests, often just a rock pile, and to raise their young. "Ice-free beaches" are the key factor for the tourist, who will be visiting Antarctica in the brief austral summer, our winter.

That also answers the inevitable question, "How cold is it?" You know it has to be above 32 degrees Farhenheit for the ice to melt a little. The temperature may not be much above the freezing point, but the long johns and the bright red parka your tour operator provides keep you comfortable. It's warmer than snow-skiing country. Maida, who lives in northern Vermont, went home to zero degrees temperature and a blizzard, weather far worse than any we encountered in Antarctica. During that

Christmastime in 1980, Miami had a bad cold spell, and one particular day, it was *only* 10 degrees colder in Antarctica than it was back home in sunny Florida.

Ice-free beaches on Antarctic and subantarctic islands are where wildlife congregates in huge numbers, as they have done since their very beginnings. There are hundreds of thousands of penguins in some colonies. Elephant Seals, looking like dirty, misshapen dirigibles, eye the visitor with supreme boredom. Southern Fur Seals glare warnings that say, "Don't you dare come closer." You don't. Weddell and Crabeater Seals lie around lazily, watching with big, round brown eyes, giving forth a low grunt if they think you'll stumble over them.

Whales don't need the ice-free beaches and therefore are seldom seen. Whale populations have not yet recovered from the devastations of the whaling industry. It is a rare sight indeed to see even the handsome Killer Whale. Occasionally, a pod will converge on a ship and put on a real show. Arching out of the water in tandem, they look like a shiny black-and-white team effortlessly pulling some mythical underwater chariot.

Even the most sophisticated traveler cannot help but be impressed with this glimpse into the world primeval. A few will yawn and say they take the voyage just because they've "been every place else." By far the majority experience the magic of sharing, for a scarce moment, the beach that these penguins and seals have been returning to for generations untold. We know we are privileged to glimpse this pristine world where perhaps only a handful of human beings have ever trespassed.

Penguins are not like the Darwin's finches on the Galapagos, so difficult to differentiate among the species. Penguins are big. It's easy to identify the different species, and everyone becomes an instant penguin expert.

Rockhopper Penguins on the Falkland Islands have long, yellow, wispy feathers hanging down from behind their eyes, looking like misplaced whiskers. They hop up and down the rocks, from the sea below to their nesting colony atop a high hill. There will be a few Macaroni Penguins among them, their yellow wisps flowing from over their eyes. "Put a feather in his hat and call him Macaroni."

Penguins peer from burrows dug under the tussock grass on the Falkland Islands. They cock their heads from side to side, better to view their strange visitiors. The white semicircular face decoration and black breastband identify them as Magellanic Penguins. Gentoo Penguins have a small white sploch over the eye and have pink bills and feet. Their demeanor suggests calling them gentle Gentoos.

Down on the Antarctic Peninsula, different species inhabit that colder place. Everybody's "basic penguin" is the Adélie. On countless calendars and greeting cards we see this one with its squared-off head and white eyelids, giving it that particularly comical look we associate with penguins.

Perhaps with more "character" is the Chinstrap Penguin, with such obvious markings that we instantly know its name. The magnificent

Emperor Penguin, standing forty-four inches high, will probably be missing from your penguin list. The Emperor breeds in the interior of the continent in the winter, *their* winter.

Chinstrap Penguins have character enough to lead a penguin parade

Penguin nesting colonies are noisy, bustling arenas. Adult penguins are constantly going to and from their source of food, often miles away. Waddling through the colony is an exercise in penguin wits, as the waddler trades bite for bite with its fellow penguins. The Adélie Penguin is particularly taken with stealing stones from a nest on the other side of the colony and bringing them back to its own nest. With a shortage of small stones, this can be a very tiresome and contentious process.

Another black-and-white bird, the Blue-eyed Shag, is often mistaken at a distance for the more familiar penguin. The pure white Sheathbill, a pigeonlike bird, stands out starkly on the dark brown beaches, scavenging perpetually. An obvious tern, the Antarctic Tern may be seen nesting near the beaches, angrily screaming at intruders. We must not disturb them, for their eggs may get cold if they are away from their nests too long.

The Cape Petrel, known familiarly as the Pintada from its black-and-white patterned wings, was a familiar follower of the ship. The avid birder, eager to add to a life list, will be thrilled to see the South Georgia Pipit, a nondescript bird, the world's southernmost land bird. Not seeing it was a big disappointment to the world birders on the 1980 trip, but wind and weather conditions precluded landing that day.

Although most landings are "wet," some on the Falkland Islands are "dry," that is, the rubber boats, or zodiacs, are able to pull up to a dock. As elsewhere in the world, there will be some old familiar birds providing reassurance to the early world birder. A funny thing happened on the way from the dock, up the hill to our first Rockhopper Penguin colony. I looked overhead and saw a "TV," an old familiar Turkey Vulture. Anticlimactic, to say the least. At another landing on the islands, it was astounding to see a roost of Black-crowned Night Herons.

Among the Rockhoppers on the top of the hill you will see Black-browed Albatross nesting at the edge of the high, sheer cliff. You see your first skua, that enormous gull-like bird found flying incessantly over penguin colonies, watching for an abandoned egg or hapless chick. The skua, which Arnold Small assures us also has babies home to feed, is the primary predator among the penguins and is often deemed "the bad guy."

Rockhopper Penguins at their nesting colony on the Falkland Islands

In the Falklands, where, mercifully, the bird life was largely at sea during the British-Argentine confrontation, one can encounter a flightless bird other than the penguin: the Falkland Flightless Steamer Duck, the Islands' only endemic species. There it was, minding its own business, sitting right next to the road in Port Stanley. One hopes it was able to hide some where during that war and that it didn't become a steaming duck.

Sanderlings and White-rumped Sandpipers might be seen. Obvious oystercatchers, the Magellanic and Blackish, will be sighted during a hike along the rocky shores. The Crested or Common Caracara will be around, and one cannot fail to meet the Striated Caracara, the dark hawklike bird known as "Johnny Rook." Leaving a camera bag unattended may encourage some unwanted attention from this curious bird. Another bird that will hardly let you alone is the small brown Tussock Bird, or Blackish Cinclodes, which doesn't hesitate to climb aboard your boots.

Not all landings are devoted exclusively to wildlife. Some are at scientific research stations operated by nations that are party to the Antarctic Treaty. There, the black-and-white reception committee is joined by a taller group, the scientists who are carrying on continuous studies to increase the world's knowledge of the last continent. They exhibit more enthusiasm for visitors; not many people just "happen by" such remote outposts.

You will likely visit Palmer Station, the United States outpost on Anvers Island, just off the Antarctic Peninsula. On such a voyage, ship's personnel will hold your passports, taking them ashore at the research stations, where they will be stamped to provide official evidence of visits to the scientific stations operated by the British, Argentines, Chileans, or Poles. The station scientists are glad to see visitors from their "other" world and are eager to show and tell about their on-going studies. After each such visit, the station personnel will probably be invited on board ship for dinner, allowing for further conversation and socializing.

Birding in Antarctica is a rare experience, rarely experienced by even the most advanced world birder. As the cradle of the continents, it nurtured a personal passion to pursue birds on those other continents to which it had given birth.

❧ *Twelve* ❧

Special Species: Birding Islands

Islands have special magic for birders, not for fantasies about tropical romances or primitive hideaways, but for the very special birds that live on islands. Islands are isolated by their encircling ring of water, which may be as wide as an ocean or as narrow as a channel. For some birds, this water is as effective a barrier against flight as a cage.

Many special species found nowhere else in the world have evolved on islands. Half the species in New Guinea are found only there. The famous Darwin's finches on the Galápagos Islands are found only there.

Island isolation has another very special characteristic. In some cases that isolation protected the unique island environment for thousands of years. When human beings finally discover an island, they bring with them foreign organisms to which they may be immune, but that may spell disaster to the fine-tuned life of these isolated lands. The rate of extinction of endemic, island birds is dramatic.

Imagine, then, the excitement of a small group of world birders in July 1985 who relocated on the island of Halmahera in the northern Moluccas of Indonesia, the Wallace's Standardwing, a bird of paradise. Little is known about these birds, seen alive in 1926 and again in the early 1980's, by David Bishop and a handful of others. The bird is named for Alfred Russel Wallace, codiscoverer, with Darwin, of the theory of evolution, and who first described the bird from specimens brought to him by natives. However, he never saw the bird alive.

Just getting to Halmahera is difficult. Boats, small and not too seaworthy, must be hired. Transportation on the island is strictly leg-powered, and one carries one's accommodations over scraggly paths. Tents set up, the group discovers, just a quarter mile away, an active lek. Quietly, but with hearts pounding, they watch about a dozen performing Standardwing males.

A handful of the top birders in the world followed David Bishop to the site: Dr. Arnold Small, Dr. James Clements, Phoebe Snetsinger, Ben King, and several others were among the distinguished group. The rareness, remoteness, and excitement quotient could hardly be beat. It's the kind of experience treasured for a lifetime.

Many of the world's islands are found in tropical waters and are often popular tourist destinations. Even though you go to soak up the sun and soak yourself in azure waters, take your binoculars. If you wander about your island, you too may just see a rare bird, found nowhere else.

Other islands are found from Arctic waters to the Southern Ocean, where some may be under hundreds of feet of ice, indistinguishable from the Antarctic continent. Surprisingly, some such islands are popular with the long underwear group. The Aleutian Islands and the Pribilofs are busy in the summer with tourists discovering that part of North America, with its many natural and cultural linkages to Russia across the Bering Sea. Even the South Shetland Islands off the Antarctic Peninsula mean a wet, penguinlike landing for a few favored tourists during the austral summer.

CLOSE RELATIONS

Islands don't have to be very far away from another landmass to develop unique flora and fauna. Even islands that once were part of a mainland, and that may be only a few miles from another landmass, can host species that have differentiated sufficiently to become separate species. If food is plentiful, if there is no reason to fly in search of it, they stay. Sometimes they even lose the ability to fly, as did the Galápagos Cormorant. Over the ages, they adapt in special ways, ultimately assuming identifying characteristics that differentiate them from their ancestors. They become restricted to their island.

Often a bird restricted to an island will include in its name the name of the island. The Jamaican Crow, jabbering its way across the "Cockpit Country," is limited in its range to that island-country. The New Ireland Mannikin is found only on that island off Papua New Guinea.

Just a seven-minute flight from Yucatán's east coast, famous for its tropical resort community of Cancún, is tiny Cozumel Island, also a popular resort with divers and diverse vacationers. Cozumel shares many birds with the mainland, yet it has species not found on the mainland. You will need to go there to see the Cozumel Vireo.

Other times there will be no indication in the name that the bird is special to a particular island or group of islands. This is particularly true in the South Pacific. The Five-colored Mannikin is found in the Lesser Sunda Islands (to the atlas, friends). The Large Lifu White-eye (really!) is found only on an island off New Caledonia.

Trinidad, like many islands, was once a part of the nearby mainland. It broke away fairly recently, in geologic time, from what is now Venezuela, just ten miles away. Some of its birds breed on the island; others migrate from the mainland or from North America. Both Trinidad and Tobago, just twenty-six miles away, share many species with each other and with the mainland. Both islands have several endemic races.

Sri Lanka, the large island broken off from the southern tip of India, shares many of the Indian species, yet has some of its own, such as the Yellow-fronted Barbet. The Andaman and Nicobar Islands in the Bay of Bengal are included in descriptions of species of the Indian subcontinent.

FARAWAY PLACES

Islands, of course, did not come into the world with a full complement of plants and animals, whether those islands were created by sudden volcanic action, slow shifting sandbars, ancient cleavages, or the actions of corals or mangroves.

Regardless of origin, the breaking of the water's surface by an island or group of islands causes the beginning of a wonderful life-process. Gradually, seeds are washed ashore or blown by the wind to new resting places. Grasping hold of a new, nurturing environment, many of the new organisms must adapt in special ways. Those adaptations often produce variations on the original theme. New species evolve.

Probably the most dramatic of these changes in species occur on oceanic islands, far away from, and never connected to, any mainland. Some are of volcanic origin, splitting the surface of a vast ocean, as a result of continuous and spectacular geologic forces. Coral reefs grow almost imperceptibly, until one day they become the foundation for a new island.

First, plant life adapts to the new land, bathed in sun and rain. Animals arrive on random waves that wash the shores. Sometimes breezes or storm winds steer mammals and birds to a new home. Over the millennia, animals and plants successively adapt and interact, often in virtual isolation. The very large number of endemic birds on the island-continent Australia is dramatic evidence of the effect of such isolation.

Hawaii

The Hawaiian Islands certainly are islands of isolation. The mere fact of their isolation conjures allure and "Aloha." They are also one of the most popular island destinations for travelers. The islands are magnificent in their combination of azure waters, sunny beaches, beautiful flowers, and active volcanos. Few visitors go specifically to look for birds.

So popular were the islands with early traders and later with colonizers that much of the bird life that evolved has fallen victim to the human penchant to dominate and tame the environment. Today's tourist finds beautiful scenery and interesting cultural history, but not the variety of bird life that once enhanced the terrestrial beauty of these islands.

In the birding world, the Hawaiian Islands are perhaps best known for the small honeycreepers—nectar-sipping birds that adapted to the different sources of food in the environment, as did Darwin's finches on the Galapagos. From a presumed single species, some twenty-two species of honeycreepers developed, having adapted to specialized environments to an even greater degree than did Darwin's finches. Unfortunately, these unusual and lovely species are one of the saddest chapters in ornithological history.

For dramatic evidence, look at the honeycreeper family, Drepanididae, in Clements' world bird checklist:

Greater Amakihi	—"probably extinct—no records since about 1900"
Akepa	—"endangered"
Akialoa	—"presumed extinct since early 1900's"
Kauai Akialoa	—"endangered"
Nukupuu	—"endangered"
Akiapolaau	—"endangered"
Maui Parrotbill	—"endangered"
Ou	—"endangered"
Laysan Finch	—"endangered"
Palila	—"endangered"

Greater Koa Finch—"Extinct since about 1896"
Lesser Koa Finch —"Extinct since about 1891"
Grosbeak Finch   —"Extinct since about 1896"
Ula-Ai-Hawane   —"Extinct since early 1890's"
Mamo   —"Extinct since 1880's"
Black Mamo   —"Extinct since 1907"

Early Polynesian settlers, bringing with them domestic animals, also brought the diseases those animals carry. Feral pigs and goats have destroyed life-giving habitats that some birds were dependent on. Forests have been felled. The lowly mosquito introduced itself and transmitted avian malaria that the native birds had little resistance to.

As on many islands, such human invasions signal the end of many species of native animals. A few honeycreepers can still be found, mostly on only a few or on a single island. Only one, the pretty crimson Apapane, is considered common. The great number of endangered species will of course attract the serious birder to the islands, hoping to see them before they are no more.

Other birds on the Hawaiian Islands will be familiar to visitors: House Sparrow, Northern Cardinal, House Finch, Mallard, Northern Mockingbird, California Quail, and Black-crowned Night Heron. The Nene will remind one of the Canada Goose, although it evolved into a different species. The endangered Hawaiian Hawk, or Io, might be seen in Volcanos National Park.

South Pacific

South and west of Hawaii are those other islands of the South Pacific Ocean that evoke Gauguinesque images: Fiji, Samoa, Tonga, New Hebrides, and New Caledonia. Other islands evoke sharper images, associated with World War II—Guam, the Marshall Islands, and Solomon Islands.

Even farther to the southwest is Lord Howe Island, far off the coast of Australia. A modern-day environmental success story occurred there. The Lord Howe Wood Rail was snatched from certain extinction by a massive habitat protection and breeding effort by the New South Wales National Park and Wildlife Services in Australia. By 1983, the Wood Rail's population was increased to 120, an 800 percent increase in three years.

The New Caledonia Wood Rail was not so lucky; it is probably extinct. Nearing extinction on that mountainous island is the flightless Kagu, the only species-member of its family. Nevertheless, New Caledonia will please the adventurous birder with its collection of ancient plants and one of the largest numbers of species of birds in the South Pacific. Although many of the island's birds will be found in Australia and in other areas of the South Pacific, some are endemic. The New Caledonia Sparrow-Hawk, or White-bellied Hawk, the endangered, beautiful, green Cloven-feathered Dove, and New Caledonian Grass-Warbler would be good to add to your island endemics list.

These islands are magnets for world birders as well as for sophisticated travelers. Bird life swings in a delicate balance between survival and extinction, a compelling reason for special attention to island birding. On Guam, several species recently have disappeared or are endangered, victims of an introduced snake.

Fiji birds are doing better. Of fifty-nine native birds, none are yet extinct. Fiji is often included as a stopover point on flights to and from Australia and New Zealand. If you have the opportunity of spending a few days there, it will be well worth a birder's effort. Most of the birds will be found on the island of Viti Levu, particularly in the forests above Nausori Highlands east of the Nandi airport. Tahiti is another favored stopover on the Australian run that will provide good birding.

During World War II, air force personnel brought back great tales of the antics of "gooney birds" on Midway Island, where hundreds of thousands of albatross breed and ride the trade winds up and down the airstrip. Laysan and Black-footed Albatross experience difficulty taking off from flatland, and they resort to sometimes hilarious antics becoming airborne.

For the ocean voyager, often it is the birds following the ship, or the possibility of spotting a rarity, that keeps boredom from becoming overpowering. Black-footed Albatross, Pink-footed, Short-tailed, and other Shearwaters, and storm-petrels are among the birds you might see. Perhaps a booby will land on the ship's superstructure, all the better to spy flying fish.

Bermuda

On the other side of North America is Bermuda, with historic ties to both North America and Great Britain. It is a favorite with tourists on both sides of the ocean. There, another success story is taking place. The Bermuda Petrel is being brought back from a presumed 300-year extinction by another habitat protection and breeding program. Bermuda has established several wildlife sanctuaries that provide good opportunities for birder/travelers; the 320 species that have been recorded there are a bonanza. The biggest bonanza in Bermuda is the White-tailed Tropicbird.

West Indian Islands

Although identified with both Americas, bird life of the West Indies is sufficiently different from that on the continents to suggest separate consideration. The West Indies are perhaps one of the best places to begin world birding. West Indian islands have lured travelers and traders, and even a famous explorer, for hundreds of years. Today they beckon vacationers, particularly those seeking sunny respite from northern winters.

People cruise the Caribbean on large ships, stopping briefly in several ports, sail on windjammers or small yachts, visit small hotels on islands favored for sunning and swimming, or stay at a Club Med. Some people have found secret islands where romantic fancies are stirred. Many islands are close to the mainland and are popular enough to warrant good air service. They make good destinations for long weekends.

Included in the designation "West Indies" is the better part of the Caribbean Sea, whose island-jewels enclose it: the Bahamas and the Greater Antilles rim the Sea on the north, and the Lesser Antilles form the eastern border of the Sea.

For the birder, there are many tropical species, and enough differentiation of species on particular islands, to entice even the most accomplished world birder seeking to fill in a long list with island endemics. Many North American migrants pass through the islands during migration and will be familiar to the North American birder visiting during that time. An old friend, the Magnificent Frigatebird, will be flying high over ship and shore. In swampy areas the usual herons, ibis, and egrets will be seen. Shorebirds, gulls, and terns will be recognized. A special treat will be the lovely Red-billed Tropicbird screaming overhead.

The magnificent Frigatebirds are a pelagic bird often seen high in the sky over islands and in coastal areas

Combining birding with more tourist-oriented activities is easy in the West Indies. Armed with the familiar "Bond" (James Bond's *Birds of the West Indies*), many interesting birds can be sighted virtually everywhere. Sometimes an inquiry at the hotel will produce the name of a native, knowledgeable of local birds, who will take you around for a few hours or a day.

Visiting historic Rose Hall in Jamaica, you are likely to see the handsome Jamaican Lizard Cuckoo and the lovely green hummingbird with the streamerlike tail, known conveniently as the Streamertail. Ocho Rios's forested hills readily produce many birds, including the Olive-throated Parakeet and the tiny Jamaican Tody, one of the really "cute" birds of the world. You can't miss the Carib Grackle cleaning up your left-over breakfast at the Club Med in Martinique.

Look for the endangered West Indian Woodpecker, the Cuban Parrot, and LaSagra's Flycatcher on Grand Cayman. Keep an eye out for the unusual Guadeloupe Woodpecker on Basse-Terre, one of the islands constituting Guadeloupe. If you're lucky, you'll see parrots: the Red-necked and Imperial Amazons on Dominica, and the St. Lucia Amazon on St. Lucia. Ruddy and Key West Quail Doves can be found in the Guánica Forest of Puerto Rico. The Bahama Woodstar, looking so much like our Ruby-throated Hummingbird, is familiar around the hibiscus blossoms on Abaco Island.

Madagascar

Looking for a really offbeat place to visit, where ghosts of birds past still live, where plant and animal life is different from anything you've ever seen before? If so, Madagascar, that giant of an island in the Indian Ocean, east of southern Africa, is your cup of "travel-tea." With nearly the land-mass of Texas, it is bisected by a range of mountains sloping down to coastal areas, with desert scrub, savannas, rainforests, and upland forests in between. Peter Alden reminds us, "The widespread destruction of the humid forests here is so nearly complete, that this huge island tops the World Wildlife Fund's list of most threatened ecosystems in the world."

For birders, it is one of the most fascinating and desirable places to visit in the world. After all, there are four families and forty-six genera there that are not found anyplace else in the world. The largest of these families is the twelve-species Vanga Shrike, of the Vangidae family. False Sunbirds of the family Philepittidae are also unique to this strange island.

In addition to the endemic birds, others are shared with Africa and a few with India, probably indicating that these land areas were joined once in long-ago geologic history. The Ground Rollers and Cuckoo Rollers, first cousins of the rollers found primarily in Africa, are the other two families of birds found only in Madagascar.

Birders visiting Madagascar will also marvel at the unique animal life for which the island is famous. A variety of lemurs, darlings of zoos around the world, are native. Insectivorous tenrecs, some of which have quills and webbed feet and look like hedgehogs or opossums, are objects of attention. Civets, a catlike carnivore, and lizards befitting nightmares may be seen.

Indonesia

Separating Australia from mainland Asia is a string of 13,000 islands hanging like a multistrand necklace between Southeast Asia and Australia. Known mostly as Indonesia, it includes Sumatra on the west, hugging the southern tip of mainland Asia, Java, Bali, Borneo, the Celebes, and Irian Jaya, the western half of New Guinea, on the east. These island are home to one of the richest avifauna in the world.

Mountains, rainforests, and coral reefs all provide special habitats that nurture some of the rarest birds. Visit the Cibodas National Park on Java and watch the mixed-feeding flocks of up to thirty different species swoop across the treetops and landing to feed, thus giving the birder a chance at sorting them out. You won't miss the Javanese Fulvetta, common on the island but confined to the highlands of this island only. Feasting on a fruiting tree may be the Pink-necked Fruit Dove, the Black-faced Cuckoo-Shrike, and the Orange-spotted Bulbul.

Few birders will try this trip alone. It is important to be with someone who is thoroughly familiar with the overwhelming quantity of birds of these islands. A birding group trip will take you to the best of the islands, most assuredly including Bali and Sumatra. On Bali, you will be looking for one of the world's most beautiful birds, the Rothschild's Mynah, only a couple hundred of which remain. Vis:.ing Sumatra you could catch a glimpse of the endemic Salvadori's Pheasant. Group leaders make special efforts to find endemics.

Philippines

Landing in the Philippines the day of the election in January 1986, Phoebe Snetsinger was in the forests when the historic coup took place. It was days before the news reached the Ben King Tours group. The birders had been concentrating on seeing half the 110 endemics, including one of the Bleeding Heart Pigeons, and the huge Monkey-eating or Philippine Eagle. (They saw an adult carrying a monkey into the nest!) The other highlight of that trip for Phoebe was reaching her goal of 5,000 species, making her the champ among women birders in North America, and perhaps the world! The Philippines, with its rich birdlife, is on the "must" list of most experienced world birders.

Galápagos

Perhaps these are the islands that have been written about the most. It is here, we believe, that we come closest to seeing some of the original unity of the animal world. Lacking terrestrial carnivores until humans arrived in 1535, the animal life still actually reaches out to touch the human visitor. The Hood Mockingbird, looking much like our Northern Mockingbird, comes up and walks on your feet as you land on Hood Island. Blue-footed Boobies and Waved Albatross look up trustingly from their nests as you carefully step to avoid disturbing them. Seals swirl around snorkelers, seemingly inviting a game of chase. The Galápagos Hawk eyes you impassively as you approach for a photograph. A Lava Gull lands on the ship's railing.

The Galápagos often are considered the cradle of the theory of evolution. It is Darwin's finches, thirteen endemic species of small brown and black birds, that attract birders from around the world. For the birder it is a challenge to spot the differences in bills between the Small Tree-Finch, the Medium Tree-Finch, and the Large Tree-Finch. There are relatively few bird species on the islands, roughly 125. Many will easily be recognized. Endemics will lure the serious birder and will delight even the beginner. Maida, one of those beginners, feared an "epidemic of endemics."

For penguin watchers, it is the Galápagos Penguin, northernmost penguin, that they want to see most. It is able to survive along the equator because of the cold Humboldt Current flowing from Antarctica. Another flightless bird is the Flightless Cormorant, which long ago gave up flying off for food, so abundant was food at its doorstep. In addition to the Hood, three other species of mockingbirds have evolved on their own separate islands.

Animals with equal fearlessness share the spotlight with the birds on the Galápagos Islands. Watch where you're walking—that brown lump you're about to stumble over is a seal or a sea lion. A Land Iguana comes out of its hiding place right on cue when your group walks by. Marine Iguanas creep out of the water and spread themselves out all over the rocks to dry. The famous tortoises, or Galápagos, for which the islands are named, are today confined to remote areas of islands, requiring a two-day hike to see them. However, at the Darwin Research Station there are several for you to admire.

How many islands in the world? No one can say. As levels of oceans, lakes, and rivers rise or fall, as sands shift, as corals grow, as mangroves become matted, as underwater volcanos pierce the ocean's surface, new islands are born or die. Within the Philippines there are some 7,000 islands. Sweden has 150,000. The answer must be millions.

Islands and their attendant plant and animal life are endlessly fascinating. Birders filling in the species of a family, or seeking to see representative species of all the families, or filling in their world bird list with endemics, must visit islands. Most islands, particularly the isolated ones, have relatively few species. Those few, however, may be so special, so rare, so endangered, that many a birder claims a willingness to sell his or her soul to see them. (Do we have the makings of an opera here?)

The next time you have a yen to get away from it all, fly or sail to some island you have never heard of before. Find out what birds are there; take your binoculars.

✍ *Thirteen* ✍

Sailing the Seas to See Seabirds:
Birding Oceans

"I'm going to California to take a pelagic trip."

"You're going to California to what?"

"I'm going to do some pelagic birding."

Nonbirding friends will be baffled by your use of this term. Sounds sort of bureaucratic. It is a common term used by experienced birders, particularly world birders, but is not commonly understood by the land-locked. Often bird watchers spend their birding lives content to watch the birds that cross their landed paths.

"Do you have to take pelagics when you go birding?"

Your friend thinks your California trip refers to some kind of drug. You quickly point out that "pelagic" means roughly "of the sea," no pun intended.

Pelagos is Greek for sea. On the ocean you will find seabirds (and an occasional misguided land bird). Peter Harrison, in his identification guide, *Seabirds*, defines "seabirds" as "those species whose normal habitat and food source is the sea, whether they be coastal, offshore *or pelagic.*" (Emphasis supplied.) Gulls are familiar seabirds of coastal waters, but they are seldom seen at sea. Albatross are pelagic, and they are found far off-shore, in the open sea.

Dr. Arnold Small, author of *The Birds of California* (Winchester Press, New York, 1974), describes the pelagic habitat as meaning "the ocean waters out of sight of the mainland and inhabited by birds that do not come ashore on the mainland or on the islands to rest or feed, except during the breeding season when they come ashore for nesting activities only."

Leafing through your field guide, you will find several pages of pelagic birds, although they may not be labeled as such. Seeing these birds is the lure that leads birders to abandon terra firma for the high seas. It was the desire to see those birds (clearly not spotted on the Texas plains) that drew avid birder Debra Love, a dental hygienist by profession, to California. Finding out what flew beyond the rocky shore, Debi was "hooked." She now operates Shearwater Journeys, an ocean touring operation that takes to sea thousands of birders and other folk curious about oceanic creatures.

It is possible to do pelagic birding without knowing it. Puffins in my bird guide were the lure for a trip to Alaska. While there, I saw puffins, auklets, guillemots (rhymes with "pots"), murres ("purrs"), and murrelets. Nothing with names like those were on my bird list; nothing I had ever seen looked like them. The tourist boat was full of glacier-watchers, not bird-watchers, so I didn't hear even a whisper of the word "pelagic."

It is possible to see pelagic birds without leaving land. There are land points that pelagic birds may fly by. Harrison, in an interview in *Birding* magazine with another pelagic expert, Ron Naveen, said his favorite seabird site was his home in Land's End, that western tip of England that juts out into the North Atlantic Ocean. This is where he developed his love for, and knowledge of, birds of the sea. The British Isles offer great coastal opportunities to spot pelagics.

Landlubbers occasionally see pelagic birds in coastal areas after storms. Birders flock there in hopes of adding a stray to their lists. In some places, ocean currents run fairly close to shore, as does the Gulf Stream off Florida. Spotting the pelagic Northern Gannet is not uncommon during its winter migration. Best to set up a scope on the boardwalk or on one of the Miami Beach beaches. Gannets will be a long way off. In England, birders have seen gannets and Little Auks as much as seventy miles inland.

The other obvious place to see pelagic birds on land is to be where they are nesting. Thousands of tourists in the Galápagos Islands, without realizing they are seeing a pelagic bird, marvel at the serene beauty of the Waved albatross sitting on its nest, next to the path. Many pelagic birds can be seen nesting on the cliffs on the Pribilof Islands, or in Newfoundland, or on coastal cliffs in Arctic waters. Penguins and Albatross will be nesting in the austral summer in the Falkland Islands and on the Antarctic Peninsula.

Pelagic birds come to shore only to breed and nest, giving many people the opportunity of seeing them close at hand, as were these Waved Albatross on the Galápagos Islands

To see many pelagic birds, it is normally necessary to board a boat or ship. It may be a deep-sea sports fishing boat if you're looking for a day trip, or an oceangoing vessel for an extended trip. One must get far enough offshore to encounter birds that live at sea. A boat must be taken even to nearby nesting places such as the Farallon Islands offshore from San Francisco, the Channel Islands off Los Angeles, or islands off the northern tip of Maine. Some breeding islands are off-limits for landing, but local nature organizations occasionally have boat trips that go close to the islands.

Visitors to Fort Jefferson in the Dry Tortugas west of Key West, Florida, often are exposed without pain to pelagic birding. Walking through the historic fort their attention may be attracted skyward by screaming White-tailed Tropicbirds, winging back and forth over the old walls. The visitor may see Brown Boobies sitting on pilings and thousands of Sooty Terns and Brown Noddies swarming over their nesting island a short distance away. Birders visiting the fort will be looking for rarities such as the Black or White-capped Noddy. If the fort was reached by boat, watch for jaegers overhead or Red-necked Phalaropes sitting on the ocean's surface.

If you are on such a trip with other passengers who are not as aware of birds as you are, be sure to tell someone of your interest. The captain, or the announcer of interesting things, or another passenger with binoculars could be the key to locating birds otherwise passed by. On the glacier-seeking tourist boats in Alaska, the person at the microphone identifying the Dall sheep up on the cliffs probably knows the birds too, but doesn't think many passengers are interested. Once you say, "I want to know what those birds are," you'll have the differences between the Horned and Tufted Puffins pointed out.

What bird best conjures up the image of oceangoing seabirds? Probably the albatross. So many of us grew up with Samuel Taylor Coleridge's "water water everywhere" in "The Rime of the Ancient Mariner." In our imagination we see the albatross following the ship and coming to the Mariner's "hollo." We cringe to hear his words, "With my cross-bow I shot the Albatross," and remember that "the good south wind still blew behind, but no sweet bird did follow."

Albatross will be found in both the North and South Pacific Oceans, the South Atlantic, across the Indian Ocean, and throughout the Southern Ocean. They are undoubtedly the best-known of the "tubenoses," those truly pelagic birds of the order Procellariiformes.

Other birds in this order include petrels, prions, shearwaters, storm-petrels, and diving-petrels. What these birds have in common, you guessed it, is a "tube nose." They have a double-barrelled nostril that enables them to carry along their own desalinization plant. Soaring as they do, sometimes for years at a time, without coming ashore, this unique device allows them to process the seawater and thus survive their salty environment.

Penguins would surely be close in rank to albatross on the pelagic recognition scale. The likelihood of seeing them on a typical pelagic birding trip is slim to nonexistent in most waters. Unlike flighted birds, which can readily be seen (if you're looking in the right direction when they're spotted), the only flying penguins do is "flying" underneath the ocean surface. While approaching a shore area where penguins breed and nest, you may see them "porpoising" through nearby waters. You might even snorkel with porpoising penguins in the Galápagos.

Although most gulls are coastal and familiar to birders and nonbirders alike, it is the kittiwakes, members of the gull and tern family, that are pelagic. Most terns are coastal or even inland birds, but some terns, such as the Sooty and Bridled Terns and the noddies, cousins of the terns, are pelagic. The auks, or alcids, of the Alcidae family, are pelagic, filling the ecological niche in northern oceans that penguins fill in southern oceans.

Many terns are coastal or even inland in their habits, but the Sooty Tern is widespread in tropical waters around the world

TAKING A PELAGIC TRIP

Although one can see pelagic birds in the course of other oceangoing activities, it is the "pelagic trip" that birders refer to as they seek to add new birds to their lists. The primary, but not sole, purpose of a pelagic trip is to see the birds of the ocean deep. Seabirds share the deep with other creatures of great interest to birders and nonbirders alike: whales. In fact, noted pelagic birder Ron Naveen calls his tour operation "Whales and Seabirds."

What is it like to take a pelagic trip?

You could charter a fishing boat, relying on the fishing boat captain for guidance (some are very knowledgeable). However, it is better to join an organized group led by an expert pelagic birder. Pelagic birds are very difficult to identify. They are often way out by the horizon, and they are often spotted in poor light, from a bouncing boat, in a strong wind that fogs your glasses with salt spray. Added to that, it may be very cold. Try holding your binoculars up to your eyes and *seeing* a bird under those conditions.

Best to be with a leader who can provide expert guidance, who knows what a bird looks like, from above, from below, and in the different stages of development. The Wandering Albatross has seven stages of development, from juvenile to old. The Common or Mew Gull has different plumages in different stages: adult breeding, adult nonbreeding, and first winter, and there are two subspecies that look slightly different.

Oceangoing birds tend to be various shades of black, gray, brown, or white. Field marks, so helpful with land birds, aren't much help on the ocean. Flight patterns, feeding habits, interaction with other birds, and what the British call "jizz" are generally more helpful in identification. "Jizz" is an imprecise word that essentially describes the essence of a bird: general size and shape, relative proportions of body and wings, attitude of wings, and movement.

Reservations must generally be made for a pelagic trip. During certain "hot" seasons that attract birders from all over, you may need to make your reservation well in advance. Based on the time of year, birds you particularly want to see, and general availability of pelagic tours, North Americans will most likely board at such places as Bar Harbor or Portland (Me.), Portsmouth (N.H.), Gloucester or Plymouth (Mass.), Galilee (R.I.), Montauk (N.Y.), Ocean City (N.J.), Cape Hatteras (N.C.) on the Atlantic; and Westport (Wash.) or San Francisco, Monterey, or San Diego on the Pacific.

Other than the selection of an expert pelagic bird guide, probably the most important thing to remember for a successful pelagic trip is the advance preparation for seasickness. *Be sure* to take a seasickness pill or apply the "patch" (a sea-sickness preventative placed behind one's ear), even if you have never been seasick. On a long ocean voyage, being seasick for a day may be no great loss. But on a one-day pelagic trip, if you spend your time hanging over the aft rail, you will miss the birds you came to see and feel miserable to boot. The boat won't turn around and take you back to shore.

Date set, you assemble at the dock—early; not because pelagic birds make their presence known early in the morning, as do many land birds, but because you can see seabirds only during daylight hours. It's a long way out to where the pelagic birds are, so you want as many daylight hours out there as possible. Your companions will probably be from all over the country. For some, it will be their first pelagic (everyone has to have a first trip once); others may be veterans, "hooked" on seabirds. Don't be surprised if some people know each other. The birding fraternity gets around.

A good leader will explain to the group what is to be expected on this trip and any special precautions that need to be taken. Most important for novices will be how to locate the bird on the vast, featureless ocean.

"We use the o'clocks," says Debi Love Shearwater.

You've used them in land birding. On the boat, the prow is always twelve o'clock, dead ahead, no matter that everyone is watching the Red-billed Tropicbird off the stern. The stern is six o'clock, although the call here is likely to be "over the wake." Nine o'clock is straight off to the left (birders, bless them, don't generally say "portside"), and three o'clock is at a right angle to mid-ship. O'clocks are even more important in pelagic birding than in land birding. In fact, greater precision is sometimes needed, and the half hour can be important in focusing on a bird.

"Two-thirty, about one-third the distance to the horizon, flying away from the boat." (This is how most birds fly!)

Where is the bird in relation to the horizon—above or below? Flying right or left? Toward the boat or away from it? Where in relation to your boat? Another boat? A cloud? Another bird? A whale spout? *Anything* that can help people spot the bird.

"Eleven o'clock flying left to right (begin to look toward one o'clock), just above the horizon, may be an albatross."

"Overhead at three o'clock, a skua!" (Eyes up and to the right.) It's the South Polar Skua—look quickly at the white "windows" in the dark wings. There, it's gone.

"Flying just over the shearwaters, to the left."

"Just beyond the spout, flying right." Here there may be a dilemma: watch for the whale to surface again (it probably will), or change your focus for a fleeting glimpse of the Red-billed Tropicbird, which likely will not reappear.

Color, shape, and size are sometimes helpful to call out, but in pelagic birding it is like the old real estate saw: location, location, location. It matters not whether the bird has pink feet or flesh-colored feet if you don't know where to look. That is secondary information to be given once all eyes are trained on that particular spot in the ocean.

Don't be concerned that you can't immediately identify the bird—just call out the location if you see one. Don't waste everyone's time by asking, "What bird is that?" unless, of course, everyone's attention is already focused on the spot. You won't need to ask. The leader, or another birder, will likely make a quick identification: "It's a shearwater—Pink-footed."

Watching one bird attacking another at eleven o'clock, the call is likely to be, "Jaeger at eleven—Pomarine." If the caller says, "A Pom," you know there's a veteran birder aboard. Jaegers customarily attack other birds to steal their food. One of them is even called the Parasitic Jaeger. All three (the third is the Long-tailed) are characterized by their piratical behavior, a good aid in identifying the bird in the distance. Actually, the jaegers are part of the skua family, Stercorariidae, but are a separate genus. The British call them all skuas. Skuas also exhibit the despicable habit of taking advantage of the good fishing practices of other birds.

Try a pelagic trip out of Monterey, California. Birders begin birding even before they board the boat. Scan the harbor for gulls and spot a Common Murre and a Pigeon Guillemot bobbing on the water. Other things will attract your attention like the 300-pound California sea lions flipping their great bulk six feet out of the water to land on a platform beneath a nearby wharf.

As you pass by the Coast Guard jetty, the boat slows and you take photographs of the California sea lions at their most important hauling-out spot. Sea otters cavort below, characteristically rolling over on their backs to crack open on their tummies the clams, abalone, or other mollusks. Overhead you'll probably see Heerman's Gulls and Elegant Terns. Brandt's and Pelagic Cormorants glide close to the water.

Farther out, an excited call: "Shearwaters crossing the wake—Sooty."

You "tick" your first pelagic bird. Shearwaters are important birds to know. Their characteristic flap-and-glide routine low over the water can be spotted at a great distance, even in poor light when field marks are not visible. The Sooty is a fairly common pelagic bird and will not only help you in identifying other shearwaters, but its general size, shape, and dark coloration are a helpful point of reference. In contrast to the Sooty, the Pink-footed Shearwater has light underparts. You may even get close enough to see the pink feet. The Buller's Shearwater has much whiter underwings than does the Sooty. With a mental fix on shearwaters, you can describe a bird, for example, as being larger than, or smaller than, a shearwater.

A little farther out, you spot an Ashy Storm-Petrel and a Cassin's Auklet in quick succession. (A nonpelagic Black-capped Night Heron flies overhead.) Then, *nothing*. Everyone is scanning all horizons, but there is *nothing*. Boredom sets in. People begin to talk to each other, find out about each other's birding experience, who they know in common. Bird books come out and the lull is used to refresh memories on appearance and flight characteristics. The leader may explain something about the ocean floor, its canyons and precipices. Notes are jotted down in bird book or notebook. Someone heads for the aft rail, just in case. Another birder dozes in the sunshine.

Suddenly, there is a shout: "Spout!" (Hardly anyone would say, "Thar she blows!") Everyone is suddenly alive, looking out at three o'clock—a Blue Whale. The boat turns to parallel the course of this magnificent mammal, the largest creature ever to live on earth. There's the spout again, misting quickly. Excitement mounts and the whale breaks the surface, slowly arching to display its great bulk. Cameras click. Everyone is fully awake.

We stay with the whale awhile, and then it disappears. A couple of Red-necked Phalaropes appear on the surface of the water, terribly tiny and fragile-looking after the massiveness of the great whale. We see a "raft" of Sooty Shearwaters and head toward them. Maybe 200 floating in the water. But boredom sets in again. People begin to eat their grapes, munch their munchies, and swig from canteens. Always scanning the waters, always alert for that instant view of the Sabine's Gull, crossing the bow in a flash, perhaps not to be seen again on this trip.

That may be the extent of the day's pelagic birding. You may have added four or five birds to your life list. If you've been out before, maybe you don't see a single new one. But you had a much better view of the Ashy Storm-Petrel and feel that you will be able to better identify it on another trip. Some views you had were distant, hazy; others were great close-ups, so that you could actually see the long tail on one of those Long-tailed Jaegers just sitting in the water ahead of the boat.

Don't feel badly if you can't remember what the difference was between the Ashy and the Leach's Storm-Petrels. It takes a lot of experience to feel comfortable with pelagic bird identification. Don't be discouraged; just plan another pelagic trip.

Enjoy your memory of the Elephant Seal, or at least its cone-shaped head breaking through the water, as it peered at your boat. It was thrilling to see the porpoises, particularly the Dall's Porpoise, swishing up and down and right and left, speeding in front of the boat, bubbles dancing and sparkling in the sunlight. And it was fun watching a crew member bring in an albacore.

Pelagic birding normally produces few species. For this reason, it is a good idea to schedule more than one trip per visit to the coast. Either coast is a considerable distance for many people to go, so it makes sense to make the most of being there. On the second trip out (or the third or fourth), you will see a different combination of birds, some you simply didn't see on the first trip.

The weather is another reason for not just flying in for a single trip and then flying out again. Be prepared for a trip to be cancelled. Better disappointed than drowned. Weather is usually more of a concern in the Atlantic than in the Pacific.

If you can choose what time of the year you want to take your first pelagic trip, choose the late summer or fall for the Pacific. Early August to mid-November is the best time to see the most species. At that time, birds are migrating down the West Coast from their summer breeding grounds in Alaskas, while others are en route to begin their breeding season off New Zealand coastal areas. Why not take a few days' vacation after your conference in San Francisco and have a pelagic adventure?

A chilling thought is an Atlantic pelagic trip in winter (November-March). However, you may see Northern Gannets, Fulmars, Black-legged Kittiwakes, Razorbills, Dovekies (Little Auks), and perhaps Atlantic Puffins. In summer and autumn, you may see Greater, Cory's, Sooty, and either Manx or Audubon's Shearwaters. You could swell your list with Wilson's and Leach's Storm-Petrels, jaegers, South Polar Skuas, and phalaropes. Spring is a better time to also see whales and dolphins. If you're in Britain at that time, watch for pelagic birds there.

In the Pacific one generally sees greater numbers and varieties of birds than in the Atlantic. In the Atlantic you find distinct species and occasional rarities such as the Black-capped Petrel and White-faced and Band-rumped Storm-Petrels.

Although only the lucky few ever get there, the preeminent place on this globe for pelagic birding is the Southern Ocean surrounding the Antarctic continent. The incredible richness of the Southern Ocean sustains a wide variety of species and incredible numbers of albatross, penguins, petrels, prions, and shearwaters. On an Antarctic expedition, it is a rare day when hundreds of birds are not within sight of the ship. Some are found nowhere else in the world.

For many birders, pelagic birding is very special. Being beyond sight of land opens up the soul to a seemingly limitless universe, yet within the confines of a boat, people often draw together in the warmth of mutual interest. For pelagic birds, oceans are home. We landed ones must sail the seas to see these marvelous creatures, for they often seek out the most distant and inaccessible points of land to secretly secure their species.

World birders are ever wondrous of all birds: those bound to a continent or to a hemisphere, those very special species that know only their own islands, those birds that call the oceans of the world their home, and those species for which the whole world is called "home." Most birders in pursuit of birding express love for the birds, joy at their flight, wonder at the intricacy of their existence, and ecstasy at their beauty.

Often the ship's wake attracts a fascinating assortment of ocean-going birds

PART III

BASICS. . .
FOR FURTHER REFERENCE

Birder/travelers will want to know a lot more about *Birding Around the World* than this quick "trip" has provided. Part III has been referred to throughout the book and basic information is provided here. You will find. . .

Basic Books and Other Birding Aids for books, periodicals, and additional information on binoculars and other aids.

Basic Book Dealers where you can find those books.

Basic Beds and Breakfasts: What to expect where; birder-friendly accommodations.

Tour Operators, birding and otherwise.

Basic Glossary

Basic Common Sense

Basic Bibliography

Good birding!

🐦 *Fourteen* 🐦

Basic Books and Other Birding Aids

INTRODUCTION

Reference books are essential for the person interested in identifying birds. Fortunately, books about birds are widely available. They cover virtually every phase of birding, from "how to attract birds to your feeder" to beautiful cocktail-table versions of raptors or shorebirds of the world. Basic books are identified here to help the early birder. These include standard field guides, standard where-to-find guides, and checklists for the world, major countries or continents, or major parts thereof. A few basic general reference books are also listed. New books about birds and birding are being published every year. Book dealers listed in the next section maintain up-to-date listings and generally have good selections of bird books covering limited or out-of-the-way places.

World birders probably will want travel guides for the countries they will be visiting. Your friendly local bookseller will be happy to help you out.

The first section below identifies books relevant to birding anywhere in the world and are designed to supplement Part I. Subsequent sections provide additional references related to specific chapters in Part II.

FIELD GUIDES

New field guides are being published each year; older guides are being updated. Nearly everywhere there is good birding, there is likely to be some type of field guide.

Experienced birders are selective about field guides. They like having the description of the bird on the page facing the plate showing the bird. The best plates are those that are drawn to show different plumages, preferably against a background that gives some idea of habitat. Photographic plates are often beautiful but seldom show varied plumages or activities of the bird.

It helps if there is a distribution map on the same page with the description, although maps often are located in an appendix. Some bird guides include a "sonogram," a picture of how the song looks, but many birders feel that songs are hard to translate into an auditory image. Good voice descriptions are imperative.

Making a field guide that includes the nearly 9,000 birds of the world would truly be impossible; you'd need a Mack truck to transport it. However, for the beginner, there is one that covers a limited number of common birds and might get you started.

Bologna, Gianfranco. *Guide to Birds of the World.* Edited by John Bull. New York: Simon & Schuster, 1978. Field guide with color plates of more common birds.

WHERE-TO-FIND GUIDES

Where-to-find guides have been published for nearly every "hot" and "not-so-hot spot" in North America and for many places in Britain, and parts of the rest of the world. If you're going to spend time in the Chicago area, check with one of the book dealers to see if there is a where-to-find guide. (There is.) Is there one for Fargo, North Dakota? Essex, England? Check local bookstores or bird clubs.

Alden, Peter, and John Gooders. *Finding Birds Around the World*. Houghton Mifflin Company, Boston, 1981. This book is out of print but book dealers may still find stock from Common Ground Book Company, 3906 Prospect Street, Kensington, Md., 20895. For individual orders from Peter Alden, P.O. Box 1030, Concord, Mass. 01742, (U.S. $20 post paid). Very good, occasionally out of date, guide to 111 great birding areas. Includes bird lists of each area, maps on how to get there, taxonomic index.

CHECKLISTS

A number of widely used checklists of the birds of the world exist, and the serious birder should look at several in order to determine which provides the level of detail desired. At present, only the Clements is designed as a list on which to make a checkmark and record other relevant data.

Clements, James. *Birds of the World: A Checklist*. 3rd Ed. New York: Facts on File, 1981. (4th edition scheduled for fall publication by Cornell University Press.) This book, widely used by North American birders, includes a list of orders and families, bibliography, and an index of scientific and common names. The checklist includes the following: Column for date of sighting, line for identifying the location for the first sighting of each species, and a one-line explanation of species distribution. The book is also coded for a computer system.

Edwards, Ernest P. *Coded Workbook of Birds of the World*. 2nd Ed. Sweet Briar, Va.: Ernest P. Edwards. Vol. 1, Nonpasserines, 1982; Vol. 2, Passerines, 1986. Loose-leaf notebook format; taxonomic list.

Howard, Richard, and Alick Moore. *A Complete Checklist of the Birds of the World*. rev. ed. New York: Macmillan Co., 1984. Systematically arranged by bird families, fully indexed with scientific and English names by species, includes every subspecies.

Walters, Michael. *The Complete Birds of the World*. London and North Pomfret, Vt.: David & Charles, Inc., 1980. Taxonomic list of all families and species, extant and extinct, with brief descriptions, range, habitat. Includes indices of Latin family names and English family names.

Convenient field checklists of the birds of virtually every place in the world have been prepared by and are available from Natural History Books, Inc. See "Bird and Nature Book Dealers," p. 225.

GENERAL

Austin, Oliver L., Jr. *Families of Birds: A Guide to Bird Classification*. New York: Golden Press, 1985. This useful little book will take up no room in your suitcase, though it is larger than original 1971 edition.

Campbell, Bruce, and Elizabeth Lack, eds. *A Dictionary of Birds*. Buteo Books, P.O. Box 481, Vermillion, S. Dak. 57069, 1985. Excellent reference work for world birders prepared under the auspices of the British Ornithologists Union.

Choate, Ernest A. *The Dictionary of American Bird Names*. rev. ed., by Raymond A. Paynter. Boston: The Harvard Common Press, 1985. Revised edition accomodates the AOU 1983 checklist.

Fisher, James, and Roger Tory Peterson. *World of Birds*. New York: Crescent Books, 1977. Revised edition covers various aspects of birds of the world. Great paintings by Peterson.

Flegg, Jim. *Just a Lark!* Origin of names of birds with a humorous touch. Photographs by Eric and David Hosking, comical illustrations by Norman Arlott.

Gotch, A. F. *Birds—Their Latin Names Explained*. Poole, Dorset, United Kingdom: Blandford Books Ltd. 1981; in U. S., Sterling Publishing, 2 Park Avenue, New York, 1981. Not all Latin names are included, but it provides interesting stories of how birds got their names. North American birds come up short.

Gruson, Edward S. *Words for Birds: A Lexicon of North American Birds*, with biographical notes. New York: Quadrangle Books, 1972. Fills in the weaknesses of the Gotch book.

Harrison, C. J. O., consultant ed. *Bird Families of the World*. New York: Harry N. Abrams, Inc., 1978. Cocktail-table size and style.

Leahy, Christopher. *The Birdwatcher's Companion: An Encyclopedic Handbook of North American Birdlife*. New York: Bonanza Books, 1982. Arranged alphabetically from "Aberrant" to "Zygodactyl." Includes a good topographical sketch of a bird; a taxonomic listing of the birds of North America by order, family, genus, and species; a list of North American vagrants and where they can be found; a list of migrant specialties and dates; and an extensive bibliography. Although the emphasis is North American, the book constitutes a glossary of much terminology useful worldwide.

Perrins, Christopher M., and Alex L. A. Middleton, eds. *The Encyclopedia of Birds*. New York: Facts on File, 1985. Good descriptions of the families of birds of the world listed in taxonomic order. Contains a glossary and extensive index. Excellent color photographs.

Readers Digest Edition. *Birds: Their Life, Their Ways, Their World*. Pleasantville, N. Y.: The Readers Digest Association, Inc., 1979. Cocktail-table–sized book. First part contains general information about birds; second part includes *Bird Families of the World*, originally published as a separate edition (Harrison).

Torres, John K. *The Audubon Society Encyclopedia of North American Birds*. New York: Alfred A. Knopf, 1980. A very big book, that emphasizes North American birds but provides a wealth of information on birds and birding terminology useful to the world birder. Contains many color photographic plates.

REFERENCES FOR CHAPTERS
FIVE THROUGH THIRTEEN

Field Guides: Chapter 5

Bull, John, Edith Bull, Gerald Gold, Pieter D. Prall, and Collier Booles. *Birds of North America; Eastern Region: A Quick Identification Guide for all Birdwatchers*. New York: Macmillan Co., 1985. Covers 253 species with brief descriptions arranged in categories for quick identification, e.g., blue birds, shorebirds.

Farrand, John Jr., ed. *The Audubon Society Master Guide to Birding*. New York: Alfred A. Knopf, 1983. Fairly detailed descriptions with photographs. Divided into three volumes: *Loons to Sandpipers*; *Gulls to Dippers*; and *Old World Warblers to Sparrows*.

National Geographic Society. *Field Guide to the Birds of North America*, Washington, D.C.: National Geographic Society, 1983. Slightly oversized, thorough descriptions, and color plates show characteristic perches and habitats, maps on same page.

Peterson, Roger Tory. *A Field Guide to the Birds*. Boston: Houghton Mifflin Co., 1980. Subtitled, "A Completely New Guide to All the Birds of Eastern and Central North America." Paperback title, *A Field Guide to the Birds East of the Rockies*. This is the bird book that made it to the best-seller list. Color plates with characteristic Peterson field marks, distribution map section, checklist.

_____ *A Field Guide to Western Birds*. 1961.

Robbins, Chandler S., Bertel Bruun, and Herbert S. Zim. *Birds of North America*, 2d rev. ed. New York: Golden Press, 1983. Widely used field guide with color plates, maps, and sonograms on same page.

Where-to-Find Guides: Chapter 5

Finlay, J. C., ed. *Bird Finding Guide to Canada*. Edmonton, Alberta: Hurtig Publishers, Ltd., 1984. Some line drawings; good information on finding birds throughout Canada.

Harrison, George H. *Roger Tory Peterson's Dozen Birding Hot Spots*. New York: Simon & Schuster, 1976. For the curious, they are: the Everglades, South Texas, The Platte, Southeast Arizona, Point Pelee, Bear River, Coast of Maine, Gaspé, Hawk Mountain, Cape May (N.J.), Horicon (Wis.), and Tule-Klamath-Malheur.

Lane, James A. *A Birder's Guide to.* . . . Revisions to most recent editions by Harold R. Holt. L & P Press, P.O. Box 21604, Denver, Colo. 80221.

> Southeastern Arizona (1984)
> Churchill, Manitoba (1983)
> Eastern Colorado (1986)
> (Revised edition covering all of Colorado due in 1987)
> Florida (1984)
> North Dakota (1979)
> Rio Grande Valley of Texas (1986)
> Southern California (1985)
> Texas Coast (1984)

Detailed guides to specific locations generally accompanied by local maps. Information on accommodations often included. Charts show seasonal distribution in different habitats.

Pettingill, Sewell, Jr. *A Guide to Bird Finding East of the Mississippi.* New York: Oxford University Press, 1977. Detailed state-by-state coverage of good birding spots.

Pettingill, Sewell, Jr. *A Guide to Bird Finding West of the Mississippi.* New York: Oxford University Press, 1981.

Stirling, David, and Jim Woodford. *Where to Go Bird Watching in Canada.* Hancock House Publishers, 3215 Island View Rd., Saanichton, British Columbia, 1975.

Tucker, Priscilla, ed. *ABA Bird-finding Guide.* American Birding Association, Inc., Box 4335, Austin, Tex. 78765. Detailed information on where to find birds, along with detailed maps contributed by members of ABA. Arranged by state in two loose-leaf binders. Emphasis on North America, but some information on other places in the world. Updated inserts are provided from each issue of *Birding* magazine.

The quick and concise *A Guide to Our Federal Lands* published by the National Geographic Society in 1984 (reprinted 1985) will be very useful to the birder. It lists national parks, forests, wildlife reserves, grasslands, etc. with reference to what birds may be found at what times of the year.

Checklists: Chapter 5

North American checklists are based on the most recent edition of the *A.O.U. Check-list of North American Birds* prepared by a committee of the American Ornithologists Union. The current edition is the sixth, published in 1983. It is used primarily as a reference work. Other checklists referred to here are abbreviated lists on which the birder "checks" (the British "tick") species seen.

American Birding Association, *A.B.A. Checklist:* Birds of Continental United States and Canada, 3rd Ed., P.O. Box 4335, Austin, Tex.

78765,1986. Booklet-size for birds of North America listed in taxonomic order. Uses Basham system of coding birds according to difficulty of finding. Updated periodically with inserts from *Birding* magazine. The A.B.A. also publishes a small, pocket-sized *Traveler's List and Check List* giving common names only. Has multiple columns for multiple travels and an alphabetical index of common names.

DeSante, David, and Peter Pyle. *Distributional Checklist of North American Birds*. Lee Vining, CA 93541, Artemisia Press. 1986. Hard-cover book lists species in taxonomic order with tables showing status and distribution by states and Canadian provinces.

Swift, Byron. *Checklist of the Birds of North America*. Including Middle America, the West Indies, and Hawaii. American Birding Association, Austin, Tex., 1986. This list incorporates the changes in definition of North America included in the AOU checklist.

General: Chapter 5

Heintzelman, Donald S. *A Manual for Bird Watching in the Americas*. New York: Universe Books, 381 Park Avenue South, New York, N.Y. 10016, 1979. General helpful information covering both North and South America.

Kress, Stephen W. *The Audubon Society Handbook for Birders*. New York: Charles Scribner's Sons, 1981. Great book for getting started and becoming proficient as a birder. Includes chapters on binoculars and spotting scopes and on photography. Reference sections include educational and research programs, periodicals, including a state-by-state listing, bird books, bird clubs, book dealers, etc.

Rickert, John E., Sr., comp. and ed. *A Guide to North American Bird Clubs*. Avian Publications, P.O. Box 310, Elizabethtown, Ky. 42701, 1978. Updated periodically by the American Birding Association.

Torres, John K. *The Audubon Society Encyclopedia of North American Birds*. New York: Alfred A. Knopf, 1980. A big book containing definitions of thousands of terms. Although emphasis is on North America, many defined terms are useful to world birders. Excellent color photographs.

Zimmer, Kevin J. *The Western Bird Watcher: An Introduction to Birding in the American West*. Englewood Cliffs, N.J.: Prentice-Hall, 1985. Both generalized and specific information on where to find birds, general information about birding, a section on western specialties, and a detailed section on bird identification.

Good sources of information for birders are books about national parks and wildlife refuges and books providing background information on places one is likely to see birds. Representative ones are listed below.

Murphy, Robert. *Wild Sanctuaries: Our National Wildlife Refuges— A Heritage Restored*. New York: E.P. Dutton & Co., 1968. Well illustrated, good descriptions.

Riley, Laura, and William Riley. *Guide to the National Wildlife Refuges.* Garden City, N.Y.: Anchor Press/Doubleday, 1979. Good information on how to get there, what to see and do, and how to get more information. Gives substantial information on birds.

Periodicals: Chapter 5

A wide variety of periodicals is available to the traveler/birder. Some provide good current travel information, some specialize in background information on countries you might be visiting, some emphasize general natural history, others concentrate on information of specific interest to birders. Most active birders will subscribe to several.

American Birding Association, Inc. Box 4335, Austin, Tex. 78765

Birding. Bimonthly membership journal of the American Birding Association, devoted primarily but not exclusively to North American birding. Subscription comes with membership.

American Express Company. 1350 Avenue of the Americas, New York, N.Y. 10019

Travel and Leisure. Much more emphasis on hotels and restaurants than on Hoatzins and Roadrunners; but occasionally a "birding is good in Xanadu" article.

American Museum of Natural History. 79th Street/Central Park West, New York, N.Y. 10024-1592

Natural History. Comes with membership. Wide-ranging natural history articles, frequently bird oriented.

Bluestone Publishing. Helen S. Lapham, publisher and editor, Box 226, Lansing, N.Y. 14882.

Wingtips. Quarterly journal providing a variety of information, book review, atlas information, etc.

Laboratory of Ornithology. Cornell University, 159 Sapsucker Woods Road, Ithaca, N.Y. 14850

The Living Bird. Quarterly journal containing in-depth but generally nonacademic articles for the serious birder.

National Audubon Society. 950 Third Avenue, New York, N.Y. 10022.

American Birds. Published five times a year; caters to the interest of the serious birder. Articles emphasize New World birding. Primary attention is given to detailed listing of birds sighted in North American regions, including the Hawaiian Islands and West Indies.

Audubon. Beautifully written and illustrated bimonthly magazine covering the environment in general; often has excellent articles and illustrations on various aspects of bird life.

National Geographic Society. 17th and M St. N.W., Washington, D.C. 20036

National Geographic. The world is its oyster.

National Geographic Traveler. Oriented to North America.

National Parks & Conservation Association. 1701 18th St. N.W.,
Washington, D.C. 20009
   National Parks. Comes with membership. What's happening in the
parks often influences bird life.
National Wildlife Federation. 1412 16th Street N.W., Washington,
D.C. 20036.
   International Wildlife. Bimonthly, often containing interesting ar-
ticles on birds and their habitats.
   National Wildlife. Bimonthly, emphasizing wildlife of North America.
Pardson Corporation. P.O. Box 110, Marietta, Oh. 45750.
   Bird Watchers Digest. Good bimonthly general bird watchers'
magazine. *BWD* also sponsors an annual series of workshops for improve-
ment of identification skills. Most are held in North America, but a few
are in selected locations around the world.
Smithsonian Society. 900 Jefferson Dr., Washington, D.C. 20560
   Smithsonian. Comes with membership. Wide range of articles on
natural and cultural history.
Western Field Ornithologists. P.O. Box 254, Lakeview, Calif. 92353.
   Western Birds. Quarterly journal providing information on bird
distribution, identification, studies, bird census, etc.
World Birdwatch. Quarterly newsletter of the International Council for
Bird Preservation, 219c Huntingdon Road, Cambridge CB3 0DL, England.
This organization is devoted entirely to the preservation of birds and their
habitats world-wide. Newsletter and other publications come with
membership. North Americans may query the I.C.B.P. at 801 Pennsylvania
Ave. S.E., Washington, DC 20003.

RARE BIRD ALERTS

   North American Rare Bird Alert (NARBA). Bob-O-Link, Inc., P.O.
Box 1161, Jamestown, N.C. 27282. Telephone: (U.S.) 1-800-438-7539,
(Canada) 1-800-438-6704. Service to subscribers alerting them to rare bird
occurrences. Publishes newsletter of rare bird occurrences.
   Most states have rare bird alerts; some local organizations have a
published number. State numbers are listed in *Birding* magazine.

Field Guides: Chapter 6

Davis, L. Irby. *A Field Guide to the Birds of Mexico and Central America.*
Austin: University of Texas Press, 1972. Standard field guide format;
available in paperback; some obsolete species designations in this edition.
   de Schauensee, Rodolphe Meyer, and William H. Phelps, Jr. *A Guide
to the Birds of Venezuela.* Princeton, N.J.: Princeton University Press, 1978.
Rather large field guide, this classic guide is used not only in the country
of the title but in other South American countries that do not yet have
their own guides.

Edwards, Ernest P. *Field Guide to the Birds of Mexico.* Sweet Briar, Va.: Ernest P. Edwards, 1972.

Ffrench Richard. *A Guide to the Birds of Trinidad and Tobago.* Newtown Square, Pa.: Harrowood Books, 1980. Thick for a field guide, this excellent book, sponsored by the Cornell Laboratory of Ornithology, includes illustrations by John P. O'Neill and several bird portraits by Don R. Eckelberry.

Hilty, Stephen, and William Brown. *A Guide to the Birds of Columbia.* Princeton, N.J.: Princeton University Press, 1986. A new guide that covers over half of all South American species. Black-and-white drawings, and color plates by Guy Tudor.

Land, Hugh C. *Birds of Guatemala.* Wynnewood, Pa.: Livingston Publishing Co., 1970.

Peterson, Roger Tory, and Edward L. Chalif. *A Field Guide to Mexican Birds.* Boston: Houghton Mifflin Co., 1973. Well-known standard guide.

Ridgely, Robert S. *A Guide to the Birds of Panama.* Princeton, N.J.: Princeton University Press, 1981. A bit large for field work, this book not only covers the birds of Panama but serves as a bridge between the Central American countries to the North and the northern South American countries.

Claudio Venegas C., and Jean H. Jory *Guia de Campo Para Las Aves de Magallanes.* Punta Arenas, Chile: Instituto de la Patagonia, 1979. Good descriptive guide with black-and-white drawings of the birds of the southern tip of South America. Spanish text.

Where-to-Find Guides: Chapter 6

Alden, Peter. *Finding Birds in Western Mexico.* Tucson: University of Arizona Press, 1969.

Edwards, Ernest. *Finding Birds in Mexico.* Sweet Briar, Va: Ernest Preston Edwards, 1968. See also 1985 Supplement.

These two volumes together along with their most recent supplements are a great help to the independent birder. Also, *Finding Birds in Panama* with 1985 supplement. See also section on finding birds in Peru in Parker checklist below.

Checklists: Chapter 6

Butler, Thomas Y. *The Birds of Ecuador and the Galápagos Archipelago.* Portsmouth, N.H.: The Ramphastos Agency, 1979. Paperback checklist; brief description of habitats.

Parker, Theodore A., III, Susan Allen Parker, and Manuel A. Plenge. *An Annotated Checklist of Peruvian Birds.* Vermillion, S. Dak.: Buteo Books, 1982. Paperback identifies birds by habitat; includes brief narrative description of habitat and black-and-white photos.

General: Chapter 6

Dunning, John S., with collabortion of Robert S. Ridgely. *South American Land Birds: A Photographic Aid to Identification*. Newtown Square, Pa.: Harrowood Books, 1982. Useful backup for standard field guides.

Skutch, Alexander F. *Birds of Tropical America*. Austin: University of Texas Press, 1983. Not a field guide, but offers excellent supplementary information.

Field Guides: Chapter 7

Because of the great interest in birding among the British, books about birding in Britain and Europe have proliferated. One can find guides to just about everywhere, along with many fine books about special birds. Most will be available from major bird-book dealers.

Bruun, Bertel, Lars Svensson, and Hakan Delin. *Country Life Guide to Birds of Britain and Europe*. Feltham, Middlesex: Newnes Books. Complete rev. ed. 1986. Excellent guide illustrated by Arthur Singer and Dan Zetter Strom.

Ferguson-Lees, Ian Willis, and J. T. R. Sharrock. *The Shell Guide to the Birds of Britain and Europe*. Michael Joseph Ltd., 44 Bedford Sq., London WC1, England, 1983. Detailed information, several drawings of each bird, distribution maps, separate section on vagrants.

Gooders, John. *Field Guide to the Birds of Britain & Ireland*. Kingfisher Books, 1986, distributed by St. John's House, East Street, Leicester, England. Introductory guide to 255 species regularly seen in Britain with color plates, distribution maps, and handy checklist of identifying key points. Full page description of each bird.

Hayman, Peter. *The Mitchell Beazley Birdwatchers Pocket Guide*. London: Mitchell Beazley Publishers Ltd., in association with The Royal Society for the Protection of Birds, 1979. Small guide fits into car glove compartment; a small model of larger *The Birdlife of Britain* published in 1976. Organized according to similar species to aid quick identification.

Hayman, Peter, and Michael Everett. *What's That Bird? A Guide to British and Continental Birds*. Bedfordshire: Royal Society for the Protection of Birds, 1986. Revised and enlarged version. Good for beginners.

Heinzel, Hermann, Richard Fitter, and John Parslow. *The Birds of Britain and Europe* (with North Africa and the Middle East.) London: Collins, St. James's Place, 1979. Typical field guide with descriptions and maps opposite color plates; lists of accidentals; separate maps of Great Britain. Covers 1,000 birds of the Western Palearctic.

Heinzel, Hermann, and Martin Woodcock. *Collins Handguide to the Birds of Britain and Europe*. London: Collins, St. James's Place, 1978. Beginner's guide to more common species.

Lovegrove, Philip, and Philip Snow. *Collins Field Notebook of British Birds*. London: Collins, 8 Grafton Street, 1986. Small guide, multiple illustrations of common birds; comes in plastic case cover with notepad.

Peterson, Roger Tory, Guy Mountfort, and P.A.D. Hollom. *A Field Guide to the Birds of Britain and Europe.* London: Collins, 1983. Update of 1974 guide; less detailed than other guides.

Where-to-Find Guides: Chapter 7

Ferguson-Lees, James, Quentin Hockliffe, and Ko Zweeres, eds. *A Guide to Bird-Watching in Europe.* London: The Bodley Head, 1975. Arranged by country, general descriptions of habitats. Includes maps of countries, cross-reference chart of birds, country, and status.

Gooders, John. *Where to Watch Birds in Europe.* New York: Taplinger Publishing Co., 1974. Arranged by country; concentrates on best spots for birds within each country. Small-scale maps of specific birding locations, brief listing of principal birds to be found in different seasons. (Currently being rewritten and revised.)

_____ *The New Where to Watch Birds.* London: Andre Deutsch, 1986. Revision of earlier edition; covers England, Wales, and Scotland, but not Ireland. Arranged by country.

Harrison, Colin. *An Atlas of the Birds of the Western Palearctic.* Princeton, N.J.: Princeton University Press, 1982. Bird descriptions, drawings, and distribution maps.

Redman, Nigel and S. Harrap. *Birdwatching in Britain–A Site by Site Guide.* Christopher Helm, London. Details best birding areas; cross-referenced checklist of species.

See also Alden and Gooders' *Finding Birds Around the World* for some locations not included in above.

Checklists: Chapter 7

The "British Birds" List of Birds of the Western Palearctic. rev. ed., British Birds Ltd. Fountains, Park Lane, Blunham, Bedford MK44 3NJ, 1984.

General: Chapter 7

Cramp, Stanley, et al., eds. *Handbook of the Birds of Europe, the Middle East and North Africa: The Birds of the Western Palearctic.* New York: Oxford University Press. Four volumes: *Ostrich to Ducks*, 1978; *Hawks to Bustards*, 1980; *Waders to Gulls*, 1983; and *Terns to Woodpeckers*, 1986. Three volumes to come in this major work.

Cramp, Stanley, W. R. P. Bourne, and David Saunders. *The Seabirds of Britain and Ireland.* New York: Taplinger Publishing Co., 1974. General discussion of seabirds and description of regularly breeding species.

Curry-Lindahl, Kai. *Europe: A Natural History.* New York: Random House, 1964. Part of "The Continents We Live On" series. It provides good overview of geography with special emphasis on birds.

Linderall, Carl-Fredrick. *The British Ornithologist's Guide to Bird Life.* Poole, England: Blandford Press, 1980. Thorough identifications; good color plates.

Lockwood, W. B. *The Oxford Book of British Bird Names*. New York: Oxford University Press, 1984.

Oddie, Bill. *Bill Oddie's Little Black Bird Book*. Methuen Paperbacks Ltd., London, 1980. Humorous account of the British birder.

Periodicals: Chapter 7

Birds. Bimonthly publication available to members of the Royal Society for the Protection Birds (RSPB), The Lodge, Sandy, Bedfordshire SG 19 2DL, England.

Bird Watching. EMAP Pursuit Ltd., Bretton Court, Bretton Center, Peterborough PE3 8DZ. Monthly general interest magazine about how and where to watch birds along with general interest features for birders.

British Birds. Macmillan Journals Ltd., 4 Little Essex Street, London WC2R 3LF. Monthly general interest magazine about virtually all aspects of birding, emphasizing Britain but containing some articles on European birding.

The Ibis. Quarterly journal of the British Ornithologists' Union, c/o Zoological Society of London, Regents Park, London.

Field Guides: Chapter 8

Borneo Smythies, Bertram E. *Pocket Guide to the Birds of Borneo*. rev. ed. by Charles M. Francis. The Sabah Society with The Maylayan Nature Society, P.O. Box 758, Kuala Lampur, Malaysia, 1984. Color plates.

China deSchauensee, Rodolphe Meyer. *The Birds of China*. Washington, D.C.: Smithsonian Institution Press, 1984. Oversized field guide; detailed descriptions, section of color plates, occasional black-and-white drawings, checklist.

Viney, Clive, and Karen Phillips, illustrator. *New Color Guide to Hong Kong Birds*. 3d ed. Hong Kong: Government Printers, December 1983. Descriptions opposite plates.

India Ali, Sálim. *The Field Guide to the Birds of the Eastern Himalayas*. New York and London: Oxford University Press, 1977. Covers 536 species, plates limited but adequate.

Ali, Sálim, and S. Dillon Ripley. *A Pictorial Guide to the Birds of the Indian Subcontinent*. Delhi: Oxford University Press, 1983. Oversized for field guide, contains color plates of all birds of India. Habitat description opposite plates.

Woodcock, Martin W. *The Birds of the Indian Sub-Continent. A Collins Hand Guide*. London: Collins, St. James Place, 1980. Small handbook to common birds.

Japan Brazil, Mark. *The Birds of Japan: A Checklist*. Terutaka Shimizu, Ebetsu, Hokkaido, Japan. 1985. *Finding Birds in Japan: Honshu*, 1985. *Finding Birds in Japan: The Tokyo Area. 1984.*

Wild Bird Society of Japan. *A Field Guide to the Birds of Japan*. Kodansha International, 10 E. 53rd St. New York 10022, 1982. Reprinted

1985. Standard size with color plates, maps; useful for identifying birds found in Alaska, Eastern Siberia and China.

Nepal Fleming, Robert L., Sr., Robert L. Fleming, Jr., and L. S. Bangdel. *Birds of Nepal*: with reference to Kashmir and Sikkim. 3d ed. Katmandu, Nepal: Nature Himalayas, 1984. Color illustrations of all birds.

Inskipp, Carol, and Tim Inskipp. *A Guide to the Birds of Nepal*. Tanager Books, Dover, N.H. 03820, 1985. Detailed guide to 835 species, color plates, maps.

Phillipines duPont, John E. *Phillipine Birds*. Delaware Museum of Natural History, 1971. Covers most birds; color plates.

Russia Flint, V. E., R. L. Boehme, Y. V. Kostin, and A. A. Kuzenetsov, by Natalia Bourso-Leland. *A Field Guide to Birds of the USSR*. Princeton, N.J.: Princeton University Press, 1984. A slightly oversized field guide with maps and color plates.

Southeast Asia King, Ben F., Martin W. Woodcock, and E. C. Dickinson. *A Field Guide to the Birds of South-East Asia*. London: Collins, Grafton Street, 1975. Field guide, reprinted several times, covers Burma, Malaya, Thailand, Cambodia, Vietnam, Laos, and Hong Kong.

Lekagul, Boonsong, and Edward W. Cronin, Jr. *Bird Guide of Thailand*. 2d ed. Thailand: Kurusapa Ladprao Press, 1974. Published under the auspices of the Association for the Conservation of Wildlife, 4 Old Custom House Lane, Banrak, Bangkok. Standard bird guide, brief description opposite plates; plates fair but useful.

Field guides are also available for other, sometimes very specific places. Check book dealer lists.

Field Guides: Chapter 9

Maclean, Gordon Lindsay. *Roberts Birds of South Africa*. 5th ed. The Trustees of the John Voelcker Bird Book Fund. 5 Church Square, Cape Town, distributed by C. Struik Ltd., 1985. Large volume with color plates, detailed information.

Newman, Kenneth. *Newman's Birds of Southern Africa*. Johannesburg: Macmillan of Southern Africa, 1985. Helpful, accurate, and practical.

Penny, Malcolm. *The Birds of Seychelles and the Outlying Islands*. London: Collins, St. James Place, 1974.

Serle, W., G. J. Morel, and W. Hartwig. *A Field Guide to the Birds of West Africa,* London: Collins, St. James' Place, 1980. Standard-sized guide containing color plates and brief descriptions. Covers the entire "hump" of Africa from Mauritania to the Congo and east to Chad and Central African Republic. Also covers the Cape Verde Islands and the islands in the Gulf of Guinea.

Sinclair, Ian. *Field Guide to the Birds of Southern Africa*. Cape Town: C. Stuik, Publishers, 1984. Covers the area from southern Angola and Zambia south to the southern coast; includes islands in the southern oceans down to Antarctica. Color photographs show good environmental background; little help with different plumages. Brief descriptions of habitats, checklist.

Williams, John G. and Arlott, Norman. *A Field Guide to the Birds of East Africa*. London: Collins, 1980. Covers Ethiopia south to Zambia, Zimbabwe, and Mozambique.

Where-to-Find Guides: Chapter 9

Britton, P. L., ed. *Birds of East Africa*, their habitat, status, and distribution. Nairobi: Natural Historial Society, 1980.

Moore, Raymond. *Where to Watch Birds in Kenya*. Nairobi: 1984. Arranged alphabetically by site with maps and useful information.

Sinclair, Ian, and A. Berruiti. *Where to Watch Birds in Southern Africa*. Cape Town: C. Struik Publishers, 1983. Paperback with photographs, descriptions of habitats, extensive status table (common, uncommon, etc.), keyed to specific localities identified in the book. The table contains a composite index indicating taxonomic order and identifies endemic species, a useful help to the experienced birder. The locational guide provides detailed directions of where to find birds, simple maps, and lists of accommodations.

General: Chapter 9

Brown, Leslie. *Africa: A Natural History*. New York: Random House, 1965. Part of "The Continents We Live On" series; provides wide coverage of natural history with considerable emphasis on birds.

Williams, J. G. *A Field Guide to the National Parks of East Africa*. London: Collins, 1981. Useful guide containing descriptions of national parks of Kenya, Tanzania, and Uganda, simple maps, and lists of birds and animals to be found in each park. The guide also includes descriptions of the principal animals, along with color plates. The bird section repeats information in the bird guide but covers only the more common species.

Field Guides: Chapter 10

Australia Pizzy, Graham. *A Field Guide to the Birds of Australia*. Princeton, N.J.: Princeton University Press, 1980. A somewhat oversized field guide, it is well arranged and easily keyed to the section of plates in the middle. Separate map section.

Slater, Peter, et al. *A Field Guide to Australian Birds*. 2 vols. Newton Square, Pa.: Harrowood Books, 1979. Good field guide, if you don't mind taking along two books. Vol. 1 covers nonpasserines; vol. 2 describes the passerines.

Papua New Guinea Beehler, Bruce M., Thane K. Pratt, and Dale A. Zimmerman, et al. *The Birds of New Guinea*. Princeton, N.J.: Princeton University Press, 1986. Covers over 700 species, most of them illustrated in color: includes natural history information.

Coates, Brian J. *The Birds of Papua New Guinea*. Vol. 1: Non-passerines. Queensland: Dove Publisher Pty. Ltd., 1986. Descriptions, photographs, drawings, and distribution maps. Apprendices on Irian Jaya and the Solomon Islands (Vol. 2, covering passerines, due in 1987.)

New Zealand Falla, A., Jr., R. B. Sibson, and E. G. Turbott. *The New Guide to the Birds of New Zealand*. Auckland and London: Collins, 1983. Standard-sized guide containing explanations of origins of birds in New Zealand, useful coverage of offshore islands.

Talbot-Kelly, Chloe. *The Birds of New Zealand*. London: Collins, St. James's Place, 1983. Introductory guide to common birds.

General: Chapter 10

Blakers, M., S. J. J. F. Davies, and P. N. Reilly. *Atlas of Australian Birds*. Melbourne: Melbourne University, 1984. An extensive text, including maps and references to detailed literature.

Cayley, Neville W. *What Bird Is That?* Angus & Robertson Publishers, 16 Golden Square, London W1R 4BN, 1984. Very large volume; excellent illustrations with general information and distribution maps on same page.

Simpson, Ken. *The Birds of Australia*. Illustrated by Nicolas Day. Tanager Books, 51 Washington St., Dover, N.H. 03820, 1984. Beautifully arranged coffee-table–sized book.

Field Guides: Chapter 11

Watson, George E. *Birds of the Antarctic and Sub-Antarctic*. American Geophysical Union, 1909 K Street, N.W., Washington, D.C., 1975. Descriptions of the species, color plate illustrations, general description of the habitat and its ecology, a number of explanatory charts, some brief history, and a good bit of geography.

Woods, Robin W. *Falkland Island Birds*. Anthony Nelson, P. O. Box 9 Oswestry, Shropshire SY11 1BY, England, 1982. A slim volume, illustrated with photographs by Cindy Buxton and Annie Price and brief descriptions. An earlier book by Woods, *The Birds of the Falkland Islands*, was published by Anthony Nelson in 1975 and contains more detailed information about the birds and their environment.

General: Chapter 11

Adams, Richard, and Ronald Lockley. *Voyage Through the Antarctic*. New York: Alfred A. Knopf, 1983. Author Adams and ornithologist Lockley took the tourist route to Antarctica aboard the *Lindblad Explorer*. Well-written account, accompanied by excellent color photographs.

Hosking, Eric. *Antarctic Wildlife*. New York: Facts on File, 1982. Photographer Hosking provides a fine visual description of Antarctica's wildlife, accompanied by brief text by Bryan Sage.

Murphy, Robert Cushman. *Logbook for Grace*. New York: Macmillan Co., 1947. Classic account of well-known scientist's voyage.

Neider, Charles. *Beyond Cape Horn: Travels in the Antarctic.* San Francisco: Sierra Club Books, 1980. Journalist Neider wintered in Antarctica and describes life in the research stations.

Parmelee, David F. *Bird Island in Antarctic Waters.* Minneapolis: University of Minnesota Press, 1980. Bird Island at the west end of South Georgia was the wildlife study area for research on penguins. Interesting text with photographs and illustrations.

Peterson, Roger Tory. *Penguins.* Boston: Houghton Mifflin Co., 1979. America's best-known bird man has provided a highly readable book, accompanied by author's photographs taken on his many Antarctic voyages.

Porter, Eliot. *Antarctica.* New York: E. P. Dutton, 1978. One of America's most famous photographers has created a splendid coffee table–sized volume with beautiful full-page, full-color photographs, accompanied by descriptive text.

Field Guides: Chapter 12

Bahamas Brudenell-Bruce, P. G. C. *The Birds of the Bahamas.* New York: Taplinger Publishing Co., 1975. Small field guide.

Bermuda Wingate, David B. *Checklist and Guide to the Birds of Bermuda.* Available from Department of Agriculture and Fisheries, Botanical Gardens, P.O. Box 834, Hamilton, Bermuda.

Cayman Islands Bradley, Patricia. *Birds of the Cayman Islands.* Published by Patricia Bradley, Box 1326, George Town, Grand Cayman, Cayman Islands, B.W.I. 1985. Beautiful little book, superbly illustrated with photographs by Yves-Jacques Rey-Millet.

Fiji Belcher, W. J. *Birds of Fiji in Color.* London and Auckland: Collins, 1972. Ornithological notes by R. B. Sigson. Brief descriptions accompany color plates.

Galápagos Butler, Thomas Y. *The Birds of Ecuador and the Galápagos Archipelago.* The Ramphastos Agency, P.O. Box 1091, Portsmouth, N.H. 03901, 1979. Annotated checklist.

Harris, Michael. *A Field Guide to the Birds of Galápagos.* London: Collins, St. James' Place, 1982. Standard field guide.

Hawaii Berger, Andrew J. *The Exotic Birds of Hawaii.* Norfolk Island, Australia, 1977. Island Heritage Ltd. Pamphlet.

Shollenbergen, Robert J., ed. *Hawaii's Birds* 3d. ed. Hawaiian Audubon Society, P. O. Box 22832, Honolulu, Hi. 96822, 1984. Illustrated pamphlet.

Pratt, H. Douglas, P. L. Bruner, and D. G. Berrett. *A Field Guide to the Birds of Hawaii and the Tropical Pacific.* Princeton, N.J.: Princeton University Press, 1987. Color and black-and-white illustrations; distribution maps.

Philippines DuPont, John E. *Philippine Birds.* Delaware Museum of Natural History, 1971. Color plates; all species illustrated.

Puerto Rico Raffaele, Herbert A. *A Guide to the Birds of Puerto Rico and the Virgin Islands.* San Juan: Fondo Educativo Interamericano, 1983. Paperback field guide with short section on where to bird.

South Pacific DuPont, John E. *South Pacific Birds.* Delaware Museum of Natural History, 1976. Some color plates; all species illustrated. Covers Fiji, Tongan, Samoan, Cook, Society, Tuamotu, Marquesas, Austral, Pitcairn, and Henderson Island groups.

Mayr, Ernst. *Birds of the Southwest Pacific.* Rutland, Vt.: Charles E. Tuttle Company, 1978. (Reissue of 1945 edition.) Field guide to seabirds and land birds on Samoa, Fiji, Tonga, New Caledonia and Loyalty Islands, New Hebrides and Banks Islands, Santa Cruz Islands, Solomon Islands, and Micronesia.

Bond, James. *Birds of the West Indies.* Boston: Houghton Mifflin Co., 1985 (reissue unrevised.) Well-known field guide covering entire West Indies.

General: Chapter 12

Amos, William H. *Wildlife of the Islands.* New York: Harry N. Abrams, Inc., 1980. Popular presentation of flora and fauna on major islands.

Martini, Frederic. *Exploring Tropical Isles and Seas.* Englewood Cliffs, N.J., Prentice-Hall, 1984. Subtitled, "An Introduction for the Traveler and Amateur Naturalist." General description is provided about origin of islands, life in the seas, and statistical material, but little information on life on the islands and no reference to birdlife.

Field Guides: Chapter 13

Harrison, Peter. *Seabirds: An Identification Guide.* Boston: Houghton Mifflin Co., 1983. An oversized guide with detailed descriptions and plates of seabirds in different phases. Also has maps. Widely used by persons with pelagic passions.

Tuck, Gerald. *A Guide to Seabirds on the Ocean Routes.* London: Collins, St. James's Place, 1980. Guide is arranged by twenty-five frequently traveled ocean routes. Black-and-white drawings.

Tuck, Gerald, and Herman Heinzel. *A Field Guide to the Seabirds of Britain and the World.* Pocket-sized guides in various editions covering different parts of the world. London: Collins, St. James' Place, 1978.

General: Chapter 13

Haley, Delphine, ed. *Seabirds of Eastern North Pacific and Arctic Waters.* Seattle, Wash.: Pacific Search Press, 1984. Several authors have written accounts of 100-plus birds, found from the Bering Sea south to the Hawaiian Islands and Baja California. Includes color photos and distribution maps.

Lofgren, Lars. *Ocean Birds.* New York: Alfred A. Knopf, 1984. Detailed information on breeding, biology, and behavior; color and black-and-white drawings, maps, and charts.

Parker, Henry S. *Exploring the Oceans: An Introduction for the Traveler and Amateur Naturalist*. Englewood Cliffs, N.J.: Prentice-Hall, 1985. Background about the oceans, interaction between geographic and geologic features, weather, and wind.

BASIC BIRDING AIDS

In addition to pursuing a variety of books to meet particular needs, the serious birder will review other aids to improving skills and enhancing the enjoyment of birding.

Audio/Video Birding

The number of tapes and records available today is beginning to match the number of available books about birds. Many book dealers listed in Part III also carry audio materials and are beginning to carry videocassettes. They'll be happy to hear from you. Special mention needs to be made of the Cornell Laboratory of Ornithology. This organization has pioneered in the taping of bird calls and has a fine collection. See the Crow's Nest Bookshop under the "Book Dealers" section of this book. A good review of records can be found in Meriwether, William M. "ABA-area Bird-sound Recordings." *Birding* (February 1986).

A few basic records, tapes, and cassettes are listed here. Audio aids keyed especially to widely used field guides are:

A Field Guide to the Bird Songs of Eastern and Central North America. 2d ed. Metromedia Producers Corporation and Houghton Mifflin Co. Available from Cornell Laboratory of Ornithology, Ithaca, New York 14850. Records or cassettes. Designed to accompany Roger Tory Peterson's *Field Guide to the Birds East of the Rockies*.

A Field Guide to Western Bird Songs. Tapes or records. To be used with Roger Tory Peterson's *A Field Guide to Western Birds*. Boston: Houghton Mifflin Co., 1961.

Guide to Bird Sounds. To be used with National Geographic Society's *Field Guide to the Birds of North America*. National Geographic Society, Washington, D.C. Available in cassettes.

A Field Guide to the Bird Songs of Britain and Europe. Sture Palmer and Jeffery Boswall. Sixteen cassettes in four packs arranged taxonomically. British birders think highly of this set of cassettes that the North American birder might want to sample if a European birding jaunt is on the itinerary. Many birds of the Western Palearctic are difficult to see; voice identification helps.

Inevitably, we're using the "boob tube" to learn about real boobies. Within the last several years videocassettes (VHS or BETA) have been used to improve one's birding skills. They tend to be relatively expensive so you might want to persuade your bird club to purchase and then loan to members one of these:

Audubon Society's VideoGuide to the Birds of North America. MasterVision, 969 Park Ave., New York, N.Y. 10028.

Techniques of Birding with Arnold Small. Videocassette available from Nature Videos, P.O. Box 312, South Laguna, Calif. 92677.

Watching Birds with Roger Tory Peterson. Videocassette available from Metromedia Producers Corporation and Houghton Mifflin Co., Boston.

Binoculars

Birders contemplating buying new binoculars are urged to read one or more of the following and to check current birding periodicals for up-to-date information.

Dunne, Peter. "Binoculars for Birders." *Birding* 17 (January 1985). A shorter version appeared in Cornell Laboratory of Ornithology's publication *The Living Bird Quarterly* (Winter 1985).

Grant, P. J., and J. T. Sharrock. "Binoculars and Telescopes Survey." *British Birds* 78 (April 1985).

Manns, Robert. "Some (New and Improved) Observations on Binoculars for Birders." *Bird Watcher's Digest* 8 (January/February 1986). Exposition of roof-prism and porro-prism binoculars. "Further Discussion" of the subject will be found in *Birding* 18, (August 1986).

Paul, Dr. Henry. *Binoculars and All-purpose Telescopes*. Revised by Greg Stone. New York: American Photographic Book Publishers, 1980.

"Shopping Tips: Binoculars." *Changing Times* (August 1985).

Computers

It seems that everything is computerized these days, and birding is no exception. Current birding periodicals advertise a variety of programs to help keep your bird lists in order. The Clements world bird checklist is computer coded.

The *Newburyport Birders' Exchange Newsletter*, published by the Newburyport Birders' Exchange, 31 Plummer Avenue, Newburyport, Mass. 01950, tries to keep readers current in the field.

Computer buffs will learn how to do their birding bookkeeping and how to adapt software for birding purposes from Edward M. Mair's *A Field Guide to Personal Computers for Bird Watchers and Other Naturalists*. Englewood Cliffs, N.J.: Prentice-Hall, 1985. It's written in a humorous tone, but it would be helpful if the reader had some knowledge of computers.

Scopes

Not as much helpful information is available about scopes as there is about binoculars, although the birder who has recently purchased a scope will likely wonder how a birder can cope without one. For guidance on purchasing this valuable piece of equipment, see Koehler, Herbert. "Is It Time You Considered a Scope?" *Bird Watcher's Digest* (May/June 1986).

General Education

There may be classes in ornithology at the local university for the birder who wants to know more about birds, their characteristics, their behavior, their flight, their nests, etc. If that is not a good option, the Laboratory of Ornithology at Cornell University has a home-study course in bird biology that provides an excellent substitute. Request information about the "Seminars in Ornithology" from the Laboratory in Ithaca, New York.

BIRD AND NATURE BOOK DEALERS

Below you will find a partial list of book dealers which specialize in books of interest to birders. Check current issues of birding periodicals for others.

American Birding Association
P.O. Box 4335
Austin, TX 78765   (512) 474–4804

Wide variety of field guides, checklists and general books available about birds of North America arranged on lists by state. Some books on foreign birding. Some audio material listed. Discounts for ABA members.

Audubon Naturalist Society Bookshop
8940 Jones Mill Road
Chevy Chase, MD 20815   (301) 652–3606

1621 Wisconsin Avenue NW
Washington, D.C. 20007   (202) 337–6062

Have perhaps the best walk-in selections of foreign bird guides on the East Coast.

Avian Publications
310 Maria Drive
Wasau, WI 54401   (715) 845–5101

Emphasis is on aviculture but contains listings of many general birding books.

Birding Book Society
c/o Integrated Distribution Services
250 Commercial Street
Manchester, NH 03101   1–800–343–9444

Book club offering current books and bonus credits toward other books.

The Bird's Nest
7 Patten Road
Bedford, NH 03102

Buteo Books
P.O. Box 481
Vermillion, SD 57069   (605) 624–4343

Extensive list of new and old books about birds and natural history.

Capra Press
P.O. Box 2068
Santa Barbara, CA 93120   (805) 966–4590

Publishes limited number of bird books.

The Chickadee
440 Wilchester Street
Houston, TX 77079   (713) 932–1408

The Crow's Nest Book Shop
Laboratory of Ornithology
159 Sapsucker Woods Road
Ithaca, NY 14850   (607) 255–5057

Gift catalog contains some books and extensive audio listings. Also available are optical equipment, T-shirts, bird feeders and the like. Members of the Laboratory receive a discount.

Flora and Fauna Books
P.O. Box 3004
Seattle, WA 98114   (206) 328–5175

Good collection of books for world birders. Separate list of used books.

L & P Press
P.O. Box 21604
Denver, CO 80221   (303) 429–1698

Publishes Lane series, *A Birder's Guide to. . . .*

Patricia Ledlie
Box 46
Buckfield, ME 04220   (207) 336–2969

Catalogs listing old and new bird books and natural history books.

Los Angeles Audubon Bookstore
7377 Santa Monica Boulevard
Los Angeles, CA 90046   (213) 876–0202

Good collection of books, checklists, and audio material for world birders. Also carries some optical equipment and miscellaneous birding knickknacks. Visit them when you're in the area.

Massachusetts Audubon Society Bookshop
South Great Road
Lincoln, MA 01773   (617) 259–9500

Major selection of overseas guides.

Nature Canada Bookshop
75 Albert Street
Ottawa Canada KIP 6B1

Natural History Books
2510 Hill Court
Berkeley, CA 94708   (415) 644–4466

Specializes in out-of-print and rare natural history books including
a good selection of ornithological books.

Natural History Books, Inc.
119 Lakeview Drive
P.O. Box 1089
Lake Helen, FL 32744-1089   (904) 228–3356

Good book lists for world birders. Specialty is checklists compiled
by owner Nina Steffe for just about every place in the world.

Natural History Book Services Ltd.
62 Tritton Road
London SE21 8DE   (01) 761–5969

Tabloid-size, extensive listings of new books; other books listed by
geographic regions.

Peterson Book Company
P.O. Box 966
Davenport, IA 52805   (319) 355–7051

Catalog contains alphabetical listings of bird books, magazines, audio
material, as well as material on other natural history subjects.

R J Books & Aviary
10540 SW 160 Street
Miami, FL 33157   (305) 232–3391

Ask for book list which covers selection of current books.

Tanager Books
51 Washington Street
Dover, NH 03820   1–800–343–9444

Attractive catalog includes descriptions of current books about birds
as well as dogs and horses and other domestic animals, horticulture, poul-
try keeping, etc.

BASIC BED-AND-BREAKFASTS:
WHAT TO EXPECT WHERE

Sophisticated travelers taking standard tours or traveling on their own are generally familiar with the standard of accommodations they are likely to find along the beaten path. They're generally familiar with the beaten path. For travelers deciding to stray, and for birders who know they must stray in order to see the bird life of a country, this information may be useful.

The quality of accommodations available to birders varies from basic camping to excellent hotels, depending upon where you're going. Accommodations tend to vary in inverse relationship to proximity to good birding; the closer you are to the good birding, the more primitive your accommodations are likely to be. The alternative to rustic (or nonexistent) quarters is getting up *very* early in order to be where the birds are when they greet the new day.

There are exceptions. Sometimes there is a luxury hotel that is used as a base of operations for day trips into nearby countryside. Here, good food is standard. It will often reflect the country's cuisine. In North America, Europe, European Russia, some parts of Africa, and Australia, you will probably find a good selection of wines and beers. "Spirits" will likely be expensive.

Although fast-food establishments, restaurants, and delightful country inns may be wonderful choices for the noonday meal, such is not likely to be the case in most of the world. Box lunches and occasionally box breakfasts are standard. Try to develop a taste for hard-boiled eggs.

If you are with an organized birding group, you will likely have the best available accommodations, but "best available," in some parts of the world, may not be up to your expectations. In major cities, you may be surprised by the elegance. You may not be accustomed to it. In smaller cities in remote areas, your room may not have been dusted in quite a while. It is likely to be too hot or too cold. The bed sheets may be torn. In more remote areas, there may be no sheets, towels, table cloths, or toilet seats.

Closer to where most birds are to be found, accommodations and transportation may be pretty basic. Sometimes sleeping space may be limited, and even though you may have paid the "single supplement," privacy may just not be possible. Fortunately, this rarely happens. There may be many people sleeping in one small building, there may only be a thin mattress on the floor, not a hook to hang anything on. There may not be an indoor toilet. There may not be running water, (fortunate for you, if there is a stream nearby for washing). Camper-types love such conditions.

Food prepared in such out-of-the-way places may be simple and lean heavily toward the local customs. Electricity, and thus refrigeration, may be available in limited supply, if at all. You may have to eat and drink things that you've never even thought of before. Dining hardware may be different from that to which you are accustomed; or fingers may be in order.

On the other hand, the native food may be surprisingly good and certainly will add variety to your dining experiences. Local beers are often most acceptable, even if they're cooled in the mountain stream. A certain comradeship frequently develops between people who must sleep in close quarters and cope together with unusual foods and customs.

North American birding poses few problems except in the most remote locations. Transportation is, for the most part, excellent, whether by land or air. Accommodations are plentiful, ranging from well-equipped camping areas to luxury hotels and elegant ranches. Hotels and motels tend to be more expensive in the east, inexpensive motels and cabins more plentiful in the west.

South American birding can include limited accommodations. In more remote jungle areas, sleeping facilities may be a thatch-roofed platform. Toilets are probably of the privy species, water limited, and hot water nonexistent. It's a trade-off: better accommodations hours away from early dawn birding (the only time many birds can be seen); or lesser accommodations virtually on top of good birding areas.

Ground transportation is highly variable. Superhighways are few and far between; dirt or gravel roads are common. Sometimes riverboats or bush planes are the only transportation available. Local vehicles in tourist areas are generally good but won't match those in most of North America. In less traveled areas, vehicles will probably be quite ancient. Anticipate an occasional breakdown.

European birding generally will be as comfortable as birding in North America. The real "bed-and-breakfast" is standard fare. Beware, however, of the peaks of tourist travel to popular destinations. If you are visiting during a peak time of the year, it's generally a good ideas to secure reservations in advance. May and June are the best months for bird song and activity.

As in North America, get off the Autobahn periodically and follow older winding roads through charming villages, woods, and fields, where the likelihood of finding birds is better, and where it is safer than in the fast lane.

Asian birding requires some tolerance. New hotels are being built in major tourist centers, generally of the luxury type. Chain hotels will typically provide the same quality of accommodation as their other hotels throughout the world. Bathroom facilities and telephone systems can sometimes be a challenge.

Much of Asia is far from the western world. Travel within Asia ranges from the superefficient to very dusty, bumpy, lengthy roads, depending upon the country. Some Asian countries have developed good highway systems, others haven't. Rest stops, standard in most of North America and Europe, are nonexistent in most Asian countries. Travel between countries in Asia is often fraught with bureaucratic inefficiencies.

African traveling and birding generally means very good accommodations. In Kenya, game lodges are most attractive and suited to their particular setting. Rooms are clean and comfortable, sometimes quite spacious. Food is generally excellent, a continental rather than native-style. It is served, buffet-style at lunchtime, in dining rooms that are often partially open-air. Contrary to popular expectations, bugs, flies, mosquitoes, etc., are not a big problem.

The locales of the game lodges are delightful and generally very close to the game, occasionally closer than you might like. That's part of the excitement. At Keekorok Lodge in the Masai Mara, as you walk to dinner, you may need to slow down while several zebras cross the path in front of you. Or perhaps they will wake you in the night, munching grass right outside your window. Many lodges provide both normal rooms and luxury tents.

Maribou Storks, normally feasting on carrion, perform an elegant dance on the lawn of the beautiful Mount Kenya Safari Club

Mountain Lodge, one of the famous "tree lodges," is built on high stilts overlooking a water hole. You walk up a long ramp to the lodge, much like boarding a ship. You watch elephants, buffalo, and other animals that come in for a muddy evening cocktail. At night the water hole is lit by floodlights, but you must have very fast film if you expect to get photographs. When you go to bed at night you can leave a wild animal call: "Wake me if a leopard comes." On the top deck, you will be eye to eye with the treetop birds of the African forest. You will likely stay at the Mount Kenya Safari Club, pure elegance right on the equator, but not very "African."

You may be on a ship, providing of course, bed and breakfast and the rest of the niceties. Lindblad and other tour operators sometimes travel to "birdy" places such as the coast and rivers of West Africa. The ship *Sirius* is currently doing such trips, accommodating both adventure travelers and birders.

Accommodations in Southern Africa generally are comparable to those in Kenya. The Berruit/Sinclair "Where to Watch Birds in Southern Africa" provides information on accommodations throughout. Egypt and North Africa tend to be more tourist-oriented, and bed-and-breakfasts are therefore good. For out-of-the-way places, get the advice of a good travel agent, or go with a good tour operator.

For those adventurous souls who like to make their own decisions, Kenya is an ideal place. You can fly into Nairobi, stay at a cosmopolitan hotel, and book your own tours with one of the many safari tour operators headquartered there.

Australasian accommodations for birders run the gamut from European-style in Australia and New Zealand, to camps in the wilds of New Guinea. Cities in Australia are among the most sophisticated in the world, and accommodations can be found ranging from the adequate to the super-elegant. Resorts specifically catering to tourists, such as those on the Great Barrier Reef and at Ayers Rock, are comparable to such places anywhere. Alice Springs is developing into a tourist center and now has a fairly wide range of small hotels and motels. Australian lodgings have the delightful custom of placing the electric blanket underneath the sleeper instead of on top, particularly welcome in the down under winter.

In New Zealand, most hotels have kitchen facilities; some tourist homes offer bed-and-breakfast. Touring by recreational vehicle is popular in both countries, and camping is popular.

Air access to both Australia and New Zealand is good from the west coast of the United States and from major European cities. Because of the vast distances in Australia, there is much air travel within the country for the traveler who wishes to see as much as possible. Roads in the eastern part of the country, where most travelers will spend time, generally are good; outside of towns you will probably find single-lane roads. Roads in New Zealand are good. On South Island they are narrow and winding due to the nature of the mountainous landscape.

Travelers and birders in Papua New Guinea will find that accommodations are surprisingly good, while the road system is typical of that in most undeveloped countries.

Oceanic touring, whether on a typical short pelagic trip, a voyage to visit islands, or to Antarctica, has the advantage of turtle-travel. It tends to be slow, but you take your "house" with you. This certainly saves packing/unpacking. Accommodations can be limited to a crowded bunk room on a fishing boat, to considerable luxury, with wine for dinner, on a longer voyage. On a short pelagic trip, you may want to bring along a sleeping bag; sleep on deck if weather and crew permit. An ocean voyage, of course, is the only way to get to some of the remote locations in the world.

BIRDER-FRIENDLY ACCOMMODATIONS

Although tourist accommodations in or near birding "hot spots" provide the birder with proximity to good birding, some are advertised in magazines read by birders in a special effort to attract a birding clientele. Recent issues of such publications have been culled, and advertisers were contacted and asked to supply basic information for this section. Some of the Lane *A Birder's Guide to . . .* series booklets provide information on accommodations, as do some other bird-finding guides. Also check campground guides.

Obviously, virtually all advertisers are geared to the North American market. However, one occasionally finds information on accommodations elsewhere that would be worthy of the birder's inquiry.

North America

Arizona

The Mile Hi and Ramsey Canyon Preserve
RR 1, Box 84
Hereford, AZ 85615   (602) 378–2785

Six housekeeping cottages available year-round in the midst of a 300-acre wooded preserve in the Huachuca Mountains, ninety miles southeast of Tucson. Bookstore and gift shop on site. Many hummingbird feeders. April through August prime birding months. Bird checklist available. Owned and operated by the Nature Conservancy. Day visitors welcome from 8:00 A.M. to 5:00 P.M.; no picnicking, pets, recreational vehicles over twenty feet.

Santa Rita Lodge
Box 444
Amado, AZ 85640   (602) 625–8746

Cottages and motel units with kitchens; available year-round in Madera Canyon, within the Coronado National Forest, forty miles south of Tucson. Service facilities twenty minutes away. Birding good year-round, but best March through June. Bird list available.

Stage Stop Inn
P.O. Box 777
Patagonia, AZ 85624   (602) 394–2211

Apartments, efficiencies and rooms with swimming pool and restaurant right in the heart of Patagonia. Very near Sonoita Creek Bird Sanctuary.

Wild Horse Ranch Resort
7501 West Ina Road
Box 35743
Tucson, AZ 85740   (602) 744–4000

Cottages available year-round in the center of a 150,000-acre game area, twelve miles north of Tucson. Restaurant, horseback riding, and swimming. Bird list available.

Florida

Bass Haven Lodge
P.O. Box 147
Welaka, FL 32093   (904) 467–2392

Ten rooms in the Lodge, including efficiencies; open year-round. Overlooking St. John's River, northwest of Crescent City. Dining room and fishing equipment available. Caters to fishers but welcomes birders.

Flamingo Lodge
Everglades National Park
Flamingo, FL 33030   (305) 253–2241

One hundred and two rooms in the Lodge and sixteen cottages on Florida Bay, at the headquarters of the park. Restaurant, small convenience store, tackle shop, and gas station. Winter is best birding season (very buggy the rest of year). Bird list available; also lists of mammals, amphibians, and reptiles.

Pelican Inn
Box 301
Carrabelle, FL 32322   (904) 697–2839

Seven efficiency rooms on Dog Island, fifty miles south of Tallahassee. Accessible by small plane, boat, or passenger ferry; limited group menus available on prearranged basis. Bird list available.

Georgia

Little St. Simons Island
P.O. Box 1078 AL
St. Simons Island, GA 31522

Lodge sleeps eight, two cottages located on privately owned island offshore from Brunswick. Guests transported to island by boat. Dining room specializes in seafood and southern specialties. Bird list available.

Maine

The Hitchcock House
Monhegan Island, ME 04852   (207) 594–8137

Five rooms, three with kitchens, located ten miles offshore from Port Clyde. Reached by mailboat. Meals available nearby. Best time: May/June and September/October; all rooms have bird feeders.

Matinicus Island cottages

Two cottages available June through September. Access by air charter from Owl's Head or from Portland. Staples available on island. Boat service available to nearby Matinicus Rock and Seal Island with its Atlantic Puffin breeding colonies. Bird list available.

(Matinicus Island bookings through Geoffrey G. Katz, 156 Francestown Road, New Boston, NH 03070, (603) 487–3819.)

Massachusetts
Red River Motel
Route 28
So. Harwich, MA 02661   (617) 432–1474

Rooms and efficiencies open year-round, located on the south side of Cape Cod. Restaurants and shops nearby. Bird tours can be arranged through Massachusetts Audubon Wildlife Sanctuary.

Seaward Inn
Rockport, MA 01966   (617) 546–3471

Rooms and suites in the Inn and cottages open mid-May to mid-October, overlooking the ocean on Cape Ann. Restaurant. Shops in nearby village. Audubon sanctuaries nearby.

New Brunswick
Shorecrest Lodge
North Head
Grand Manan
New Brunswick EOG 2MO   (506) 662–3216

Lodge containing a dozen guest rooms plus space in attached annex, open year-round. Access via car-ferry from Black's Harbour, family-style meals. Boat access to Machias Seal Island; good bird and whale watching. Bird list available.

New Mexico
Bear Mountain Guest Ranch
P.O. Box 1163
Silver City, NM 88061   (505) 538–2538

Bed-and-breakfast cottages and four rooms in main house, open year-round. Services available in nearby town. Good birding on property and in nearby preserves. Owned by well-known birder Myra B. McCormick. Birding good all year, especially during migration: mid-April to early May and late September to early October. Birding tours available. Bird list available.

Texas
Indian Blanket Ranch
P.O. Box 206
Utopia, TX 78884   (512) 966–3525

"Bed-and-breakfast for Bird-Watchers." Two rooms and cabin in-the-woods, open year-round on 250-acre ranch on the Edwards Plateau, ninety miles west of San Antonio. "Folksy Gourmet" meals available. Owners knowledgeable birders. Birding good year-round, especially during migration. Bird list available.

Beyond North America

In Britain, prevalence of bed-and-breakfast places makes finding accommodations relatively easy. They're generally inexpensive and near "birdy" areas, and proprieters generally are understanding of birders' needs and often have suggestions of where to go. Birding publications occasionally advertise accommodations that particularly welcome birders.

Australia

Cassowary House
Black Mountain Road
P.O. Box 252, Kurando
Queensland 4872
Australia   (070) 93 7318

Two double and two single rooms in guest house located in forested hills above Cairns. Birding trips to varying habitats available with local guides.

Gipsy Point Lodge
Gipsey Point, Victoria 3889
Australia   (051) 58 8205

Twin and double rooms with full board in remote location on southern coast near Melbourne. Special package for overseas birders available on request; write to John and Marg Mulligan.

Costa Rica

Las Ventanas de Osa
(Inquiries and bookings through Natural History Books, Inc.,
P.O. Box 1089, Lake Helen, FL 32744–1089)

Lodge accommodations located in virgin rainforest 500 feet above Pacific Ocean, open January through April. Reached by four-wheel-drive vehicles from San José. Six double rooms, four single rooms; restaurant, bar, and swimming pool. English-speaking staff. Bird list and birding tours available.

TOUR OPERATORS

Birder/travelers have a great range of organized tours from which to choose. We identify below a good selection, but the list is not intended to be comprehensive. Although birding tour operators are separated from nature tour operators, it is recognized that there is a fine line separating several, and some arbitrary designations were made. Readers interested in rigorous birding trips, or birding/natural history trips, are urged to review the catalogs of both. Look also in recent publications read by birders for other tour operators going to places you want to go.

Birding Tour Operators

Some birding tour operators specialize in particular areas. Others offer a wide variety of destinations. Some trips have waiting lines; others are canceled because of lack of interest. Inquire early, but don't hesitate to call at the last minute to see if there are cancellations.

Bird Bonanzas, Inc.
P.O. Box 611563
North Miami, FL 33161   (305) 895–0607

Led by Joel Abramson, listed in the American Birding Association as the number-three world birder in 1985; advertises economical tours, featuring expert bird leaders from the countries visited on the tour. The 1986 tour program included India, Japan, Yemen, Hawaii, Puerto Rico, Philippines, Minnesota, Scandinavia, Fiji/New Caledonia/New Zealand, Australia, New Guinea. Its 1987 program includes Southern India/Sri Lanka, and West Africa.

Birding
Lattenden's Farm, Ashburnham
Battle, East Sussex TN33 9PB
England   (0323) 833245

John Gooders and Robbie Chapman will lead birding tours in 1987 to European and North African destinations.

Birdquest, Ltd.
8 Albert Road East
Hale, Altrincham
Cheshire WA 15 9AL
England   (061) 928–5945

Led by Mark Beaman, Steve Madge, Nigel Redman, and Iain Robertson; takes participants on birding trips, emphasizing Asia and Africa. Leaders are often joined by local experts for particular countries. Some trips are conducted annually; others are scheduled every several years. The 1987 program includes Thailand, India/Nepal, Sikkim/Darjeeling/Kashmir/ Ladakh, Kenya, Malaysia, Israel, Poland, Japan, Zimbabwe, Turkey, Siberia/Central Asia/the Caucasus, Costa Rica, Austalia, and Madagascar.

Caligo Ventures, Inc.
405 Greenwich Avenue   (203) 622–8989
Greenwich, CT 06830   1–800–235–1216

Arranges birding and natural history tours to Trinidad and Tobago. Participants stay at Asa Wright Nature Center.

Cardinal Birding Tours
P.O. Box 7495
Alexandria, VA 22307   (703) 360-4183

Led by Don Peterson; concentrates on South Florida but includes expanding tours to Mid-Atlantic states, and possibly farther afield. Utilizes experts in particular areas. Emphasizes small groups focusing on "early birding."

Cornell Laboratory of Ornithology
159 Sapsucker Woods Road
Ithaca, NY 14850   (607) 256-5056

Sponsors limited number of tours led by ornithologists. The 1986–87 program includes Kenya, the Hawaiian Islands, and Borneo/Malaysia/Hong Kong/Singapore, Papua New Guinea, New Zealand and Costa Rica.

Cygnus Wildlife
96 Fore Street
Kingsbridge, Devon TQ7 1PY
England   (0548) 6178

Birding tours for 1987 include Europe, Asia, Africa, and the Falkland Islands.

Field Guides, Incorporated
P.O. Box 160723
Austin, TX 78746   (512) 327-4953

Led by Jan Erik Pierson, John Rowlett, Rose Ann Rowlett, and Bret Whitney; 1986 program emphasized New World birding but includes some other trips. The 1986–87 program includes various birding "hot spots" around the world.

Four Points Nature Tours, Inc.
744 McCallie Avenue, Suite 105
Chattanooga, TN 37402   (615) 267-5580

Benton Basham, Noble Proctor, and others lead Atlantic Ocean pelagic trips and tours to North and Central America; other destinations in the planning stage.

Great Britain Birding
18 Old Woman's Lane
Cley next the Sea
Holt, Norfolk NR25 7TY
England   (0263) 740127

Led by Steve Gantlett; tours focus on Great Britain and emphasize small groups.

Joseph Van Os Nature Tours
P.O. Box 655
Vashon Island, WA 98070   (206) 463-5383

Led by Joe Van Os; other expert leaders for particular areas. Emphasizes general interest in nature study, especially birds. The 1987 program concentrates on North American "hot spots," Great Britain, Switzerland, Hungary, Costa Rica, Panama, Trinidad, Patagonia, Kenya, Australia, and Yucatán/Cozumel.

King Bird Tours
P.O. Box 196
Planetarium Station
New York, NY 10024   (212) 866-7923

Led by Ben King, eminent authority on Asian birds and coauthor of *A Field Guide to the Birds of South-east Asia* (currently, he is working on *A Field Identification Handbook to the Birds of the Indian Region*). The 1987 program includes West China and Indonesia. The 1988 schedule emphasizes intensive birding in Thailand/Burma/Southwest China, West China, and Indonesia.

Massachusetts Audubon Society
South Great Road
Lincoln, MA 01773   (617) 259-9500

Sponsors tours to "birdy" places led by expert birders.

McHugh Ornithology Tours (MOT)
101 West Upland Road
Ithaca, NY 14850   (607) 257-7829

The 1987 schedule of tours led by experts includes Venezuela, Brazil, Trinidad/Tobago, Alaska, and several other North American locations. Also sponsors nature photography workshops.

Nature Alaska Tours
P.O. Box 10224
Fairbanks, AK 99710

Dan L. Wetzel leads both birding and nature study tours in his home state, particularly Arctic Alaska.

Ornitholidays
1/3 Victoria Drive
Bognor Regis
West Sussex PO21 2PW
England   (0243) 821230

Run by Lawrence G. Holloway; has staff of expert birders. Emphasis on Europe, Asia, and Africa. The 1987 program includes Kenya, Sri Lanka, Northern India, Kashmir/Ladakh, Morocco, Zimbabwe, Seychelles, Turkey, Jordan, Thailand, France, Spain, Majorca, Greece, Australia, Yugoslavia, Andorra, Norway, New Zealand, Madagascar, Israel, Cyprus, Egypt, Iceland, and Ethiopia.

Peregrine, Inc.
P.O. Box 4251
Seattle, WA 98104   (206) 767-9937

Led by Ben Feltner, with associates Robert A. Behrstock, Mary Ann Chapman, Linda M. Feltner, Dr. David Mark, and David J. Markley. The 1986 program included the Pacific Northwest, Texas, South Florida/Dry Tortugas, Southeast Arizona, Alaska, Venezuela, Panama, Israel, and Kenya. The 1988 schedule features the Philippines. Also provides "short notice" trips (to see special species), private guide service, and field identification seminars for groups.

Sunbird
P.O. Box 76 Sandy
Bedfordshire SG19 1DF
England   (0767) 82969

Birding tours to European destinations including Cyprus and Majorca, Morocco, The Gambia, Kenya, Siberia, Trinidad, Mexico. Some tours run in conjunction with Wings, Inc.; others in cooperation with *British Birds* magazine.

Victor Emanuel Nature Tours (VENT)
P.O. Box 33008
Austin, TX 78764   (512) 477-5091

Led by Victor Emanuel and other birding experts, extensive tour schedule emphasizes New World birding, but includes trips to Africa, Australia, Japan, and Europe. The 1987 schedule includes major birding "hot spots" in North America, Baja California, Southern Oaxaca, western Mexico, Palenque/Yucatán/Cozumel, Costa Rica, Panama, West Indies; Venezuela, Colombia, Suriname, Ecuador, Peru, Brazil, Chile, Argentina; Gabon/The Ivory Coast, Namibia/Botswana, Kenya, Tanzania, Zambia/Zimbabwe, Japan, India/Sri Lanka, Papua New Guinea, Australia, Spain, and Israel. Photographic trips are also offered.

Wings, Inc.
P.O. Box 31930
Tucson, AZ 85751   (602) 749-1967

Led by Will Russell and other expert leaders. Offers extensive worldwide program. The 1987 program includes major birding "hot spots" in

North America, Mexico/Yucatán, Panama, Trinidad/Tobago, Venezuela, Ecuador, Brazil/Paraguay, and Argentina, Great Britain, Sweden, France, Spain, Majorca, Greece/Turkey, Israel, Egypt, Kenya, northern India/Nepal, Siberia/Mongolia, Thailand, Malaysia, and Australia. Also provides leaders for private tours, weekend trips, and bird-drawing workshops.

Wonder Bird Tours
500 Fifth Avenue
New York, NY 10036   (212) 840–5961

Operated by Manny Arias; provides birding tours of Trinidad for individuals or groups. Participants stay at Guest House of Mount St. Benedict Monastery.

Pelagic Birding Trip Operators

These tour operators are known for their emphasis on pelagic birding. For other tour operators that offer opportunities for oceanic birding, see "Nature Tour Operators."

Four Points Nature Tours (see "Birding Tour Operators")

Paul G. DuMont
4113 Fessenden Street N.W.
Washington DC   (202) 363–8994

Operates periodic Atlantic Ocean pelagic trips May through October.

Shearwater Journeys
P.O. Box 7440
Santa Cruz, CA 95061   (408) 688–1990

Led by Debra Love Shearwater; utilizes additional pelagic birding experts. Offers extensive year-round calendar of one-day and several-day trips for Pacific Ocean birds. Most frequent trips: August to October.

Sirius
P.O. Box 16682
1001 RD Amsterdam
The Netherlands   (020) 255104

The ship *Sirius* is available for ocean voyages all over the world; can accommodate up to twenty guests. Can be chartered by individuals, as well as birding tour operators.

Whales and Seabirds
2378 Route 97
Cooksville, MD 21723   (301) 854–6262

Led by Ron Naveen; provides Atlantic Ocean birding trips out of Ocean City, Maryland, in spring and fall. Also sponsors trips in cooperation with scientific research organizations for special species.

Pelagic trips are often offered by Audubon Societies and bird clubs in coastal areas. Contact organizations directly for information on ocean trips out of major coastal cities.

Nature Tour Operators

Many travelers seeking respite from standard capital city tours are turning to the nature or adventure tour operators. Some tour operators plan visits to places where participants may see interesting birds. Emphasis, however, tends to be on general nature appreciation, rather than a total focus on birding, characteristic of birding tour operators. There may or may not be competent birding leaders.

Alaska Fishing and Wilderness Adventures
P.O. Box 102675
Anchorage, AK 99510–2675   1–800–544–2219

Natural history safaris and cruises. Opportunities for pelagic birding.

Alaska Wild Wings
Goose Cove Lodge Box 325
Cordova, AK 99574

Limited accommodations for travelers interested in natural history, fishing, and birding. Owners Belle and Pete Mickelson advertise the "best spring migration birding spot" and often have birding experts available.

Baja Expeditions, Inc.
P.O. Box 3725
San Diego, CA 92103   (619) 297–0506

Whale watching and scuba diving; tours emphasize Baja California and natural history trips to Costa Rica.

Biological Journeys
1876 Ocean Drive
McKinleyville, CA 95521   (707) 839–0178

Led by Ronn Storro-Patterson, naturalist and marine biologist, Ron Levalley, naturalist and bird expert, and John Kipping, naturalist; general nature tours with birding orientation. The 1987 program offers trips for whale watching and pelagic birding in Baja California. The Pacific Northwest, Alaska, and the Galápagos. One-day pelagic trips operated out of San Francisco.

Cheesemans' Ecology Safaris, Inc.
20800 Kittredge Road
Saratoga, CA 95070   (408) 867–1371
                                                   741–5330

Led by Doug Cheeseman, zoologist and ecologist, and Gail Cheeseman, naturalist and birder; emphasis on birding, natural history, and wildlife photography. Participants must be nonsmokers. The 1987 program includes Kenya with Terry Stevenson, Galápagos, Brazil, Hawaii with Bob Western and Rick Palmer, and Papua New Guinea/Queensland, Australia. Pretrip and post-trip seminars when possible.

Earthwatch
Box 403N
Watertown, MA 02272   (617) 926–8200

A unique organization providing field research opportunities in a number of disciplines around the world. Although research unrelated to birding in a particular country might provide opportunities for the birder, several programs are led by ornithologists engaged in research projects. The 1987 program includes studying shorebirds and mergansers in Scotland, gannets in New Zealand, and shearwaters in Scotland.

Holbrook Travel, Inc.
3520 NW 13th Street
Gainesville, FL 32609   1–800–345–7111

General natural history and cultural trips, including some especially designed for birders and led by birding specialists. The 1986 tours of interest to birders were Galápagos Islands, East Africa, and Costa Rica.

Nature Expeditions International
P.O. Box 11496, Dept. 418
Eugene, OR 97440   (503) 484–6529

Natural history tours with some emphasis on bird life. The 1986–87 program includes trips to Alaska, Hawaii, Amazonia, Galápagos Islands, Mexico, Baja California, West Indies, East Africa, India, Nepal, Japan, Australia, Easter Island, New Zealand (walking tour), Papua New Guinea, and Polynesia.

Questers Tours and Travel, Inc.
257 Park Avenue South
New York, NY 10010–7369   (212) 673–3120

Worldwide nature tours with strong birding orientation. Organization says all leaders are ornithologists. 1986–87 program includes Everglades/Dry Tortugas/Southwest Florida, Okefenokee Swamp/Georgia (south coast), Hawaiian Islands, Alaska, Pacific Northwest, southern Mexico/Yucatán, Panama/Costa Rica, Venezuela, the Amazon, Ecuador/ Galápagos Islands, Peru, Brazil, Argentina, Trinidad/Tobago, Iceland, Ireland, Scotland, Norway, Spain, Switzerland, Greece, Turkey, Japan, Burma/Thailand, Nepal/Sikkim/Bhutan, East Africa, Zimbabwe/Botswana, Madagascar/Réunion/Mauritius, Australia, New Zealand, and Papua New Guinea.

Worldwide Holidays, Inc.
7800 Red Road, Suite 112   (305) 665–0841
South Miami, FL 33143   1–800–327–9854

Galápagos expeditions aboard the M/V *Bucaneer* with local guides, customized natural history tours of Costa Rica; both have good birding opportunities.

EXOTIC TRAVEL

Some major tour operators specialize in travel to places where there are good opportunities for travelers to sample the bird life, as a personal activity, incidental to the planned itinerary. Expert birding guides are not normally available unless indicated.

Abercrombie & Kent
1420 Kensington Road   (312) 954–2944
Oak Brook, IL 60521   1–800–323–7308

Major tour operator offering multiple departures to France, Scotland, England, Ireland, the Orient, India, Nepal, Tibet, Egypt, and Africa. Advertises Ben King birding safaris. (See "Birding Tour Operators.")

Condor Expeditions International Ltd.
53 East 67th Street, Suite 3-A
New York, NY 10021   (212) 628–8043

Takes passengers by ship and helicopter to Antarctic Peninsula for 12-14 day cruises. No particular birding orientation, but you can't avoid the penguins.

Hartours, Inc.
20 Park Plaza
Boston, MA 02116   1–800–821–0800

Flexible touring programs to Europe, the Middle East, and Africa, with capability of setting up "special ornithological-interest tours with expert guides" outside the United States; specialty is Kenya, East Africa.

International Expeditions, Inc.
1776 Independence Court, Suite 104   (205) 870–5550
Birmingham, AL 35216   1–800–633–4734

Worldwide tours with wildlife emphasis, many of which visit habitats of interest to traveling birders. Frequent departures to the Amazon, Andros Island, Australia, Belize, Costa Rica, Galápagos Islands, Hawaii, Kenya, Peru, East Africa, and Venezuela. Uses local birding experts on some trips.

Lindblad Travel, Inc.
P.O. Box 912
Westport, CT 06881   1–800–243–5657

Charters ships for cruises to the Galápagos and operates a changing schedule of cruises to Antarctica, the Amazon, and Africa yearly. Usually has scientific lecturers aboard.

Metropolitan Touring
c/o Adventure Associates
13150 Coit, Suite 110   1–800–527–2500
Dallas, TX 75240   (214) 357–6187

Several tours to the Ecuadorian Amazon offer many opportunities to the adventure traveler for tropical birding. Partial bird list available. Trekking tours offered. Galápagos tours available. Local guides.

Mountain Travel
1398 Solano Avenue
Albany, CA 94706   (415) 527–8100

Emphasis on trekking and hiking. Destinations are often places where there is good birding. Multiple departures for Asia, South Pacific, Africa, Europe, USSR, Central and South America, Alaska, Antarctica, and Hawaii.

Oceanic Society Expeditions
Fort Mason Center, Building E
San Francisco, CA 94123   (415) 411–1106

Land and ocean trips led by naturalists, with emphasis on birding and whale watching. The 1987 program includes Patagonia/Chile/Tierra del Fuego, Kenya/Seychelles, Botswana/Zimbabwe, Baja California, and Sea of Cortez (aboard motorized vessel). The program also includes sailing cruises of Vancouver Island, the San Juan and Gulf Islands, Southeast Alaska, Bahamas, Hawaii, and Bay of Fundy (with local boat trips for whale watching and island birding).

Ocean Voyages
1709 Bridgeway
Sausalito, CA 94965–1994   (415) 332–4681

Worldwide sailing trips, emphasizing cruising, island-hopping, diving, and snorkeling. Many island destinations of interest to birders, good opportunities for pelagic birding. Some areas of interest to birders are the Galápagos Islands, Cocos Island, the Grenadines, Hawaii, outer islands of

Tahiti, and New Zealand. Also sponsors sailing trips to South Pacific islands, the Caribbean, Mediterranean Sea, and Indian Ocean.

Pacific Sea Fari Tours
2803 Emerson Street
San Diego, CA 92106   (619) 226–8224

Emphasizes Baja California whale watching but also provides opportunities for ocean birding. Bird list available. Charter trips available.

Quabaug Bird Conservation Foundation
315 Palmer Rd.
Ware, MA 01082   (413) 967–7519

Tours to Amazon led by scientists.

Society Expeditions Cruises, Inc.
3131 Elliott Avenue, Suite 700
Seattle, WA 98121   1–800–426–7794

Designs and markets worldwide sailing trips on expedition ships: the *World Discoverer* and *Society Explorer*. Voyages include Antarctica, the South Pacific, and other exotic places. Natural history experts, and sometimes ornithologists, are on staff.

Special Interestours
3430 Evergreen Point Road, P.O. Box 37
Medina, WA 98039   (206) 455–1960

Specializing in the Arctic, Skip and Susan Voorhees offer several trips of interest to birders, including trips to the North Poles, Greenland, Nova Scotia, and Newfoundland. Some trips have birding emphasis.

Travcoa
875 N. Michigan Avenue
Chicago, IL 60611   (312) 951–2900

Tours to Antarctica in combination with other trips; good combination of exotic travel programs.

Wilderness Expeditions, S.A.
c/o Peruvian Amazon Tours
310 Washington Avenue, S.W.
Roanoke, VA 24016   (703) 342–5630

General natural history orientation, no particular birding emphasis, but just being in Amazonia provides great birding opportunities.

Wilderness Travel
1760 Solano Avenue
Berkeley, CA 94707   (415) 524–5111

Wildlife and trekking emphasis; some leaders may be good birders. Worldwide adventure trips, including some of particular interest to birders. The 1986–87 tours feature multiple departures to wilderness locations in Central and South America, Europe, Africa, India, the Himalayas, China, Japan, Australia, and New Guinea.

National Audubon Society and various state and local Audubon groups offer nature tours, some of which are led by ornithologists and have a strong birding emphasis. Many other organizations, such as the Smithsonian Institution, The Nature Conservancy, and Sierra Club, offer great nature trips that may provide some opportunities for birding without the intensity of a typical birding trip.

BASIC COMMON SENSE

Sophisticated travelers generally have stored up a good cache of common sense. Many common sensitivities apply to places beyond the beaten path and some special ones apply to birders in habitats in which they find themselves.

Valuables

The most important thing for world travelers and world birders is: *always know where your passport is.* Make sure it's valid for several months after your intended trip. Some travelers habitually put their passport in a hotel safe. Birders in the bush might better keep it on their person. Passport checks occasionally occur, particularly near border areas in Third World countries; therefore, it is important keep your passport with you. It's a good idea to make a photocopy of essential pages in the passport and keep it separately. Many birders carry passport, a small amount of the local currency, and sometimes a traveler's check and credit card on their person at all times. Major credit cards are useful in most cities.

Avoid carrying an obvious purse, handbag, etc., in crowded places. American dollars and British pounds are particularly attractive to the light-fingered. Anyplace in the world, *watch your valuables.* Avoid leaving a purse in a locked car where it can be easily spotted. Preferably don't take one along. Ratty old canvas bags generally don't invite unwanted curiosity. World birders generally leave good watches, gold jewelry, and diamond rings at home. Don't invite problems.

If you will be aboard ship, these admonitions are probably not so important. Your cabin or the ship's safe is safe. You needn't worry when you go ashore in an outboard-motor-powered zodiac or rubber boat.

One comic exception occurred on the *Lindblad Polaris* trip to West Africa. We had left the ship early one morning in the zodiacs to explore the coastal area of the Delta de Saloum National Park. As we sighted flamingos and spoonbills, we also sighted a native canoe approaching us, filled with Senegalese park wardens. With the assistance of one of our group members, who spoke some French, we discovered the local agent had failed to secure a needed permit, the fee for which was payable on the spot. Who would have thought we'd need money in such a remote area early in the morning? It was a struggle before nineteen bathing-suited birders were able to pool enough cash to pay the modest fee.

You need not keep your "powder dry," but do *keep your binoculars and cameras dry*. Birders do bird in the rain, and a rain guard for binoculars is a good idea. Holding them under arm or tucking them inside your jacket can help. A plastic bag for equipment not in immediate use not only will keep it dry, particularly important on ocean trips, but will keep out fine dust from rough country roads in the dry season.

In some places in the world, binoculars and cameras arouse suspicion and nervousness among the local militia. Keep them in an inconspicuous place if you're anywhere near a military establishment. Heed the signs. In some countries, don't take pictures of government buildings, bridges, or at airports. When in doubt, don't. Peter Alden points out that in many foreign lands natives don't know the difference between a Polaroid camera and your binoculars. They may think you're taking a picture of them (without permission or payment) when you're just spotting a sand grouse.

Health Precautions

In tropical areas, *don't drink the water* unless you're told it's safe. However, *do* drink lots of liquids to help keep you on a regular schedule. If you know the water isn't safe to drink, forsake the ice too. Birders often carry iodine crystals or other water purifiers with them. Fortunately, plastic bottles with screw-tops containing pure water are becoming available in many countries.

Many birds love bugs, and some bugs love birders. *Insect repellent is generally a necessity*. In the forest, it's best to apply repellent before you go out birding. Which repellent you should use is a matter of opinion and experience; try several. The antibug campaign can range from a casual spraying, if you're not going into very buggy territory, to an elaborate routine in the tropics. Most birders in the tropics apply repellent to their legs and feet before putting their clothes on; some cover virtually all their body. After dressing, apply repellent to shoes, socks, and pants.

To prevent the "creepies" and the "jumpies" from crawling up your legs, it's a good idea to stuff the bottoms of your pants into your socks. Long pants and long-sleeved shirts are often imperative. If chiggers are in the area, some people shake sulphur powder on their shoes. If you know you're going to be in mosquito-infested areas, you may want to invest in a mosquito-netted hat. Check your local camping store.

What to do after you've been bitten? Don't scratch; tough it out. Few bites will cause a reaction more serious than mild annoyance. If you do tend to be allergic to bug bites, ask your doctor for an antihistamine, or try Benadryl, an over-the-counter remedy. Watch for drowsiness.

Adventure traveling and world birding can appeal to people of all ages, provided they are in reasonable good health. Birders typically do a lot of hiking, often some climbing. If you aren't into a regular exercise routine, spend a few weeks getting into shape.

If you are going into remote areas, be sure your health is such that you won't cause inconvenience to your companions. This is particularly important for any traveler contemplating a voyage to Antarctica, or other places far from a good range of medical help. If in doubt, don't go. Although there will be a doctor on the ship on a long voyage, any serious illness will be a problem not only to you, but to the other passengers as well.

Age, however, for a normally healthy person, should not dissuade anyone from going to Antarctica, probably the most remote place in the world. There was a couple in their early eighties on my trip, and they seldom missed a trip to shore. My roommate was a near-octogenarian, and she was usually first in line for boarding the rubber boats.

Travel magazines and travel sections of major newspapers run periodic articles on the disease dangers of overseas travel. Sometimes it seems they are trying to keep everyone home. Medical precautions, for the most part, are uncomplicated in North America, Europe, and Australia.

Beyond there, always check with your family doctor and public health physician before traveling. They may suggest a variety of vaccinations for hepatitis, measles, meningitis, polio, rabies, typhoid, tetanus, and diphtheria. Your public health doctor should be up to date on what shots or other preventive medication is required, depending on the country you will be visiting. Don't wait until the last minute to do this; some medication must be taken well in advance of your intended departure.

If you're taking medications regularly, be sure to take an adequate supply with you. You just won't find a corner drugstore in the rainforest. Waterborne diseases can be disastrous, and I certainly would not advise swimming anywhere, except in a game lodge or hotel swimming pool. *Seasick medication is a must* if you're going to be waterborne. It can even be helpful in mountain driving or on long trips over very bumpy roads. Always carry medication with you; don't pack it in your suitcase.

Getting off the beaten path may result sometimes in getting "off your feed." The best antidote is preventive; *don't overeat*, even if the buffet is laden with wondrous culinary achievements, as it may be on a Lindblad ship or in a Kenyan game lodge. In some countries the menu will include foods you've never seen or heard of, and you may not like them. It is unlikely, however, that you will go hungry. "Montezuma's Revenge" is as vengeful in India as it is in Mexico. Be careful about unpeeled fruits and vegetables, and be sure to have a supply of Lomotil.

Clothing

Clothing on all birding trips should be comfortable. Subdued colors are recommended; some say it's because animals don't like bright colors, but really it's because they don't show the dust. Everywhere, wear closed-toe shoes rather than open sandals.

Comfortable shoes are, of course, a must for the active traveler and birder. Good walking shoes or boots will be welcome on tough terrain. It is often necessary to hike fairly long distances to see the "good" birds. Sometimes waterproof boots are recommended. An alternative is a pair of sneakers you don't mind getting wet, and bring an extra pair to wear while one is drying.

Clothes, of course, will be dictated by the climate of the country to be visited. Extremes of temperature will be encountered in many places, and "layering" is the general rule. Most birders carry a day pack, or rucksack, in which to stuff a sweater, if the day warms up. Birders dress casually, even saving particularly scruffy pants and shirts for birding trips. If nice hotels are on the itinerary, pack a few appropriate clothes. *Pack lightly.* Minibuses and dugout canoes have limited storage space, and you may be limited to one suitcase. In most of the world, some kind of laundry service is available, particularly in areas catering to tourists. In the more remote parts, count on doing your own, or (horrors!) going dirty.

Special Cautions for Birders

On the forest trail, *keep one eye on the treetops, the other eye on the ground.* Admittedly impossible, but you get the idea. After looking up too long, tropical bird expert Ted Parker looked down to find himself straddling a snake. Bird tour leader Mort Cooper, after admonishing his group to *always* look before advancing or retreating, stepped backward without looking, lost his balance, and fell into a muddy puddle.

Of course, follow the leader's rules about staying together on the forest trail, or staying in the vehicle on a game run. If you're birding the periphery of the lodge grounds in Africa, watch where you're walking and heed the signs warning you not to go beyond bounds. Always remember, wild animals are dangerous; treat them with caution and respect. If you're making shore landings from small boats, be particularly careful. Because of rough seas, wet and sometimes rocky landings, and slippery snow, it is more important than usual to heed the advice of those in command. Their task is to prevent accidents and to insure that passengers enjoy their experience.

Birders are subject to some special ailments not known to more traditional travelers. "Birditis" of the neck afflicts 99.5 percent of birders. Remember to stretch your neck down frequently. There is also the more insidious "birder's burnout" to be aware of. Birders, particularly world birders who really want to bash the hell out of a country, knowing they will probably never return, tend to bird themselves into the ground. They *never stop*. Watch for symptoms of "burnout" when you decide that the Scarlet Macaws are all "trash birds."

Courtesy

Finally, sophisticated travelers and world birders know that common courtesy is important wherever you are. A smile is generally a passport to friendly treatment. Hone your sense of humor. Traveling to remote locations often requires large doses. Don't expect anything to be "like it is at home." You'll get pleasant surprises every so often, but be prepared to accept what *is*; if you don't like it, just remember it won't last long. A sense of humor will get you through many a tough time, whether a buggy bed or a batty roommate.

Respect local customs. It is a pain in the foot to remove your boots every time you enter a Buddist home or temple, but the observance of this ritual is important to your hosts and will reduce potential unpleasantness.

Birder's Checklist

Experienced travelers and world birders know, as a result of experience, what things they'll need to pack in order to make life tolerable. Just as a reminder, here's a checklist geared especially to the world birder

> Binoculars
> Telescope and tripod if you think they'll be useful
> Bird guide(s) (but don't take the library)
> Bird checklist for the country you'll be birding
> Notebooks—a small one for the field, a larger one if you keep a log
> Pencils and pens
> Maps
> Kleenex and/or toilet paper; either may be nonexistent when you most need it
> Hat
> Sunscreen
> Insect repellent
> Flashlight ("torch" as the British say) with extra batteries
> Alarm clock/watch
> Washcloth in a plastic bag; maybe an old towel
> Extra plastic bags (for muddy boots and socks that didn't get dry, to cover the camera exposed to road dust or ocean spray)
> Poncho, the kind that folds up compactly
> Scarf/bandana, sometimes useful on very dusty roads
> Copy of your itinerary (leave a copy home in case of an emergency)
> Customs certificates for binoculars, cameras, lenses, and anything else that might be questioned on your return home

Spare eyeglasses, and prescription for same, if you can't read your bird guide without them

First aid supplies: Band-Aids, antacid, laxative, Lomotil, water purifier, cortisone cream, eye drops

Cosmetics (bare minimum) and items of personal hygiene

Survival kit (for the really well prepared): string, glue, rubber bands, spare shoe laces, needle and thread, scissors, small pencil sharpener, safety pins

Basic advice: relax and enjoy it.

Basic Glossary

"Early birders" will gain an understanding of some terms used in this book and heard on a typical birding trip. Anatomical parts of birds are not included; every standard bird guide contains a labeled diagram of the standard bird. For more extensive information, refer to Bibliography.

ACCIDENTAL. Standard terminology for describing frequency of a species' occurrence. Occurs in a particular place infrequently and irregularly—rarer than rare in particular areas. See also RARITY, VAGRANT.

AMERICAN ORNITHOLOGICAL UNION (AOU). The scientific organization that publishes the authoritative *Checklist of North American Birds,* on which most field guides are based. An AOU committee makes periodic decisions on combining or separating species (lumping and splitting) based on the latest scientific knowledge and makes official changes in the American names of birds. Publishes *The Auk*, a quarterly journal.

ATLAS. A census of species, usually breeding birds, occurring in given geographic areas, generally of a state. Results are published.

AUDUBON SOCIETY. Originally identified as a "bird-watching" organization. Audubon Societies, at the national, state, and local level today, focus their attention on wide-ranging environmental issues. The National Audubon Society publishes *Audubon* magazine and *American Birds*.

BIRD OF PREY. Generally refers to Osprey, hawks, eagles, and falcons, sometimes to vultures and owls.

BOREAL. Northern life zones of North America: Arctic, Hudsonian, and Canadian.

CANOPY FEEDING. 1. A peculiar habit of some herons that hold their wings out to shade the water around them, presumably to attract fish to the ensuing shade. The Reddish Egret can be distinguished at a great distance by this behavior. Other egrets, particularly the Louisiana Heron, occasionally exhibit this behavior. 2. The habit of vast number of birds in the tropics that feed only in the crowns of trees, rarely descending to afford birders' good looks at them.

CENSUS. A periodic count of the number of birds of each species in a given geographic area. Periodic census counts provide time-lines for determining changes in bird populations.

CONSPECIFIC. Belonging to the same species. For example, formerly two separate species, the Mexican Duck is now considered conspecific with the Mallard.

CONVERGENCE/CONVERGENT EVOLUTION. Evolution of structural and behavioral similarities in birds and other living things in unrelated species or families. The longclaws in Africa look and behave very similarly to North American meadowlarks, yet they belong to different families.

DIHEDRAL. In birds, the angle at which the wing meets the body. A good reference point is the angle at which Turkey Vultures' wings are raised when soaring. The Black Vulture's dihedral is less pronounced; the Bald Eagle's is virtually flat.

DIMORPHISM. Occurrence of two distinct forms. Sexual dimorphism describes different plumages of the male and female of a species. Dimorphism may also refer to differences in characteristics such as size between male and female. See MORPH.

DISPLAY. Any activity engaged in by a bird designed to induce a desired behavior by another bird. Males often display their feathers or engage in specific behavior designed to attract the female. Males of some species construct elaborate display grounds for such activity. See LEK.

ECOLOGICAL NICHE. See NICHE.

ENDEMIC. Restricted to, or found only in, a particular geographic area. The Galápagos Hawk is found only in the Galápagos Islands.

FAUNAL. Relates to animal life of an area. Faunal regions—see Zoogeographic.

FLYWAY. The air-highway over prominent topographic features, along which large numbers (but certainly not all) of birds migrate. The Atlantic and Pacific flyways follow the coast, the Mississippi flyway follows that river.

FOOD CHAIN. Succession of food by successively larger organisms. For example, krill is at the bottom of the food chain for all Antarctic animals. Penguins eat the krill, Leopard Seals then eat the penguins, etc.

IMPRINTING. The rapid learning phenomenon occurring soon after birth by which the young of a species attaches itself to its larger parent. Baby ducks in close early association with a human often learn to follow the human rather than the parent duck.

INTERNATIONAL ORNITHOLOGICAL CONGRESS (IOC). International organization of ornithologists that, among other activities, seeks to resolve differences in nomenclature of birds.

IRRUPTION. Irregular mass movement of birds after breeding to areas beyond their normal range. May be due to inadequate food supply in regular range or to a superabundance of food, leading to supernesting success, thus encouraging large numbers to move into new areas.

LEK. A place where a number of male birds gather to display for the females. It may be a forest floor area, cleared by the males to provide a place to "dance," such as made by White-bearded Manakins, or a forest soundstage, as is the case for Screaming Pihas, or a hillock in a marsh, where the marvelous male ruffs show off.

LIFE ZONES. North American designation of areas of roughly 400 miles of north-south direction, or 2,500 feet of elevation, within which a particular combination of flora and fauna may be found. Ranges from lowest and hottest to highest and coldest. Bird guides often provide maps showing life zones.

MELANISM. Unusual dark coloration of a bird's plumage. Also known as "dark phase," particularly common with hawks.

MIST NET. A finely woven net, set up on poles close to vegetation, into which birds fly. Birds become harmlessly caught in the net and can be removed for banding or other study purposes.

MONOTYPIC. A taxonomic category that contains only one representative of the next lowest category. For example, a monotypic order would contain only one family; a monotypic family would contain only one species.

MORPH. A phase or variation of color, size, or other characteristics that is different from the norm. Many hawks are recognized as dark phase or light phase. The Eastern Reef Heron, customarily white, also has a dark phase, or morph. Red phase Eastern Screech-Owls are more commonly found in the South. Species are known as POLYMORPHIC if they have two or more phases, e.g. light and dark, and intermediate has both.

NICHE. The place or function an organism plays in the ecosystem. Some birds occupy a physical niche, such as the top of the forest canopy. Others may only eat a particular insect. The nectar-sipping sunbirds in Africa are said to fill the same niche filled by hummingbirds in North America. Auks in northern oceans fill the ecological niche filled by penguins in southern oceans.

NIDIFICATION. Relates to nests and nest building.

NOMINATE. In effect, the first officially documented species in a genus. The Latin name may repeat the name, e.g., the Eastern Kingbird, *Tyrannus tyrannus*, the nominate species of the genus *Tyrannus*. A good birding leader might urge you to become familiar with the nominate species in order to better identify other related species.

ORNITHOLOGY. Scientific study of bird life. A birder is not an ornithologist. An ornithologist is a person who by scientific background is qualified to make scientific studies of birds. Amateurs routinely make considerable contributions to certain facets of ornithology to an extent not customary in other scientific disciplines.

PASSERINE. Member of the order Passeriformes, the largest of the orders; includes half the bird species. In North America this is roughly translated as "perching bird." The order is derived from the Latin *passer* for sparrow. British birders define the term as meaning "sparrowlike."

PELAGIC. Relates to the ocean or open sea rather than to coastal waters. Pelagic birds spend their lives on the ocean, coming ashore only to breed and nest.

PHYLOGENIC. Roughly, the evolutionary sequence of an order, family, or species arising from a common ancestor. Virtually synonomous with TAXONOMIC. The sequence of listing species in a bird guide is by the phylogenic or taxonomic order.

RARITY. A bird uncommon in a particular area, although it may be common elsewhere.

RATITE. Flightless birds lacking a keel down the breastbone, e.g., Ostrich, Emu.

RIPARIAN. Relates to plants or animals that live in areas influenced by the presence of rivers, streams, and ponds.

ROOKERY. Nesting colonies of birds such as herons.

SONOGRAM. Visual representation of what a bird's song is like. Shown in some bird guides.

TAXONOMY. The systematic ordering of plants and animals based on similarities and differences. Birds are sorted by orders, families, genera, and species.

TUBENOSE. An extra nostril, or salt gland, that enables seabirds to extract and secrete the salt from seawater, thus enabling them to live far from a source of fresh water. Refers to members of the order Procelariiformes, the albatrosses, shearwaters, petrels, and storm-petrels.

VAGRANT. A bird that wanders, or perhaps is blown, beyond its normal range.

ZOOGEOGRAPHIC. Relates to the distribution of flora and fauna of large geographic areas. (See Introduction to Part II.)

Basic Bibliography

To provide a formal bibliography would be to virtually duplicate the list of books and periodicals that opens Part III. Many of those publications were used and reused for reference purposes during the preparation of this book.

Of particular interest and value to me were the periodicals that are listed in Part III, Chapter 5: *Birding, Bird Watcher's Digest, American Birds,* and *Living Bird.* I urge everyone with even a moderate interest in birds to subscribe to one or more. After joining the Royal Society for the Protection of Birds in Britain during the book's preparation, its quarterly publication, *Birds,* joined that list.

Some information on faraway places, particularly relating to endangered birds, was derived from several issues of *International Wildlife. Audubon* magazine and *National Geographic* were frequent reference sources.

Three primary reference books provided answers to most of my questions. James Clements' *Birds of the World: A Checklist* (3d ed.) was in constant use and was my primary authority for both common and scientific names of birds. This is the checklist most familiar to North American birders traveling the world. It was often the arbiter between two or more field guides that used different common names for the same species, and was nearly always my authority for the spelling of common names.

The Audubon Society Encyclopedia of North American Birds contains a wealth of useful information and was in constant use. Christopher Leahy's *The Bird Watcher's Companion* provided quick explanations of many aspects of birding.

A conscious decision was made not to include books on "the wrens of the world," or any other "bird species of the world." Because of the "tip of the iceberg" nature of this current work, the many fine books of this genre were generally not used as reference sources. Three exceptions should be mentioned.

Peter Harrison's *Seabirds: An Identification Guide* was an essential reference and is listed in this section for Chapter 13. It was useful in work on other chapters as well.

Late in this work's preparation, a new book became available that, because of the excellence of its descriptions and color plates, deserves special mention: *Shorebirds*, subtitled, "An identification guide to the waders of the world," by Peter Hayman and John Marchant and Tony Prater; Croom Helm, 1986.

The third "family" book often relied upon was the monumental *Parrots of the World* by Joseph M. Forshaw; T.F.H. Publications, 1977.

Index